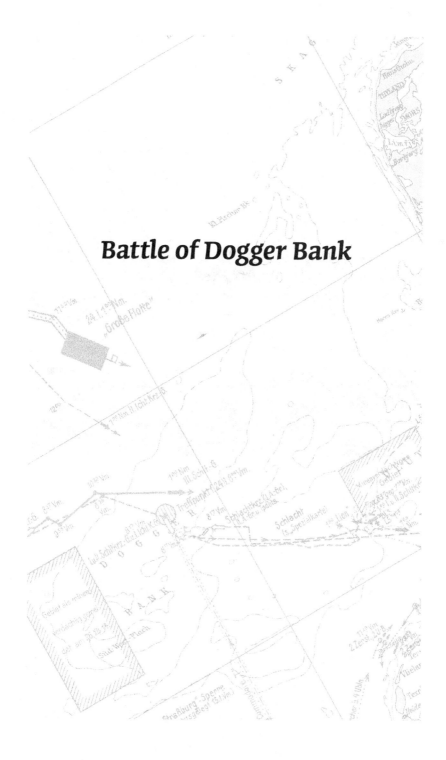

Battle of Dogger Bank

TWENTIETH-CENTURY BATTLES   *Spencer C. Tucker, editor*

BATTLE of DOGGER BANK

The First Dreadnought
Engagement, January 1915

TOBIAS R. PHILBIN

INDIANA UNIVERSITY PRESS   *Bloomington & Indianapolis*

This book is a publication of

INDIANA UNIVERSITY PRESS
Office of Scholarly Publishing
Herman B Wells Library 350
1320 East 10th Street
Bloomington, Indiana 47405 USA

iupress.indiana.edu

Telephone 800-842-6796
Fax 812-855-7931

Manufactured in the
United States of America

Library of Congress
Cataloging-in-Publication Data

Philbin, Tobias R.
  Battle of Dogger Bank : the
first dreadnought engagement,
January 1915 / Tobias R. Philbin.
    pages cm. – (Twentieth-century battles)
    Includes bibliographical
references and index.
  ISBN 978-0-253-01169-5 (cloth : alk.
paper) – ISBN 978-0-253-01173-2 (e-book)
  1. Dogger Bank, Battle of the, 1915. 2.
Germany. Kriegsmarine – History – World
War, 1914–1918. 3. Great Britain.
Royal Navy – History – World
War, 1914–1918. I. Title.
  D582.D6P55 2014
  940.4'55 – dc23

                        2013038546

2 3 4 5   19 18 17 16 15 14

This book is dedicated to Bryan Ranft,
Professor Pater, educator, and scholar.

What the country needs is the annihilation of the enemy.

Vice Admiral Horatio Nelson

Gaining military victory is not in itself
equivalent to gaining the object of war.

Captain B. H. Liddell Hart

Contents

Illustrations

Preface

THIS BOOK IS DESIGNED TO PROVIDE NEW INSIGHTS INTO THE
first battle between the largest fighting machines of the early twentieth
century. It seeks the reasons for the battle in the context of what was basically a stalemate on the ground in the opening phases of World War I.
The ships involved were novel, powerful, and regarded as national assets
that were not to be risked lightly, but which could be gambled in an attempt to even the odds for the battle fleets for which they scouted. The
prestige and competence of Imperial Germany and the British Empire
were at issue. Efforts of the previous twenty years and the investments of
hundreds of millions in gold were at risk. Dogger Bank involved dozens
of ships and it was a large, cold, and desperate battle, but it was both novel
and a precedent for engagements to come.

It is instructive to understand the roles which time and distance
played in the North Sea Theater. To this event, the Germans have left
posterity with a remarkable little chart showing the distance in *Seemeilen,* or nautical miles (2,000 yards or 6,000 feet instead of 5,280 feet on
land), between all the key points on the chart. This enables us to view the
problems faced by the combatants both in time and distance. The North
Sea is shallow and treacherous, providing a challenge to simple navigation, much less naval warfare. It is hostage to incredibly foul dangerous
weather and low visibility which affected both combatants throughout
the war. It is not possible or wise to ignore the role of the other half of
the geography of the north German Coast – the Baltic. Germany faced
the prospect of a naval campaign against Russia during the First World
War. The subordination of the Russian navy, like the German, to the land

campaign, and the lack of coordination or imagination on their part for most of the war, despite Russia having significant resources, meant that the Germans did not have to concern themselves with Russian initiatives. They could resort to a purely defensive strategy, which retained Baltic sea-lanes for German use, especially support of German raw material imports for her war industries from Sweden, throughout the conflict. To a great extent however, the Germans were able to deter an active Russian fleet policy which might have contested control of the Baltic and opened the German North Sea coast to a Russian amphibious assault – Berlin was only ninety miles from the Baltic littoral. The Germans were able to do this because of the Kiel Canal, which would allow transfer of the High Seas Fleet from the North Sea to the Baltic, or the other direction, in a matter of a day. There was always danger from mines, and later from British submarines, but no British Baltic operation was ever attempted. The Baltic was always relevant to German sea power, as this map shows, but it was never operationally decisive, except to prolong Germany's ability to conduct the land war on two fronts and to deny victory to the Russians.

The map in figure A.1 illustrates some basic numbers. From the German main naval bases in the Jade River around Cuxhaven, the distances were: to Scapa Flow – 490 nm (the principal Grand Fleet base); to the Firth of Forth – 470 nm (the normal British Battle Cruiser Base, and sometimes the Grand Fleet locus); to Hull – 310 nm (and most targets on the British east coast); to the Thames – 340 nm; to Dover – 290 nm; to Portsmouth – 400 nm (main British naval base and repair facility). Distances of this magnitude, involving strategic operations either strictly naval or amphibious, would involve planning and logistics on scales unprecedented, but not impossible. The real issue was how to win the war and impose the will of either side by force. The British knew they would eventually win a war of distant blockade with little risk; but they could not know the cost in time or lives while the generals and politicians gambled on other fronts. Fisher and Churchill's Baltic ideas were not such chimeras as they have appeared. A battle which deprived the Germans of any significant portion of their fleet would alter the calculus for success or failure in the Baltic, thus potentially upsetting what was

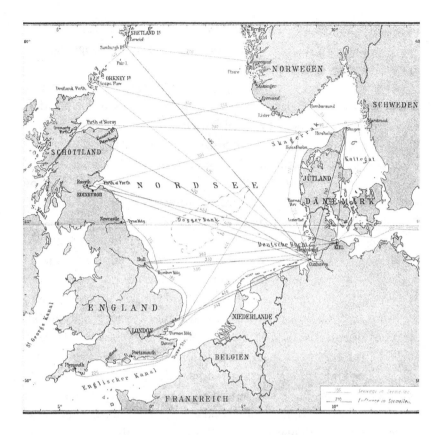

A.1. Map of strategic distances in the North Sea as illustrated in the German Official History.

for the German army a front that, as long as it was guarded by the navy, contained no risk or threat, but for which there was no reserve or effective defense. The risks in the actions which resulted in Dogger Bank thus contained danger not heretofore obvious.

The first battle between dreadnoughts took place on 24 January 1915 in the southeastern North Sea. The Germans were frustrated because the British, who possessed what Clausewitzian strategists called "brutal superiority," were supposed to attack.[1] Because of this mind-set, and the "vaunted British offensive spirit," the Germans believed they would attack. Instead, the war settled down into a series of feints and counter feints, in each of which the other sought to trap their antagonist and resolve the issue with a favorable outcome.

In his foreword to *The War Plans of the Great Powers*, Fritz Fischer advances the belief that the German body politic and its military leaders were essentially motivated by social Darwinist ideology to fight the First World War. The German army had to get the balance of German national resources because the army would determine the continued existence of Germany in the midst of a hostile Europe. Germany was surrounded by enemies. So, from about 1912 onward, the army was at the head of the line for resources, and the German navy had lower priority.

Grand Admiral Alfred von Tirpitz and Admiral of the Fleet Lord Fisher had coincidentally realigned the British Empire to a regional power from a global power by the time of the outbreak of World War I. Tirpitz was the hammer who metamorphosed both the Royal Navy and the British Empire into a Eurocentric naval entity by forcing a consolidation of British naval strength in the North Sea, where the Battle of Dogger Bank occurred. That consolidation resulted from a confluence of economic and political circumstances which no war could actually have brought about. The rise of other powers, including Japan and United States, and the development of second echelon naval challenges in the Mediterranean, particularly Austria-Hungary and Italy, as well as others in South America, meant the Royal Navy had to neglect the rest of the world to focus on what was a serious threat to the center of gravity to her commerce – the home islands.

The High Seas Fleet, because it existed as a real and growing force, regardless of its actual numbers and its poor geographic situation, had already altered the balance of naval power forever from as early as the fulfillment of Tirpitz's first Navy Law in about 1908. Britain abandoned the two-power standard in 1911–1912, because she could focus only on Germany. The Royal Navy was designed and built to have 60 percent superiority over that country. In addition, the British army was being recapitalized to overcome the deficiencies revealed in the Boer War, and so it could support France in a conflict with Germany.

To some extent, Dogger Bank was an accidental battle in a war of miscalculation fought by a navy which was not really needed. But Dogger

Bank was fought as was its sequel Jutland. This engagement was documented by both sides as part of war propaganda efforts, as part of subsequent official histories, and then in both multi-volume analysis and in
published papers on the British side. On the German side, it has been a
subset of the larger Tirpitz/German sea power debates, some of which
revolve around the Imperial German desire to achieve world power sta-
tus. Most of the literature in the attached bibliography is at least 20 years
old. There is no recent work on Dogger Bank per se rather several other
works which contain examinations of the battle.[2] Of those, the most
complete and comprehensive is the analysis by Gary Staff in *Battle on
the Seven Seas*. This is full of both insight and flavor of what it felt like
to live as a German admiral, officer, petty officer, or seaman in the full
scope of German World War I cruiser battles. It is a complement from
the German perspective to the Australian James Goldrick's *The King's
Ships Were at Sea*, albeit 20 year later.[3]

Two principal decision makers with impact both on and off the battlefield were Grand Admiral Alfred von Tirpitz and his British opposite
number Admiral Sir John Fisher. These two men reflected their nations
and societies during two decades of the first modern arms race which
culminated in the invention of the dreadnought type battleships, whose
battle cruiser sisters comprised the principal combatants at Dogger Bank.
The context here is social, economic, political, scientific, industrial and,
of course, military. The social context is that of an evolving global system
which contained the roots of conflict both vertically among classes and
horizontally among nation states. Those roots comprised both fear and
ambition on the part of every nation which eventually became involved
in World War I. A common element was, of course, jingoistic nationalism
reflected in both the press and middle classes of Britain and Germany,
and used by Tirpitz as a lever to impose his vision of navalism on his
own country, and by Fisher and Winston Churchill to manage the British response. The nature of the competition was at first political within
Reichstag, *Kaisertum*,[4] Parliament, and Empire. It then manifested itself
in industrial products which harnessed the science of the day. Dogger
Bank showcased the military and naval production of each side, which
was the product of the "Anglo-German arms race before the First World
War [which] was the most celebrated arms race in modern history."[5] On

both sides, the ships and the navies evolved over time reflecting almost
16 years of industrial, strategic, and tactical decisions and experience, the
results of which clashed on a cold January morning in 1915 in the North
Sea. Although the tools of war evolved along relatively incremental lines
as succeeding classes of battleships and battle cruisers were built, the
argument can be made that the submarine, long thought too technologi-
cally immature for an impact on traditional naval operations, played a
critical, even decisive role in this battle. It was in fact a submarine which
did not exist, but the threat of it in Admiral Beatty's mind, which caused
him to turn away from the Germans at a critical moment, and allowed
them to escape. There was in fact no submarine, just what looked like
a periscope wake in the midst of several hours of combat on that cold
January morning.

As Lambert puts it, the British high command on the outbreak of
World War I was so myopic as to fail to reconsider the fundamentals of
their naval strategy, resulting in the Royal Navy going to war in 1914
"with an outdated strategic doctrine."[6] However, there is new evidence
that Churchill and the Admiralty, had they not been distracted by the
war, were about to shift away from dreadnoughts to mine and torpedo
carriers, which would be cheaper, leave the Germans in the "mud banks
of the Elbe," with their dreadnoughts immobilized by the threat of underwater attack, and shift the larger British shipbuilding capacity to submarines by 1917. Whatever the outcome of that issue, it was true that,
both before and after Dogger Bank, the British did not have to come to
the Germans to enforce the distant blockade; the Germans absolutely
did have to come to the British if they wished to break the blockade.[7]
This strategy would have threatened the rest of the world's dreadnought
battle cruisers and battleships, and driven navies in a wholly different
direction. Both the Japanese and the Americans were building dreadnoughts and the Japanese proceeded to build the four ship *Kongo* class,
the first of which was built by Vickers. The *Kongo's* superior design drove
improvements in the British battle cruiser *Tiger,* the newest ship at Dogger Bank.[8] For their part, when the United States Navy (USN) discovered
Kongo was to be one of four, which made the current armored cruisers
of the Pacific Fleet obsolete, it began working on its own battle cruiser
designs. But the USN did not consider the type worth building until

the Japanese decided to build battle cruisers. The early American battle cruisers would have resembled the USS *Wyoming* but would have had four 12-inch turrets on a very long hull, with battleship like protection and high speed.[9] After the *Kongo* class appeared, U.S. designers and the General Board considered an enlarged *Kongo* class with 8–14 inch guns, a speed of 30 knots and armor on the scale of the *Nevada* class. In essence, these were high speed battleships, which was the eventual direction U.S. capital ship construction followed. The USN preferred to build battleships so if they found the enemy fleet or it found them, numbers and sheer power would tell the tale, at least for the period 1906–1915. There were additional designs, but worthy of note was the comparison of U.S. design philosophy to everybody else: "US Ships were not comparable to their foreign rivals, they had a far greater radius of action; displacement was calculated on an entirely different basis; the US armoring scheme was entirely different and far more extensive."[10]

For the story of the battle itself, sources include the logs of almost all the ships and after action reports for Admiral Beatty and Admiral Hipper, as well as the papers in their respective admiralties. The construction details of the ships on both sides, including the compromises are also available. Eyewitness reports, prisoner interrogations, and war diaries are also available on both sides.[11] There is no ultimate consensus yet on the nature of the context – the fall of the Soviet Union and the collapse of communism have severely undermined the left-wing model advanced by twentieth-century political scientists and historians. A recent review of the literature summarized the dialectic as less than determined or open to final interpretations.[12]

What has now begun to emerge is another interpretation of the context of the Battle of Dogger Bank. What we have come to understand about the First World War and its context is perhaps more about its tragic consequences than its actual chronology. Even the chronology bears more scrutiny, as this work shows. The truth is hard to find, particularly when it is buried in paper and enshrined in issue-based dialectical analysis of the last century. With an eye towards history, which he and his adherents have energetically embraced, Tirpitz provided a summary of the naval race in his work *Deutsche Ohnmachtspolitik im Weltkreig* [German Appeasement Policy in the World War]. His purpose was to document

Anhang 6

Schiffstabellen

Großkampflinienschiffe.

Jahr	England	Größe t	Deutschland	Größe t
1905	1. Dreadnought 10:30.5 cm	18190		
1906	2. Bellerophon	18900	1. Naffau 12:28 cm	18600
	3. Superb	"	2. Weftfalen	"
	4. Temeraire	"		
1907	5. St. Vincent	19560	3. Rheinland	"
	6. Collingwood	"	4. Pofen	"
	7. Vanguard	"		
1908	8. Neptune	20220	5. Helgoland 12:30.5 cm	22400
			6. Oftfriesland	"
			7. Thüringen	"
1909	9. Coloffus	20320	8. Oldenburg	"
	10. Hercules	"	9. Kaifer 10:30.5 cm	24310
	11. Orion 10:34.3 cm	22860	10. Friedrich der Große	"
	12. Conqueror	"		
	13. Monarch	"		
	14. Thunderer	"		
1910	15. King George V.	23370	11. Kaiferin	"
	16. Centurion	"	12. König Albert	"
	17. Ajax	"	13. Prinzregent Luitpold	"
	18. Audacious	"		
1911	19. Iron Duke	25400	14. König	25400
	20. Marlborought	"	15. Großer Kurfürft	"
	21. Benbow	"	16. Markgraf	"
	22. Emperor of India	"		
1912	23. Queen Elizabeth 8:38.1cm	27500	17. Kronprinz	"
	24. Warfpite	"		
	25. Valiant	"		
	26. Barham	"		
	27. Malaya	"		
1913	28. Refolution	29800	18. Bayern 8:38 cm	?
	29. Ramillies	"	19. Baden	?
	30. Revenge	"		

A.2. Appendix 6 to Grand Admiral von Tirpitz's *Deutsche Ohnmachtspolitik im Weltkreig* [German Appeasement Policy in the World War]. This is a comparative table of British and German capital ships in the Naval Race.

A.3. The bottom of the capital ship comparison table, this time enumerating the battle cruisers of both sides.

662   Anhang 6

Jahr	England	Größe t	Deutschland	Größe t
1913	31. Royal Sovereign	29 800		
	32. Royal Oak	„		
	33. Agincourt 14:30.5 cm	27 500	Beschlagnahmte fremde	
	34. Erin 10:34.3 cm	23 000	Schiffe	
	35. Canada 10:35.5 cm	28 000		

Schlachtkreuzer.

Jahr	England	Größe t	Deutschland	Größe t
1905	1. Indomitable 8:30.5 cm	17 250	(Scharnhorst)	
	2. Inflexible	„		
	3. Invincible	„		
1906			(Blücher) 12:21 cm	15 500
1907			1. von der Tann 8:28 cm	18 700
1908	4. Indefatigable	18 750	2. Moltke 10:28 cm	22 640
1909	5. Australia	„	3. Goeben	„
	6. New Zealand	„		
	7. Lion 8:34.3 cm	26 350		
	8. Princeß Royal	„		
1910	9. Queen Mary	27 000	4. Seydlitz	24 640
1911	10. Tiger	29 000	5. Derfflinger 8:30.5 cm	28 000
1912			6. Lützow	„
1913			7. Hindenburg 8:35 cm	?

Die während des Krieges in Dienst gestellten Großkampfschiffe.

Am Tage der Indienststellung besteht naturgemäß noch nicht Frontbereit=schaft; diese wird erst nach einer Übungszeit von mehreren Wochen bis Monaten erreicht.

Etat	England	In Dienst	Deutschland	In Dienst
1911	21. Benbow	Okt. 1914	14. Großer Kurfürst	Aug. 1914
	22. Emperor of India	Okt. 1914	15. König	Aug. 1914
			16. Markgraf	Okt. 1914
	10. Tiger	Okt. 1914	5. Derfflinger	Sept. 1914
—	23. Agincourt	Aug. 1914		
—	24. Erin	Aug. 1914		
—	25. Canada	Nov. 1914		
1912	26. Queen Elizabeth	Okt. 1914	17. Kronprinz	Nov. 1914

the comparative naval efforts in capital ship construction. This was to support the argument that Germany was not really the aggressor – British "brutal superiority" prevailed – and that the driver of the arms race was Britain not Germany.

What is obvious is the smaller number of German ships listed in each category by Tirpitz on a year-by-year basis and the lighter caliber of guns and the increase in displacement on both sides. The list provided of ships placed in service during the war ends with the program year of 1913 for both sides. The battleship and battle cruiser race ends, with the British ahead by a length. The battle cruiser "race" can be seen in figure A.3. Most interesting is the inclusion of the last German armored cruiser *Scharnhorst,* and the transition ship *Blücher.* What it does not do is provide a similar list for all the other powers and show where they were politically in relation to each other and to Britain. It is reproduced here as it is very useful in understanding the balance of power that led to the battle.[13]

This book posits the view of history that individuals, even if heavily influenced by their context, were very important in determining both the way the battle went and the events which were affected by the battle. Human beings were involved in making key decisions which determined the design, capabilities, and limitations of the ships that fought, the strategic context in which the battle was fought, the actual fighting itself, and, of course, the issue of war itself. The imposition of war on the ships and navies which fought Dogger Bank upset all sorts of compromises made in design, operations, naval planning, and strategy. As Field Marshal Helmuth von Moltke the elder once said, no plan ever survives contact with the enemy. Dogger Bank, like any battle, was determined by the merit of combatants' action and the impact of earlier decisions which turned out to be serious miscalculations, or more bluntly put – mistakes. The unappreciated risks and potential losses to British and German fleets of a greater engagement in the Jade estuary and its concomitant threat to German naval power in the Baltic can now be appreciated, if not absolutely understood. The risks imposed on both sides' admirals were not always obvious, even to the admirals.

Acknowledgments

AN AUTHOR'S RETURN TO GROUND COVERED AT THE OUTSET OF a career in many things other than history must have in that return the gifts of many scholars and institutions. Of the scholars, I would list Volger Berghahn, Keith Bird, Patrick Kelly, Rolf Hobson, Paul Kennedy, the late Dr. Gert Sandhofer, the late Antony Preston. Of the institutions, I would list the U.S. National Archives, the UK National Archives (late Public Record Office), the UK Ministry of Defense History Branch (Navy), the UK National Maritime Museum, the Federal German Military Archives, and the German Military History Office. Above all, I would like to acknowledge the late Professor Bryan Ranft, without whose inspiration and insight this historian would never have left the graving dock.

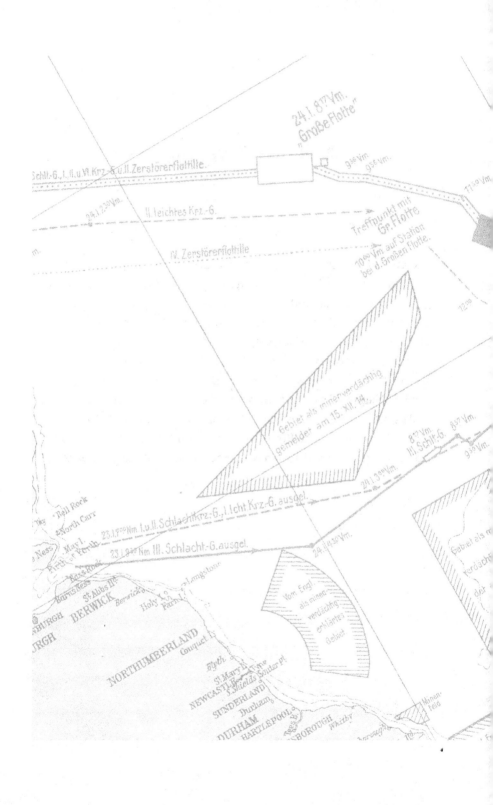

Battle of Dogger Bank

1

Decisions beyond the Battlefield

DOGGER BANK WAS FOUGHT AGAINST THE ADVICE OF THE MAN who commanded the German force. Rear Admiral Franz Hipper believed "the expected success is not worth the effort." It was intended only to sort out British intelligence sources among the numerous fishing trawlers of the Dogger Bank and to roll up any unsuspecting British light forces which might be scouting the North Sea.[1] It was fought in the twilight of the *Pax Britannica* at the end of nearly two hundred years of British supremacy at sea.[2] The antagonists were Imperial Britain and Imperial Germany. The latter was a continental power with aspirations to sea power which threatened the vital interests of Britain, at the time the preeminent sea power on the planet. Imperial Germany risked national aspirations of a secure place as a great power as well as commercial and military success in a bid for sea power at the rise of the Second German Empire.[3]

There are many explanations as to why this happened: it could have been an exercise in Social Darwinism[4] or nationalism[5] or imperialism.[6] Grand Admiral Alfred von Tirpitz was both the architect and the apologist for the fleet that Germany possessed in 1915; Grand Admiral Erich Raeder, chief of staff for the principal German flag officer conducting the battle, Admiral Franz von Hipper, was another apologist and staunch defender of the fleet Tirpitz built. Today there is another defender of their legacy afoot in the German naval establishment – *Kapitan zur See* Jorg Hillmann.[7] Vice Admiral Wolfgang Wegener, however, was the most significant German naval strategist in the twentieth century and he saw the Battle of Dogger Bank in very different terms than the Grand Admiral's. What Tirpitz did originally was to take Clausewitz to sea, which in fact could not be done. Raeder did the same thing with the same result. He was more successful in achieving geographic position with Hitler's Wehrmacht behind him – Brest was German for four years, as was the Norwegian coast and virtually all of the Baltic. This was not so in World War I. As Wolfgang Wegener noted, the High Seas Fleet always had two tasks – to control the sea in the Baltic to assure Swedish supplies of the German war effort and defend the north German coasts. If the Imperial Navy were to succeed in defeating a large portion of the British Grand Fleet by depriving it of "brutal superiority," the British would still have had superior geographic position. In Wegener's view, the Grand Fleet would be able to cut off German trade and access to the Atlantic. Admiral Reinhard Scheer agreed:

> If the enemy ever succeeded in securing the command of the Baltic, and landing Russian troops on the coast of Pomerania, our Eastern front must have collapsed altogether, and brought to naught our plan of campaign which consisted of a defensive attitude in the East and the rapid overthrow of the French Army. The command of the Baltic rested on the power of the German Fleet. If we had destroyed the Russian Fleet our danger from the Baltic would by no means have been eliminated, as a landing could have been carried out just as easily under the protection of English forces, if the German fleet no longer existed ... for such a purpose the English Fleet had no need to venture into the Baltic itself ... they could compel us to meet them in the North Sea, immediately they made an attack on our coast. In view of such an eventuality we must not weaken ourselves permanently as we could not help doing if we attempted to eliminate the danger which the Russian Fleet represented in the Baltic.[8]

Dogger Bank could have been a disaster for the Germans and a significant victory for the British. If Britain had managed to bring von Friedrich von Ingenohl's two squadrons (about 70 percent of the German fleet including Hipper) and Hipper to battle, there would have been only one modern squadron (about a third of the German fleet) left. That would have to be split between the Baltic and North Sea. Should the Germans have destroyed the major portion of the Grand Fleet with mines and torpedoes and survived in repairable condition due to robust construction, Germany's strategic position would have been preserved. England's strategic position would have been at risk. But a decisive battle required almost impossible risks. Naval power required two things: geographic position and a fleet. In 1914, the Germans vis-à-vis the British had a weak geographic position and only about two-thirds of the fleet they needed. The Battle of Dogger Bank took place in the first months of the war when both the High Seas Fleet and the Grand Fleet were growing stronger[9] as the pre-war programs of 1912 and 1913 were coming to fruition; the British had added a pair of dreadnoughts taken over from Turkey for what was to be a terrible price. The Russians were not able to deploy a fleet which threatened Germany because of their isolation and technological dependence for key elements of their new fleet on foreign sources. The Imperial Russian Navy suffered from greater constraints and bureaucratic lethargy than the Germans – the new dreadnought could not be moved without permission from the Czar himself and the rest of the navy was subordinate to a second echelon land forces commander.[10] The overarching reasons for the battle and the war are to some extent only now being appreciated. Wegener long ago appreciated the German military position, which without any fleet, if successful, would gain the navy both Brest and the French coast. This would erase the British position of total geographic superiority and threaten British sea-lanes as well as reopen the Atlantic to German shipping.[11]

In the battle, upwards of a thousand seamen died. One British battle cruiser, HMS *Lion*, was damaged as was the German flagship SMS *Seydlitz*. One German armored cruiser, SMS *Blücher*, was sunk. The battle occurred because the Germans believed a reconnaissance in force might reveal some critical information on the whereabouts and operations of the Grand Fleet; the British successfully intercepted and read German communications and laid a trap for the German force.[12]

STRATEGIC THINKING AND DOGGER BANK

If a general engagement had developed and had been decisive, what would the implications be? The real significance of the battle was its indecisiveness which guaranteed that, regardless of the outcome, the ground war would continue, unless the results spilled into the Baltic. Most would say that a naval engagement ill compares to the losses of any day in the trenches of the western front. Yet the context of the battle became the context of the war. The battle occurred in the context of the German General Staff's belief that war must be fought no later than by 1917, lest Germany be overwhelmed by a rearmed Russia and a revanchist France. The German navy itself was a lot less ready for war in 1914 than it would be in 1917. German naval victory early in the war might have had more of a political effect, as the re-deployments of British naval forces after the German bombardments of the coastal towns indicated. At a minimum, it would have given the politicians pause and perhaps time to avoid the great bloodletting which had begun on the western and eastern fronts. At most, the real cost of the war would have been brought home to publics and elites not inured to the cost of endless dreadnought construction.

That the calculus of the German General Staff was entirely based on ground forces is one of the statements of the obvious in the period. It did not involve the Imperial German Navy in any meaningful way. This was probably because at the time the Schlieffen Plan was created, and later even as it was amended, the German dreadnought battle squadrons and battle cruisers were still on drawing boards and Tirpitz was competing with the army to get the fleet through the Reichstag. The competition for resources among the German services and the concomitant lack of parity with the British in battle cruisers dictated the outcome of the battle as much as anything else. Tirpitz's fleet laws had headed toward 20 battle cruisers by 1920 allowing for replacements of older armored cruisers and the increase of the battle fleet to forty ships. In order to get there, the fleet had to successfully compete with the army to keep its guns. After Jutland, the Second Battle Squadron, composed of the surviving eight pre-dreadnoughts, was decommissioned and lost its guns to the army and coastal defense. Much earlier, in 1911, *Seydlitz* had lost her natural sister ship to Tirpitz's stillborn disarmament negotiations with the British. At the time of Dogger Bank, the Germans had *Lützow* and *Hindenburg* as well as *Ersatz Freya* (actually *Prinz Eitel Friedrich)* and *Mackensen* under construction. All were slowed by wartime shortages, especially of construction workers, called up to the front or active service in the navy. In peace, the Germans could have built three or even four dreadnoughts a year, although this was never actually Tirpitz's plan; and if half the production had been battle cruisers, Hipper would have had ten more by 1920. But that was not to be. *Mackensen*'s very powerful 35 cm guns went to the army as did those for all the rest of the capital ships under construction after *Bayern*. In peace, Hipper would have had three more ships and by 1916 perhaps as many as five more. Ultimately, had peace held, the High Seas Fleet itself at the four ship annual construction rate, was headed for forty battleships by 1925, which at that point would have brought it abreast of almost any foreseen British naval order of battle. That order of battle never materialized. Now is the time to wonder what another *Seydlitz* would have meant in this battle, and to understand the consequences of failure in arms control negotiations.

The wartime battle cruiser program of the British included two *Renown* class which were high-speed, lightly armored versions of the *R* class slow dreadnought design, with only six 15-inch guns. They were followed by three more lightly armored "tin cans" of the *Courageous* class. This last gasp of the Admiral Sir John Fisher philosophy of speed over safety fortunately never faced Hipper's ships in action. These five ships were not ready until after Jutland so play little part in the narrative about Dogger Bank. Nevertheless all five were available by the end of the war, whereas the last reinforcement Hipper got was the *Hindenburg*, which according to Tirpitz actually had 35 cm guns, not the 30.5 cm usually attributed to her.[13]

We now know that the British in 1914 were at a crossroads in naval strategy having settled on distant blockade and having become aware of the economy of force offered first by dreadnoughts and then by the submarine. This combination of technological evolution and economics would have posed a major challenge to Tirpitz and his creations. Tirpitz had all but ignored the U-boat until the last minute in favor of battleships. But a combination of Serbian ambitions and Austrian pride, as well as the interlocking secret treaties and alliances plunged the continent and the world into conflict ahead of Tirpitz's fleet laws and building schedule. Winston Churchill was distracted from the North Sea and his Baltic schemes by what would become the disaster of the Dardanelles. Thus, major strategic change was stillborn on one side and the distant blockade made the twenty battle cruisers of the last German Navy Law (Novelle) a pipedream. Cost might also have made them prohibitive, but this presumes a stagnant economy and frozen tax base through the first half of the 1920s. What mattered for the battle was that the issue was clearly about a shortage of money by 1913/14.

Even so, Dogger Bank was important. The relation of the land war to the perceived stalemate at sea was just being recognized, and the U-boat loomed large as the best way the Imperial German Navy could affect the outcome of the war, and U-boat construction accelerated after Dogger Bank.[14] This was the principal conclusion of the German High Seas Fleet command's assessment of the state of the war after Dogger Bank. The Germans did not understand the consequences of doing nothing with the fleet. The British understood that the Germans must be convinced that decisive naval action was unlikely and suicidal. This understanding was also behind the engagement; even if the British did not recognize this aspect of the action's origins at the time, it can be taken as implied in their setup of the action.

To achieve an understanding of the motives and policy formulation which underlies the battle, it is relevant to look at the influence of Alfred Thayer Mahan, the doyen of naval history, who wrote his books because he was concerned that mainstream historians did not understand and did not effectively chronicle the role that sea power played. It was as Sir Herbert Richmond put it: "Mahan . . . explained that the definite object he had in mind was an examination of the general history of Europe and America with particular reference to the effect of sea power on its course."[15] Richmond's thoughts are helpful in understanding the origins, issues, and ultimate meaning of Dogger Bank. He distills Mahan as asserting that control of the sea "had exercised an influence, not merely in deciding some particular issue but in giving a definite direction to the whole course of events . . . he aimed at making an estimate of the effect of sea power and the course of history and a chimera of naval social Darwinism."[16] There is absolutely no question of Mahan's influence of the *Kaiser*, Tirpitz,[17] and the higher echelons of the German navy. As Andrew Lambert said: "Historians must look below the surface of contemporary debates over naval policy. This does not mean adopting intuitive reasoning or a counterfactual approach to history. Rather it is necessary to examine a full spectrum of sources, rather than just so-called policy documents and to understand the range of options open to decision makers before . . . attempting to analyze . . . intentions. This approach to naval and strategic history will reveal a more complex yet more fascinating picture of strategic policy-making during this period."[18]

DECISIONS AFFECTING DOGGER BANK

There were deliberate decisions on and off the battlefield that shaped the outcome of Dogger Bank.

Off the battlefield, these can be broken down into several decisions: the politico-military decisions to allocate resources to fleets; the decisions to support certain industries and technologies which equipped those fleets; and, the decisions regarding the training and equipping of navies of which the units at Dogger Bank were especial representatives. Lastly, there were decisions made at higher military and naval echelons other than the fleets which directly impacted the course and outcome of the battle, but it was never this organized, deliberate, or even rational. It only appears so with the clarity of 20/20 hindsight. Politico-military decisions made with regard to fleet resource allocation were basically three on both sides: the decision to have navies as instruments of national power; the decision to allocate resources for navies within those allocated to war as a pursuit of policy; and the decisions to build certain types of ships to challenge or counter those of the opposing powers. After Dogger Bank, Tirpitz believed that a fleet action that would fatally weaken the British navy was the route to success, but by then Tirpitz had lost power. Although even partial results were better than leaving the fleet at anchor, the Germans ultimately decided that submarine warfare was the way to obtain results the fleet could not.

As Halpern puts it: "It is against this background of dissatisfaction within the German Navy and the search for a viable naval strategy that the Germans seem almost to have stumbled into the submarine war against commerce."[19] The German U-boat's principal mission was to function as a scout and operate in support of the battle fleet until the first U-boat campaign in 1915, which commenced shortly after Dogger Bank. In 1915, the Germans did not have sufficient numbers of long-range submarines to blockade the British Isles effectively. There were about twenty-five deployable U-boats, with another thirty or so useful in coastal roles, training, or in the yards. About twenty-four were under construction.[20]

Before Dogger Bank, Vice Admiral Reinhard Scheer twice opined positively on submarine warfare. On 20 November and 7 December 1914, Scheer submitted private memoranda favoring submarine warfare. He did so, however, with the idea of submarines forcing the British Grand Fleet to give battle on German terms – inflicting so much pain that the Royal Navy would have to resort to close blockade.[21] This supported German tactics of using U-boats to sink British battleships.

With regard to decisions to support certain industries and technologies, there are also three areas of importance. The first was the decision to invest in large armor plate and steel manufacture. The second was the decision to invest in heavy gun manufacture. The third was the decision to develop communications and control devices which allowed these ships to function together. Other decisions also influenced the outcome of the battle. They included the training and equipping of both navies, the selection and training of officers, the organization of navies and fleets, and the training and logistical support of navies and fleets, including development of technical intelligence arms. There also were the decisions of those in higher echelons, ashore and afloat, which affected the combatants: the crafting of the missions of the combatants within national military strategies; the deployment of the units involved including the setting of the Dogger Bank interception and ambush by the British; and, the selection and grooming of the commanders and key participants.

The Germans responsible for U-boat construction in Tirpitz's Reischmarineamt (RMA) believed that World War I at sea would be a short war, like everybody else in authority, on all sides, and therefore they aimed construction to support peacetime plans and peacetime needs, which were to construct and support the battle fleet. Submarines would have lower priority unless in the context of competition with the Royal Navy.

KEY BATTLEFIELD DECISIONS

During the battle itself, the key decisions were the German deployment of a reconnaissance in force to snap up smaller British units in the North Sea and the British the counter deployment in force to crush it. Sequentially there were: the pursuit of the German main body by British light forces until it was time to turn around; the British decision not to pursue German heavy units by the British naval second in command; the German commander's decision to leave *Blücher* to her fate. Then there were subsequent decisions after the battle, including the relief of the German fleet C-in-C, Admiral Friedrich von Ingenhohl, the continuance of the strategy of distant blockade and fleet deterrence, and the conduct of the first U-boat campaign as an end run to strategic stalemate. There were of course the technical lessons on both sides; long-term lessons including the intended and unintended consequences of the battle and finally the interpretation of the battle by historians from both sides.

Parenthetically, history as practiced in the twenty-first century benefits from both archival science and technical knowledge, which, in retrospect, almost always allows a fair degree of hindsight, so accuracy is possible to some degree on some issues; but regarding the human element it remains an art, neither definitive[22] nor absolute. Oddly, knowledge which could have been presumed of an interested readership a generation ago cannot be assumed today: today's readership is not certain what a battleship is much less the difference between it and a battle cruiser. The process by which these ships came to be and by which they were sailed and fought remains the province of specialists. The reasons for which the dreadnought battleship and battle cruiser were built and therefore their prospects in battle are now arcane. Nevertheless, research and analysis have given the writer and reader new tools and a greater understanding than perhaps even the creators of these behemoths commanded. So, there is a great deal of merit in knowledge of the context of the 1915 Battle of Dogger Bank.

There is something else about the assumptions that Mahan made, and the lessons of the First and Second World Wars, and even of the Cold War, about the concept that maritime power is now no longer relevant to conflict. To summarize, it was (and is in many quarters today) thought that all future wars would be fought over a very short time, thus eliminating the principal effects of slow-acting sea power.[23] Other reasons the potential obsolescence of Mahanian sea power included the introduction of new instruments of war above and under the water. These deprived traditional sea power of its ability to control the sea from the surface alone as it had from the beginning of warfare; in addition, there have been land and air communications developments which make sea control irrelevant. Neutral actions could negate the effects of belligerent sea power.[24]

All of these may be true, but it is the first which is most relevant to what happened at Dogger Bank. German grand strategy as orchestrated and stated by Chancellor Theobald von Bethmann Hollweg considered: "It will be a violent storm but very short; I count on a war of three or four months and I have organized my policy on that assumption."[25]And yet the purpose of the policy for which Germany built a fleet, the tip of which fought its British equivalent at Dogger Bank, was "to render Germany secure by making others insecure . . . it made others insecure and therefore stimulated growth, caused alliances and made its contribution in this way to war."[26] A policy which makes others insecure also drives the growth of navies and ships. There is no question that all who mattered, down to the battle cruiser commanders on both sides, thought it would be a short violent war, over by Christmas. Navies would have a short time to justify their existence.

Richmond concludes that what dictates the size of a ship is the object of its existence. If you do not define the ship consistently with the objective in mind, then it makes no sense. He put it this way: "The questions therefore, what dictates the size of a navy? And what dictates the size of the ship is essentially practical: for if there is one unpractical thing to do it is to proceed upon any undertaking without having clearly defined one's objective. Having defined the end, the means of attaining it become more clearly indicated."[27] The time in which it took to render Germany or Britain secure did not matter. It was to be whatever it would take. As to the ships which made up the battle, their size and capabilities became the subject of political self-justifications on both sides of the Channel with Tirpitz and Churchill making their retrospective cases for their policies. Churchill's and Fisher's special pleadings focused on armor and speed as armor – this only works if the other guy cooperates and decides on weaker and slower ships. In hindsight, this was a very bad and deadly British Fisher/Churchill decision. If on the other hand there were still more British battle cruisers than German after catastrophic losses, it represented a reasonable risk, even if it was potentially and ultimately expensive in human life.

On the other side of the North Sea, Tirpitz's Reichsmarineamt made decisions on the range of German naval guns based on the principle of limited North Sea visibility – German heavy guns were calibrated to 18,900 meters and a relatively low twenty degree maximum elevation.[28] This was later increased. Krupp actually built its guns for a twenty-five degree maximum elevation, but this was limited by the navy's orders for turret builds which were not always in Krupp's hands.[29] The decision to build for lower elevation and lesser ranges was RMA driven, no doubt by Tirpitz's short range North Sea myopia. Considering Scheer was secretary to Admiral Tirpitz in 1906 when the decisions were made on German dreadnought specifications, the latter's unwillingness to criticize German ship construction designs or decisions become patently obvious.[30] Scheer had been involved in all the key decisions on dreadnought construction. As a Senior Commander, or *Fregattenkapitan*, Scheer had been head of the Zentralabteilung, along with then Captains Harald Dahnhardtand Admiral Eduard von Capelle, and in the summer of 1905 decided the *Nassau* and *Westfalen* were to be propelled by reciprocating engines with 28 cm [11-inch] guns and a speed of 18.75 knots at 18,000 tons. The 1906 cruiser, *Blücher*, was to be about 15,000 tons and armed with 12–21 cm [8.2-inch] guns.[31] Scheer was a key member of Tirptiz's staff in the RMA, as opposed to the Admiralty Staff which had relatively little influence on the navy until the war began. In 1906, Scheer reported to Admiral Capelle, who was director of the Administrative Department of the RMA. Scheer also "wanted to increase the size of the large cruisers only if the British did so first. To do otherwise would leave a bad impression of Germany at the upcoming Hague conference. He believed that German restraint would expose the falsely 'humanitarian' British purpose in supporting the conference, and leave the RMA open to criticism of 'appeasement' in the Reichstag. He felt that Britain's real reasons were more about the economy than propaganda."[32] Scheer was indeed a player in the game of battleship chess. The ultimate objective was a fleet of forty battleships, comprised of three active squadrons and two reserve and twenty large cruisers, the equivalent of four or five First Scouting Groups.[33]

The British did not increase the size of their battle cruisers until the *Lion* class of 1911, although Lord Fisher was extremely sanguine about his repeat *Invincibles:* "By the way, I've got Sir Philip Watts into a new *Indomitable* that will make your mouth water when you see it! (and the Germans gnash their teeth!)."[34] Indeed, it was Tirpitz over Fisher in this one: the ship at issue, HMS *Indefatigable,* was sunk by SMS *Von der Tann,* Tirpitz's first battle cruiser, at Jutland in 1916. And yet if we accept the strategic thinking of Fisher, there really needed to be two fleets for the UK. To defend Britain's imperial interests, he developed the battle cruiser: a conceptually new type of warship designed to engage enemy warships at relatively long-range before coming under effective fire itself, capable of either forming line of battle or being deployed independently on trade protection missions. Also, he formulated the concept of "flotilla defense," a "sea denial" strategy that depended upon torpedoboats and submarines whose capability to inflict heavy losses on troop transports and their escorts would deter or prevent invasion. The traditional dreadnought based battle fleet would have no part in this strategy.[35]

The reality is that there were by 1915 all these dreadnoughts on both sides and both sides were full of admirals who wanted to do *something.* If one looks at what actually happened in the first few months of the war, albeit not perfectly, Fisher's battle cruisers were deployed overseas in precisely such a way as he intended. The use of the battle cruisers overseas fits precisely this strategy, and it can be argued the lack of sufficient destroyers and smaller ships allowed the Germans to get away with their East Coast raids. In the teeth of opposition from the Admiralty, Churchill suggested a temporary close blockade of German ports with destroyers and submarines. They rightly dismissed the idea of "any close blockade of Germany with surface ships as lunacy."[36] It is interesting to note that there was little battle cruiser construction during World War I: the *Repulse* and *Renown* were regarded as light battle cruisers more fitted to global foreign stations and the three large light cruisers of the *Coura-geous* class were totally unsuited to operations in any line of battle and designed for a special purpose. The *Hood* and her three stillborn sisters were the real replacements for British battle cruiser losses and they received little attention in wartime in the face of the submarine menace.[37]

While all this was going on, Churchill was busily setting up to build large numbers of submarines as a cost saving measure and substitute for battleships – he could get 14 submarines for the price of one battleship.[38] He was not above stacking the archives, just like Tirpitz, for posterity: "None of the official dockets relating to the battleship substitution policy ... have survived in the Admiralty archives. . . . Evidently all the documents relating to these proposals and plans were placed in a file that was kept by Churchill's personal private secretary." Had war not occurred until 1917, Hipper would have found himself facing long-range submersible armored torpedoboats envisioned by Churchill and designed to attack a battle fleet within close range, capable of surviving even the heavy 15 cm [5.9-inch] secondary batteries of German dreadnoughts.[39] In fact, had the war not occurred until January 1915, Churchill's battleship substitution policy would have been enshrined as Admiralty doctrine and policy and construction would have followed.[40]

Of course there would have been an "Admiral's rebellion," unless swift victories were forthcoming from the new generation of materiel. Indeed, the stillborn Canadian dreadnoughts were to be replaced by Canadian built submarines as an end run against the inevitable opposition to such a radical change in naval policy.[41] Moreover, to pull off the change in policy, Churchill proposed a repeat of the deception surrounding *Dreadnought* and thus suckering the Germans into continuing their 1914 dreadnought plans as planned and being caught in the British changeover to submarines. This policy change could have thoroughly hobbled German plans for global equality with the British, much less dominion. And it could have been done without stressing the British budget – in fact relieving it. A squadron of eight battleships would have yielded 112 submarines with about the same level of manning or less. Game, set, and match to Churchill. But it was not to be, at least not the way Churchill envisioned it. Moreover, he had the Admiralty professionals on board in favor of the submarines![42]

GERMAN SUBMARINES AND THE FLEET THAT
FOUGHT AT DOGGER BANK AND JUTLAND

It should come as no surprise that the Germans, too, were looking for a way around this conundrum of battleship expense and effectiveness. The Germans reexamined their strategy after Dogger Bank and sought to find a way around the functional immunity that the British enjoyed by playing a game of distant blockade and shutting up the Germans in the North Sea.

Returning to Scheer and his role in creating the High Seas Fleet, he served with a number of others in the R M A, including Adolph von Trotha who later became chief of staff to Scheer in the High Seas Fleet, then Chief of the Admiralty under the early Republic, and lastly a national socialist. Trotha's role in the navy was key as he understood the nature of compromises Tirpitz had to make with both the Reichstag and the Kaiser to get as much as he could for the navy.[43] This is important as, before and after Dogger Bank, the officers commanding the fleet were wielding an imperfect but important instrument, the nature of which made it almost impossible to accomplish much in the Mahanian tradition. Scheer was to face these difficulties squarely when he assumed command of the High Seas Fleet. In 1911, Scheer was still in the R M A, working on Tirpitz's ultimate fleet law. After the Agadir crisis, Tirpitz decided he wanted a new navy law built around big cruisers, with larger guns in 1912.[44]

By November 1911, Tirpitz's ideas had crystallized and a draft law had emerged, still focused on cruisers but aimed at a final fleet strength of forty dreadnought battleships and twenty battle cruisers. The rationale for the new Novelle was replacing old cruisers and increased readiness. But 1912 was a bad year for the German defense budget – the Germans had an army to recapitalize and the navy now absorbed 33 percent of the budget. But, it turned out two brothers, August von Heeringen and Josias von Heeringen, headed up the Admiralstab and Prussian War Ministry respectively and refused to argue the point, with the army agreeing "to make the Army's request small enough not to jeopardize the Navy's request."[45] In the end, the Haldane Mission[46] could not upend the altar of Tirpitz's adherence to the concept of the navy law and keep their supremacy at sea. Beyond this obstacle, there remained the political rationale

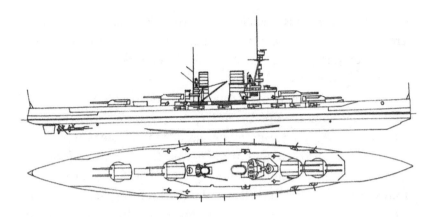

1.1. SMS *Mackensen* – This class of ships would have been the German fast battleships built after *Hindenburg*. They would have replaced *Blücher, Scharnhorst, Gneisenau, Friedrich Karl, York* and older cruisers, and *Lützow*. Reproduced from Friedrich Forstmeier and Siegfried Breyer, *Deutsche Grosskampfschiffe 1915–1918.*

which justified the German navy in the first place – national security and removal of a British threat to German naval establishment.[47] In the end, the German navy was only justifiable as a fleet against England,[48] which by 1917 would include eight battle cruisers. Whatever other fleet types, tactics, approaches, or weapons might offer prospects for victory over the British, Tirpitz would oppose to the end in the name of the sanctity of the law. New strategic thinking of any kind was anathema.[49] Scheer was not exactly a partisan of the truth in his allocation of responsibility for the failure of the Imperial Navy – he was a Tirpitz adherent. This even went as far as his *Memoirs*. Although Scheer believed Tirpitz did not fight the *Reich* Chancellor Bethmann Hollweg and his cabal as fiercely as he should have, Scheer told Admiral von Trotha that "he would follow the Tirpitz line in his own *Memoirs*."[50] As noted in the discussion above (p. 15), under the 1912 Novelle, the wartime Scouting Forces would receive only the *Lützow* and *Hindenburg; Mackensen* and *Ersatz Freya/ Graf Spee* were never completed. Parenthetically, Tirpitz says the *Hindenburg* had 34 cm guns. If she did, she was a tremendous asset and it is fortunate Admiral Sir David Beatty's ships did not have to engage her. As far as the rest of the program, the Germans were consistently out-built and out-gunned, because their follow-on *Mackensen* class and *Yorck* class were never delivered. These latter would have had everything the front desired, but wartime priorities, basically the demands of the army and U-boat war, intervened.

The British counters to German naval construction through the war years included the five *Queen Elizabeth* class fast battleships, the battle cruisers *Tiger, Renown,* and *Repulse* and the five ships of the *Royal Sovereign* class, all armed with 15-inch guns. The *Queen Elizabeth* class represented the finest combination of speed, heavy armor, and firepower of any ships in the British order of battle. There were no German equivalents. Fortunately for Hipper, they were not with Beatty at Dogger Bank.

UNDERSTANDING THE BATTLE OF DOGGER BANK TODAY

Understanding this battle needs to be accomplished in terms of both trends and people. These represent the biographical and the ideological schools of history: the people who were involved in the battle as well as the bigger historical trends. In his exegesis on the Great War, Churchill explained: "War between equals in power . . . should be a succession of climaxes on which everything is stacked, towards which everything tends and from which permanent decisions are obtained. . . . A battle means the whole of the resources of either side that can be brought to bear are, during the course of a single episode concentrated upon the enemy."[51] Here Churchill is talking about ground forces engagements which lasted months and whose casualties were hundreds of thousands. Naval battles were analogous but on much smaller scale in terms of resources; Dogger Bank only directly involved the heavy scouting forces of both sides directly, but ultimately both main fleets were involved even though they did not come to grips. And in his assessment of the circumstances of Jutland, the next big naval battle, Churchill observed that a decisive naval battle involved a "far greater stake . . . to Britain than Germany." What was important about Dogger Bank was as much the time at which it was fought as the actual numbers. The great popular historian Barbara Tuchman painted the year of 1907 when *Blücher* was laid down[52] as possessed of three characteristics – "a bursting economy, a burst of creative vigor in the arts, and the sound of a steady drumming like a noise in dreams." For many who did not hear it there were many who did, not all with dread. In the German navy, it was the custom of officers to drink to "the day."[53] *Der Tag,* of course, referred to the day when the Germans would meet the British navy in battle and supplant them as the rising power of the epoch. On the day of the surrender of the High Seas Fleet, the British fleet presented a broadsheet to every captain and flag officer of the victorious fleets; it depicted the order of surrender, ship by ship, as the Germans sailed to their doom at Scapa Flow.

A quick glance at a key Admiralty document, as well as the subsequent analysis of Arthur J. Marder and Patrick Kelly, underlines this terrible combination of determinism, *sangfroid,* and hubris which gave us the war and the battle. In a letter to British Foreign Minister Sir Edward Grey, dated Berlin 30 July 1908, British Captain Philip Dumas, who was the Naval Attaché in the British Embassy in Berlin, assessed German intentions as less than favorable to England. He discussed three aspects, including the aristocracy, the military and "[t]he learned and professional classes [which] are on the other hand so far as I can learn, rather anxious for a forward policy, although I also thoroughly believe that that they realize, that it must in the long run lead to a collision with England, and as they exercise a very considerable power in the political world, they are I suppose the most dangerous enemies to England within the Empire."[54] The other two classes were, in his view little less sanguine about an "inevitable" conflict. This letter was written after the Hague Conference of 1907, and in the midst of the Naval Crisis of 1908 in England, which resulted in the doubling of the annual program of dreadnoughts to be built in response to an alleged secret German dreadnought crash building program which would have brought about near parity in that type of ship by 1912. Arthur J. Marder's magisterial work, *From the Dreadnought to Scapa Flow,* Volume 1: *1904–1914: The Road to War,* deals with the crisis in detail and concludes in chapter seven: "The Navy Scare of 1909" that the British perceived [without much justification as we now know the fiscal realities would not have allowed it] that the Germans were going to out-produce the British shipbuilding program and pull even of what was an extraordinary UK effort.[55] Their analysis was presented in public, in Parliament, and in the end the British procured eight instead of four dreadnoughts in response to a pre-emptive estimation of

German capabilities. The Germans were believed to be capable of building and in fact were building twice as many ships as they would admit to doing. The British evidence came from the Krupp facilities and shipyard expansions not ships actually under construction.[56] It also came from an overestimation of Tirpitz's capabilities, though not his intentions, and ultimately from a lack of appreciation of interest group politics in the Kaiser's Germany.[57] Perhaps an old comrade in arms, Admiral von Usedom, who had been with then Captain John Jellicoe during the Boxer Rebellion in China, could have raised doubts in the latter's mind about German capabilities to say nothing of Tirpitz's intentions. Von Usedom was in charge of the Baltic Naval Station and wrote Jellicoe from Kiel in February 1909:

> You are quite right in wondering that I did not answer your two cards with the Christmas wishes. I don't know if you have seen Captain Widenmann [the German Naval Attaché] since his return from Berlin and have told you the real cause of my not answering. It was my intention of not sending a card in return to yours but to write you a sensible letter. I have tried to several times but found it so very difficult as being not able to express myself in a foreign language about matters of such a complicated nature as the misunderstanding between our two nations that I found myself obliged to give it up.... In a similar sense I wrote four weeks ago to Admiral Seymour who asked me my opinion about the big modern ships. I tried then to give my opinion about the so-called race of our nations in building such ships, which I always said quite absurd [von Usedom meant the naval race not the ships], because we are wanting the money, and that therefore there is no possibility for us and never will be of our attacking you or trying an invasion of England.... But we don't want to be a *quantité negligible* and are therefore building as fleet as large as we can pay for. That Germany is not able to build a fleet like yours or one of much more than a third part of yours cannot be doubted, as we are obliged by our open frontier on all sides to have an army ready of more than two millions of soldiers.[58]

Actually, the issue turned out to be more one of parsimony on the part of Tirpitz in dealing with the triple headed German dragon of industrial greed, class warfare, and conservative designers at the RMA. In deciding to build the *Dreadnought*, the British calculated that the increase in cost from the previous pre-dreadnought class was £181,000 (*King Edward VII* class) or actually £142,800 less than the *Lord Nelson* semi-dreadnoughts.[59] But then the Agadir incident arose and the fleets never met again until after the war broke out.[60] The same was true for the Germans, but this was only true for the first classes of that kind of ship. Prices tended to rise dramatically as did the size and weaponry of subsequent classes of dreadnought. As Rafael Scheck points out, Tirpitz's shipbuilding program came to represent not a solution to German domestic conflicts, but a serious threat to the established order because it threatened to raise taxes on the agrarian landowners and on the workers as well, probably generating social unrest. The German government heard the no new taxes objections loud and clear from the aristocracy and did not wish to impose taxes on the workers because of the depressing effect this would have on spending ability and upward pressure this would have on wages and ultimately shipbuilding costs.[61] But in the end no naval reduction could be agreed to because the British would not sign a political agreement which was meaningful to Germany – that is, ensure British neutrality "come what might" in a war between Russia and France.[62] Tirpitz's ultimate intention was to effectively check the British and satisfy German political ambitions, but in addition to the taxes on workers and agrarians, Tirpitz by 1911 faced one immutable counterweight: the army. Germany could not afford the best fleet in the world *and* a two million man, two-front army.

The British had the resources of an empire at their disposal, including the Dominions of Canada, Australia, and New Zealand. Each promised to provide help for the mother country, most of it in the battle cruiser category: Australia promised a battle cruiser, manned by Australians; Canada promised three dreadnoughts, paid for but manned by the Royal Navy; and New Zealand another battle cruiser. Over and above that there was the *Queen Elizabeth* class fast battleship *Malaya*. Tirpitz had no such resources or dominions at his disposal to build what could have amounted to the equivalent of another entire First Scouting Group. As *Blücher* and *Von der Tann* were taking the water and the ways respectively,[63] negotiations were under way with the Dominions on reinforcements to British capital ship strength. At that time the battleship, particularly the dreadnought type, was considered the ultimate measure of national power.[64] Tirpitz understood this was going on, and handled it as yet another little obstacle to his vision.[65] But it was not as simple as it would appear. Australia, Canada, and New Zealand, although members of the British Commonwealth and Dominions, were functionally independent countries and as there was a need for capital ships for the Empire, the issue of a common imperial foreign policy in whose service they would be used inevitably arose. This policy would ultimately decide the number, type, and shape of Commonwealth capital ships. Needless to say, whatever differences there were, the end result would not benefit Tirpitz. To give some perspective, the actual support for the Royal Navy provided by the Dominions including New Zealand, Australia, Canada, and the Federated Malay States, included: *New Zealand* at £1,795,166; *Australia* at £1,705,000 and other light cruisers, submarines, destroyers etc. at £4,372,266; and the Federated Malay States for HMS *Malaya* at £2,647,000.[66] The Admiralty actually initiated Dominion involvement in the Empire's naval strength, under the aegis of Churchill, because of the "increased interest in the Royal Navy by countries of the British navy and abandonment of the two power standard."[67] Due to fiscal limitations even on the British, the calculation of 60 percent superiority over the German fleet, advanced by Sir John Jellicoe, while Royal Navy Comptroller, was the de facto standard.

The story of the additional battle cruisers and *Malaya* merits recounting if only to provide the reader with a better understanding of just how steep the odds were against Tirpitz's underlying intention of overturning British naval superiority. In fact, in 1908 there was no Royal Australian Navy, Royal Canadian Navy, or Royal New Zealand Navy. What there would emerge was an Australian naval force which could be deployed to support British naval requirements in wartime with the permission of the Government of the Commonwealth of Australia.[68] The same applied to Canada and New Zealand. What those forces would comprise, who would man, command, and pay for them were issues at their infancy. Churchill was pushing things to get them to either build or fund capital ships. But two of the battle cruisers, *Australia* and *New Zealand*, ended up under Admiral Beatty's flag, and one, *New Zealand* was at Dogger Bank. The Norwegian scholar Rolf Hobson provides a perspective of the context of a World War I sea battle in a view of history from 1840 to the present. He analyzes the evolution of international rivalry, the unwinding of naval strategic thought from 1865–1895, the origins and objectives of Grand Admiral Alfred von Tirpitz's plans from

1895 to 1914, and the intellectual history of those issues up through the beginning of this century.[69] Even more direct to the issue is the update of Hobson on Tirpitz which Kelly provides. The tragedy was that there were in the British domestic policy of the day the same seeds of inevitable clash of interests as there were in Germany. Neither side could have anticipated the cost.

As Sir David Beatty put it when war came: "The longed talked of and much dreaded has happened and now we are to be put to the test after all. I can hardly realize that it is so and it seems as it were only a dream that I ever heard of such a thing. It is a cruel war because there has never been any reason for it we have been forced in entirely through the rapacity and thirst for power and a large portion of the world by Germany. Never in the history of the world has there been so little reason or so little cause."

Lest the reader think Beatty was ambiguous about the weight of command or his ability to shoulder it: "We are making history now, so courage Sweetheart and it shall be a page that will not be behind those of the glorious past. All will be well in the end."[70]

Six months after Dogger Bank, Beatty wrote to his wife and observed that the long drudgery of war and paperwork was worse than combat itself: "I think we are all getting rather hipped [expression of the time meaning exhausted] and I am sending the Secretary for a few days to have a night in bed and a rest. 8 months on the same spot, the same faces, and the same atmospheres is trying to anybody and we are beginning to dislike each other."[71] Beatty had no direct role in procuring or building his ships, but his role as their commander was clearly decisive in their development as a force. As for the others, there were the previously examined aboveboard contacts among the British and German, as well as other allied officers who were involved in the Boxer Rebellion and the relief of Peking at the turn of the century, but these became more and more difficult as the political situation deteriorated. In addition, Beatty and Hipper did not meet in China as the latter was in home service at the time, but there were contacts between Jellicoe, Beatty's boss, and Usedom and, perhaps even more interestingly, Tirpitz himself prior to the war. There was to have been a meeting between the German High Seas Fleet and the British Atlantic Fleet during the latter's cruise to Norway in 1911, but the meeting was canceled because of the Agadir crisis. Other visits, notably the visit to the Kiel Yacht Club races were affected, but did come off, as did the visit by the Second Battle Squadron under Admiral Warrender during Kiel week in 1914, just before the war.

Jellicoe is important to the story, however, as he was Controller of the Navy and Third Sea Lord during a critical part of the Anglo-German naval arms race. He made decisions which directly affected the size and strength of the British battle cruisers, including all those which fought at Dogger Bank.[72]

2

Building the Battle Cruisers

GERMANY AND BRITAIN BUILT A WHOLE SERIES OF WHAT WERE very fast dreadnoughts designed to scout enemy battle fleets and obtain advantage for their main bodies with speed and firepower. They were designed to take risks and escape while inflicting major punishment on adversaries. Both sides saw the battle cruiser as an evolution of the cruiser as fleet scout, as Beatty put it: "it is now accepted that there are two principal duties for the battle cruisers to perform that is (a) Supporting cruisers, (b) Acting as a fast division of a battle fleet."[1] Hipper for his part clearly understood and practiced these two when operating with the fleet; however, he had another mission, which was to operate independently as a lure for British forces which might be overwhelmed and thus allow defeat in detail for the British fleet. This latter was a function of the High Seas Fleet's geographic position and strategic inferiority. Ultimately, the loss of either side's battle cruisers would have been serious but not decisive. Only the loss of the dreadnought battleships, which were the ultimate measure of maritime power, would have been decisive. The British initiated the battle cruiser type and thus draw pride of place in this analysis. After that it is the German response, except for the *Blücher,* which is a case in its own right.

THE BRITISH

There has been a great deal of ink spilled about the battle cruiser in World War I as the brainchild of the erratic visionary Admiral Jackie Fisher of the Royal Navy.

When the revolutionary battleship HMS *Dreadnought* was conceived, the Royal Navy decided that it would require a cruiser complement, thus the battle cruiser emerged. The principal designers and
builders of the British battle cruiser fleet included a number of naval
constructors, architects as well as several shipyards. There were three
and a half classes of British battle cruiser at the time of Dogger Bank
and all classes were represented. There were the *Invincible* and *Indefatigable* classes, which were too slow to keep up with the *Lion* class and the
Tiger. Of the full war program, only two other battle cruisers, *Repulse*
and *Renown* would join after Dogger Bank and before the war ended. In
addition, three hybrid super-light cruisers of the *Courageous* class would
also be commissioned.

There is no doubt that the revolutionary *Queen Elizabeth* class were
considered part of Beatty's forces, but they were not battle cruisers per-
se, and were not present at Dogger Bank as they were either deployed
elsewhere or just coming into service. The *Queen Elizabeth* class is important to the story of the battle cruiser or fast battleship type which is
an integral part of any analysis of Dogger Bank. They were unique, as
afterwards the British reverted to the slower heavily armored *R* class and
the lightly armored *Renown* and *Courageous* classes.

The key British personality in the drama of the Anglo-German naval
arms race, of which Dogger Bank was the first battle, was Admiral Sir
John Fisher.[2] Fisher was brought into the Royal Navy as the cadet of
the last of Admiral Horatio Nelson's captains, and as Fisher put it "curi-
ously my first ship of war was the *Victory*, Nelson's flagship. She had her
sails bent in those days and was kept ready for sea with a regular crew."[3]
Fisher ultimately was responsible in large part for the navy and the battle
cruisers which fought at Dogger Bank, including both their capabilities
and limitations. By the time John Fisher became First Sea Lord of the
Admiralty, he had decided what was right, what was wrong, and what
needed improvement and had a course in mind as to how to bring the
Royal Navy into the twentieth century. Like Tirpitz, he was a gunnery
and torpedo man, both were pioneers in torpedo tactics and materiel.
The principal difference between the two is the former was a reformer
and the latter was a pioneer. Fisher also collected a brain-trust along the

way to help him achieve his goals, although Sir David Beatty, the British battle cruiser commander at Dogger Bank was not one of those; Sir John Jellicoe, the Grand Fleet commander at the time of Dogger Bank, definitely was one of Fisher's protégés.

Jellicoe had many key assignments in his career including that of Third Sea Lord or Controller, which meant he played a critical part in constructing the ships Beatty led at Dogger Bank. In Jellicoe's autobiographical notes, he observed that from the British perspective the key variable in the construction of new ships was the fabrication of guns, turrets, and mountings.[4] Moreover, Jellicoe also observed that in order to provide ships which were either equal to or better than German competitors, the British Admiralty reverse engineered known costs from the amount spent on the German ships. Interestingly enough, this proves Tirpitz's contention that the British knew more about the German shipbuilding effort than they admitted.

When Jellicoe and the rest of the Fisher brain-trust were designing the *Dreadnought* in 1904, they concluded going to all big gun ships clearly enhanced accurate fire control, because it eliminated the confusion of fall of shot from different caliber. More important to Dogger Bank, was Jellicoe's later decision and that of the Admiralty in 1911 to design ships of a larger size. This British design philosophy was adopted because once the German dreadnoughts (battleships and battle cruisers) started to appear, it was obvious the Germans equaled or exceeded British ships' displacement of the same date, and the Germans could look at what the British had and then counter it for their side. The British did not know how politically difficult it was for the Germans to build accordingly. They saw the Germans as following British designs and improving on them. Jellicoe decided: "It may well be here to state that the only true criterion of power in a capital ship, or indeed a ship of any class is size or displacements, provided that one may conclude that the designers of ships in different countries are of more or less equal skill."[5] In addition to Jellicoe, whose role in battle cruiser production turned out to be pivotal, there were several officers who played key roles in getting the fleet out to where it was on 24 January 1915. They belonged to an ad hoc organization invented by Fisher:

THE COMMITTEE ON DESIGNS

The membership of the original 1904 *Dreadnought* and *Invincible* brain trust, the Committee on Designs, included Rear Admiral Prince Louis of Battenberg who was later Atlantic Fleet Commander and First Sea Lord on the outbreak of war. Prince Louis was an important officer and offered both command and staff experience to any civil Lord of the Admiralty. Battenberg's role in designing the strategy and writing the Admiralty policy which underlies the battle cruisers was significant. Despite a career which was dogged by political fights over his German ancestry, Battenberg played a decisive role in determining that Germany was likely to be the principal enemy and was the country against which Britain should build her fleet. As Marder put it: "Prince Louis of Battenberg recommended, in November 1904, that England maintain a superiority in battleships of at least 10 percent over each of these most likely combinations against us . . . in order of probability, 1. Germany and Russia, 2, France and Russia, 3, the United States being regarded throughout as friendly." Lord Fisher concluded in a subsequent memorandum: "There remains Germany. Undoubtedly she is the possible enemy."[6] Later in his career, because of fears his German ancestry would compromise the public image of what the Admiralty would do in the war, Battenberg was replaced by with the superannuated Sir John Fisher who was brought out of retirement by Churchill when the war broke out. If Marder is to be credited, this change was not merited at all: "Prince Louis was by 1914, generally considered to be the outstanding flag officer on the active list"[7] It was one of Churchill's worst decisions.

The next officer on the board was Engineer Rear Admiral Sir John Durston. Albert John Durston was a Fellow of the Royal School of Naval Architecture, entering in 1866, and rose through the ranks as an Engineer Officer until his retirement in 1905. The committee was his last assignment. Durston had taken the Royal Navy from steam powered wooden ships of the line when he entered, then generations of ironclads, through the height of Pax Britannica. He experienced the overwhelming British fleet of pre-dreadnought battleships, which was the model for the world's navies at its time. Durston was a pioneer in the adoption of more efficient types of water tube boilers which were the core of fleet propulsion and engine efficiency. An insight to the man is a record of his focusing the Admiralty on the need for professionalism in the Engineer Officer branch, requiring engine room watch keeping standards as early as 1890.[8] In addition, he oversaw the introduction of steam turbines and oil fuel, which later became the global standard in capital ships. In Durston, the committee had an innovator of extraordinary experience.[9]

Rear Admiral A. L. Winsloe was another of the Fisher brain-trust. Winsloe was actually commanding the torpedo and submarine flotillas before becoming Fourth Sea Lord whence he was drafted onto the committee. His subsequent duties in that post included managing all supplies, and medical support, for the fleet of the day. He later commanded the China station before retiring in 1913.[10] The parallel to Franz Hipper is interesting with torpedoboats and submarines. Winslow brought a perspective of the new naval environment of underwater weapons to the board which designed the Committee on Designs.

Captain Henry B. Jackson, later Admiral of the Fleet Jackson, was another innovator, having been involved in the development of modern day wireless communications. This work included overseeing the development of the installations and the training of those who would use it, from its inception in the late nineteenth and early twentieth centuries. He went on from this work to be chairman of the Committee on Electrical Equipment in 1892, and then Assistant Director for Torpedoes. As recognition for his scientific work, he was made a fellow of the Royal Society in 1902. Thus he was both an innovator and responsible for getting new technology into the fleet. He also commanded several ships including a new battleship, the *Duncan*. While commanding HMS *Duncan*, Captain Jackson was also involved in the Committee on Methods of Controlling Gunfire in Action. After leaving *Duncan*, he was assigned to HMS *Vernon* (the gunnery school for the Royal Navy), for more developmental work in communications. He then reported for duty at the Admiralty and, while serving on the Committee on Designs, was appointed Third Sea Lord and Controller responsible for money and budgets. He went on to be an admiral and served as Chief of the Admiralty War Staff and First Sea Lord, among other assignments. In terms of the battle cruiser, Jackson's time on the committee represented the application of scientific expertise, research and development experience and fleet service combined to apply to the issues surrounding the battle cruiser's development.

Captain John Rushworth Jellicoe was the future Lord Jellicoe, Commander of the Grand Fleet, who later served as First Sea Lord of the Admiralty in World War I. Jellicoe, as a captain, was director of Naval Ordnance, which designed, built, and maintained the navy's inventory of guns, and thus Jellicoe was responsible for the development and deployment of the main weapons of the fleet. His presence on the committee made eminent sense. He respected Fisher, but did not always agree with him.[11] Marder's assessment of Jellicoe illustrates how Jellicoe was suited for the committees' work: "No unsound however attractive proposal had a rabbit's chance when he turns his searchlight brain on it – it's riddled by a dry fact or two that he knows but that no one else seems to."[12]

Captain Charles E. Madden, who was Jellicoe's brother-in-law, and was regarded as a "very composed man of few words whose record as a brilliant torpedo officer and a fine executive officer inspired confidence,"[13] also served on the Board. Again, there was recognition of the importance of underwater weapons in Madden's experience. Madden also served as Chief of Staff in the Grand Feet under Jellicoe and was acknowledged by Fisher as one of the five best brains in the navy.[14] He retired as an Admiral of the Fleet.

Captain R. H. S. Bacon was in 1904 Inspecting Captain of Submarine Boats working extensively with the first five *Holland* class submarines in the Royal Navy order of battle. Fisher at that time already thought Bacon "the cleverest officer in the navy." Bacon was working on the idea of submarines being a more effective defense against mines. This was in 1903.[15]

The committee decided on a battle cruiser which would have a "speed of 25 knots; armament of 12-in guns and anti-torpedo guns. Nothing in between; 12-in guns to be as numerous only as is consistent with the above speed and reasonable proportions; armour on a similar scale as *Minotaur*[16] class; docking facilities were to be carefully observed."[17] Oscar Parkes goes on to recount the committee looking at five different designs for the battle cruisers of which two were selected as finalists: both had eight guns mounted on the weather decks, of which four could fire forward and four aft, and eight on a broadside. The constructor was John Narbeth. The final design had obsolescent reciprocating engines, which were replaced by turbines when the ships were actually built.[18] The ships had the highest freeboard of any warships of the time, were the fastest warships of the time and had the highest horsepower of any ship afloat in 1908. They were planned and constructed at the same time as *Dreadnought*, with that ship having priority of the contractor's time.[19]

DESIGN AND CONSTRUCTION

Of the oldest battle cruisers, only *Indomitable* was at Dogger Bank, and by then she could not keep up with the newer battle cruisers, and thus took little part in the action.[20] In hindsight, it is always interesting to find that opposing sides in a contest in war suffered from the same difficulties although they did not realize it at the time. The British Admiralty financial officers were constantly faced with the limits of their resources almost as often as the Germans, but that was and is the nature of an arms race. To begin with, when British 1905–06 estimates required three battle cruisers in addition to the *Dreadnought*, it was found that the Royal Navy's shipyards did not have the capacity to build battle cruisers so they had to be built in private yards. *Inflexible* was built at Clydebank, *Indomitable* at Fairfield, and *Invincible* at Elswick.

A case can be made that, because of overarching geopolitical problems, the British heavy ship building industry was by no means in flush times during the naval race prior to World War I.[21] Because of the destruction of the Russian fleet at Tsushima, the Anglo-Japanese alliance and the focus of France on the German military threat, Germany was left as the only enemy for Britain to worry about. The United States was seen as a near ally. In addition to this natural slowdown and abandonment of the two power standard, there was the British Admiralty's determination to retain a capacity to build major warships in Government yards, which led to a major slowdown on the Clyde after the *Inflexible* and *Indomitable* were finished in 1909. But by 1910, the British navy buildup began in earnest with five capital ships or more per year, until 1914–15.[22]

The Director of Naval Construction for all British battle cruisers at the Battle of Dogger Bank was Sir Phillip Watts. Watts was regarded as technically talented. He graduated from Kensington School of Naval Architecture, and he was at ease with both the mathematics of naval architecture and the "common sense questions" which had to be dealt with while building warships. He was an Edwardian gentleman of that age, who: "Lived in a fine house on the Chelsea embankment ... was fond of riding ... in the park before setting out for his office which he reached about 11:30. He remained there until nearly 8 in the evening, though he did not need any staff beyond one shorthand typist."[23] The Kensington School was founded in 1864 to replace the one closed in the 1830s which had operated at Portsmouth. The school was subsequently moved to Greenwich Royal Naval College and then in 1967 to Imperial College London. The significance was that British naval architects had a common grounding in the technical mathematics and specialized sciences needed to build ships of modern era. The evolution of naval architecture in the previous thirty years from wood and iron to steam and steel was a major technological benchmark. What it does signify is that the battle at Dogger Bank represented an operational manifestation of technology's rapid evolution and displayed a microcosm of mankind's ability to handle new tools of war.

The builders of the British battle cruisers included: J. H. Narbeth, W. H. Whiting, and E. L. Atwood for *Invincible* class; W. T. Davis for *Indefatigable* class; W. T. Davis and E. L. Atwood for *Lion* class; and E. L. Atwood for *Tiger* class. Detailed oversight responsibilities were not absolutely prescriptive. Narbeth was responsible for the construction of the last pre-dreadnoughts, *Lord Nelson* and *Agamemnon,* which were actually more expensive than *Dreadnought.* He was also responsible for the follow-on first generation dreadnoughts *Bellerophon, Superb,* and *Temeraire.*

Narbeth was a character. He "was remembered for having an absolute fearlessness in confronting authority on matters of principle and a complete stubbornness if he believed he was right."[24] In later years he became regarded as the father of the institution of naval architects, and was the designer of HMS *Dreadnought.* He was awarded the MVO in 1906 for work surrounding this achievement. The MVO, or Member of the Victorian Order, was a decoration personally bestowed by the Sovereign for achievement redounding to the credit of the Crown. He retired in 1923.[25]

Of all the constructors, Atwood was the most involved in the battle cruisers. Edward Louis Atwood was a distinguished naval constructor.

Atwood wrote *The Geometry of Shipbuilding* (Cambridge, 1899), which was an authoritative text on theoretical naval architecture. A member of the Royal Corps of Naval Constructors, he was a graduate of the Royal Naval Constructors course and a subsequent lecturer at the college. Next after Atwood was W. T. Davis, who retired a Commander in the Royal Naval Volunteer Reserve (RNVR) and died in 1936. He was decorated with the Order of the British Empire (OBE) for his work during World War I. He was recognized in having made a "very substantial contribution to the British battle fleet at Jutland."[26] Davis was distinguished early, as he was first in his class at the Royal Naval College Greenwich in 1887; by 1903, he had been appointed an Assistant Constructor at Portsmouth and was shortly thereafter promoted to Constructor and assigned to the Admiralty.

John Harper Narbeth was even more distinguished receiving a Companion of the Bath (CB), Commander of the British Empire (CBE), and a Member of the Victorian Order (MVO); he lived from 1897 to 1944. For those not familiar with the British honors systems, these letters translate CB (not quite a knight, but distinguished), Commander of the British Empire (very distinguished); Member of the Victorian Order (done something so distinguished as to merit personal recognition by the Royal Family).

W. H. Whiting became an assistant director of naval construction.

Of the British battle cruiser program afloat by Dogger Bank, only *Lion* and *Indefatigable* had been built in a naval dockyard (Devonport). The others were built in private yards as laid out in the particulars below. The Committee on Design provided essential requirements for which the constructors had to actually design and then build the ships.[27] While involved in the design process as Controller, Jellicoe found it:

> difficult to ascertain the particulars of the German ships under construction during the years (1908–11) of my service as Controller. More especially, did this apply to German battle cruisers? Our vessels of this class already built or building consisted of the *Invincible* class with a displacement of 17,250 tons and the *New Zealand* class displacing 18,800 tons. The design of the next ship came under discussion in 1909, such information as was obtainable from our intelligence department being to the effect that the Germans were not exceed in this size. But secret information reached me from another private source that the horse power of the projected German ships very largely exceeded that of our

earlier battle cruisers, so the presumption was that the new German vessels must be far larger than anticipated. I accordingly had the design of our new ship (the *Lion*) altered, her size, armament, horsepower being greatly increased, with a displacement of 26,350 tons. It was fortunate that his was done, as it turned out that the corresponding German ship, the *Moltke,* displaced 22,640 tons, whilst the ship next to her, the *Seydlitz* displaced 24, 610 tons.[28]

As the international situation continued to deteriorate, Jellicoe eventually paid a visit to Berlin in May 1913, and had dinner with the Kaiser and Admiral von Tirpitz. Jellicoe says he and Tirpitz and the Kaiser discussed both fleets, engineer training and the latter turned down an invitation to visit Jellicoe because Tirpitz believed his policy was so unpopular it would lead to his murder in the street! [Jellicoe's exclamation point].[29] Tirpitz wrote to Jellicoe from Berlin 23 October 1913 in response to condolence on the crash of the airship *L 11* Berlin on 17 October and the concomitant loss of life. Tirpitz kindly accepted the condolence.[30] It is of more than passing interest the only time Jellicoe gets mentioned in Tirpitz's *Memoirs* is the reported expression of admiration of the German Ambassador Freiherr Marshall von Bieberstein presented his credentials in July 1912 when Jellicoe was present.[31] The tragedy was that there were the same seeds of inevitable clash of interests in British domestic policy of the day. Neither side could have anticipated the cost.

The *Invincible* class, the first battle cruiser, had her origin in Admiralty conferences surrounding the creation of the revolutionary dreadnought type battleship, and there is in the record a final section devoted to the creation of an analogous cruiser type. The ultimate tactical justification of an all big gun, high-speed capital ship was arrived at in 1905. The fleets of the day were composed of ships with four heavy guns and a dozen or more medium caliber guns; the belief was concentration of fire would overwhelm the opposition, provided the fire was rapid and accurate. The ranges at which this would occur were roughly 6,000 yards, or only three times the range of a 32 pounder in the age of sail. The battle speeds in 1905 were likely to be only 12–15 knots. A dreadnought would raise the speed to 18 knots or better and the range to 12–15,000 yards or more. The concentration of fire in fewer ships would simplify the problems inherent in very long lines of pre-dreadnought or so the thinking went. So the decision was taken to build both types.

Thus, the British had assembled the very best array of talent to create the dreadnought battle cruiser and her like. They made the best decisions they could at the time. And yet, as Jellicoe put it later:

> Hence as German followed us in constructing Dreadnoughts, and her ships equaled or in some cases exceeded our vessels of similar date in displacement so we were forced to design ships of a larger size. It may be as well to state here that the only true criterion of power in a capital ship or indeed of a ship of any class is size or displacement, provided of course that one may conclude that the designers of ships in different countries are of more or less equal skill.... Some people (of whom Mr. Churchill was one) were in the habit of stating that British ships were of greater power than German ships, because the caliber of the guns was larger ... any naval officer who inspected the German ships salved from Scapa Flow, when in dock at Rosyth (as I did) could clearly see their immense underwater protection ... I certainly as Second Sea Lord before the war – pointed out to Mr. Churchill the fallacy of his arguments.[32]

By Dogger Bank there were four classes of battle cruiser in the British navy: the *Invincible* class of three ships, the *New Zealand* class of three ships, the *Lion* class of three ships and the *Tiger*. The reader needs to understand that these ships were large and powerful, yet held serious weaknesses and hardships for their crews and commanders. Those who fought in them were often cold, frightened, and sometimes killed. British battle cruisers in particular had a very high casualty rate.[33]

THE *INVINCIBLE* CLASS (*figure 2.1*)

LOAD DISPLACEMENT: 17,250; 19,000 deep.

DIMENSIONS: 567' overall; 78'6" beam; 27' draught.

MACHINERY: coal and oil-fired boilers, driving turbines developing 25,000 shaft horsepower, to 25 knots (3,000 tons coal and 700 tons oil).

ARMOR: Belt 6" amidships, 4" forward extending 7.3" above and below load water line; barbettes and turrets, 7"; bulkheads 7".

ARMAMENT: 8–12-inch, 45 caliber breech loading guns, first proof tested in 1905, maximum range was 18,850 yards at 13.5 degrees elevation, eighty rounds per gun carried; sixteen 4-inch anti-torpedoboat guns; 5–18-inch submerged torpedo tubes.

THERE WERE THREE SHIPS: *Invincible, Indomitable, Inflexible*.

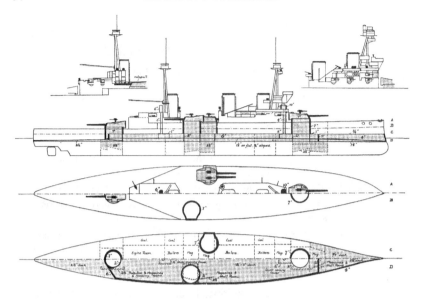

2.1. Oscar Parkes's rendition of the first British battle cruisers of the *Invincible* class from *British Battleships. Plan and caption by permission Seeley Service Publications from Oscar Parkes,* British Battleships.

THE *NEW ZEALAND* CLASS (*figure 2.2*)

LOAD DISPLACEMENT: 18,750 tons.

DIMENSIONS: 590' overall, 80' beam, 26'6" draught.

MACHINERY: coal and oil fired boilers, driving turbines developing 43,000 shaft horsepower, to 25 knots (3,000 tons coal and 850 tons oil).

ARMOR: Belt 6", amidships, 4" at ends; fore and aft, extending 7'6" above the waterline and 3.6" below load water line; 7" and 7–10" barbettes and turrets, bulkheads 3 and 4" forward and 4.5 and 4" aft.

ARMAMENT: 8–12-inch, 45 caliber breech-loading guns, maximum range 18,850 yards at 13.5 degrees elevation, eighty rounds per gun carried. The projectile weighed 850 pounds and muzzle velocity 2,275 feet per second; sixteen 4-inch anti-torpedoboat guns, two 18-inch submerged torpedo tubes.

THERE WERE THREE SHIPS: *Indefatigable, Australia, New Zealand.*

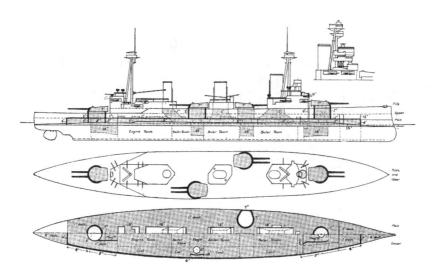

2.2. Oscar Parkes's rendition of the second British battle cruisers of the *New Zealand* class from *British Battleships*.

THE *LION* CLASS (*figure 2.3*)

LOAD DISPLACEMENT: 23,350 tons light, 29,580 deep draft (for
   Lion – others varied slightly).

DIMENSIONS: 700' overall; 88'6" beam; 28' mean draught.

MACHINERY: coal and oil fired boilers driving steam turbines developing 70,000 shaft horsepower to 28 knots.

ARMOR: 9" main belt with 6" upper amidships, extending 16' above
   and 3'6" below the load water line; bulkheads 5" forward, 9" aft;
   turrets and barbette armor 9" and 8", gun-shields 10" and 7".

ARMAMENT: 8–13.5-inch, 50 caliber breech loading guns first proof-
   tested in 1909 maximum range was 23,000 yards at 20 degrees
   elevation; eighty rounds per guns carried, the projectile the
   projectile weighed 1,250 pounds with muzzle velocity 2,500 feet
   per section; sixteen quick firing 4-inch anti-torpedoboat guns; two
   21-inch submerged torpedo tubes.

THERE WERE THREE SHIPS: *Lion, Princess Royal,* and *Queen Mary.*

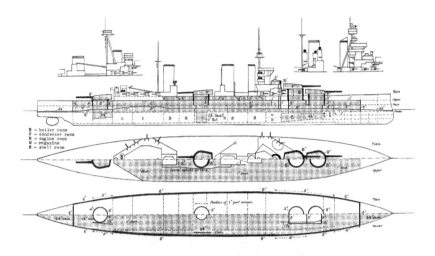

2.3. Oscar Parkes's rendition of the third class of British battle cruisers of the *Lion* class from *British Battleships*.

THE TIGER (*figure 2.4*)

LOAD DISPLACEMENT: 28,500 tons, 31,160 tons deep.

DIMENSIONS: 704' length overall, beam 90'6", draught 28'5".

MACHINERY: steam driven turbines developing 85,000 shaft horse-
    power producing 29 knots (3320 tons coal and 450 tons oil).

COMPLEMENT: 1121.

ARMOR: BELT: 9" tapering to 6" bulkheads 4" tapering to 2"; barbettes
    9" tapering to 8", shields 9" backs 4".

THERE WAS ONE SHIP.

*The British and German light cruisers and destroyers which participated in
the Battle of Dogger Bank are covered in detail in the order of battle later in
this work.*

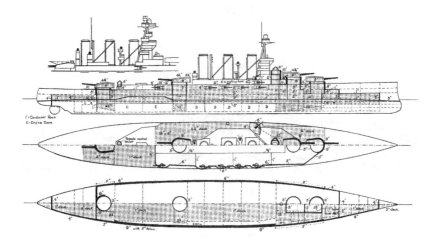

2.4. Oscar Parkes's rendition of the fourth class of British battle cruisers of the *Tigers* from *British Battleships*.

THE GERMANS

Before we discuss the true battle cruiser types, the participation of the *Blücher* a transitional armored cruiser in Dogger Bank almost overshadows the other ships as the photo of her end which is so iconic of the battle.

The characteristics of *Blücher* were the result of a major disinformation effort by the British. But they were also the results of deliberate decisions on the part of Tirpitz's staff. The *Blücher* was a transition ship whose capabilities were determined by money – Tirpitz was always operating on a shoestring.[34] Interestingly, when the decisions were made regarding *Blücher*, she was a compromise created by Tirpitz,[35] Dahnhardt,[36] Capelle,[37] and Senior Commander Reinhard Scheer.[38] The *Nassau* and *Westfalen*'s cost, size, speed, and armament were also decided at this conference. Thus, the responsibility for *Blücher*'s smaller armament size, lower speed, and lighter armor belonged to Tirpitz, Dahnhardt, Capelle, and Scheer. As Kelly put it: "it is fair to say that Tirpitz opposed building dreadnoughts until the combined pressure of Emperor and Fisher forced him to."[39] In the case of *Blücher*, Tirpitz let himself be talked into a "floating coffin" for a thousand German sailors. In subsequent discussions

2.5. SMS *Blücher* stern quarter view, much as she looked departing for the battle (source unknown).

2.6. SMS *Blücher* sinking at Dogger Bank.

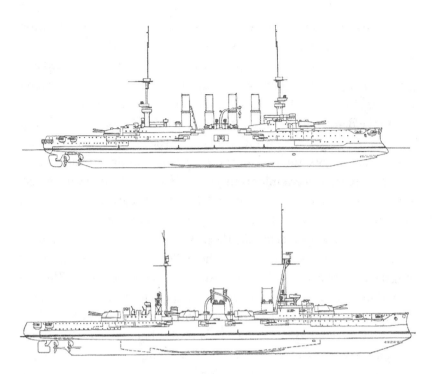

2.7. Scale representation of *Scharnhorst* and the *Blücher,* both as sunk. From Erich Gröner, *Die Deutschen Kriegschiffe.*

about the German dreadnoughts to follow *Blücher,* Tirpitz was reminded that during the *Novelle* debates the German navy had stipulated it would only build ships "of equal value to other nations," which of course *Blücher* was not. She was an embarrassment to Tirpitz even before her launch.[40]

One of the post–World War II chroniclers of the German navy was Paul Schmalenbach, the former gunnery officer of the Reichsmarine's heavy cruiser *Prinz Eugen.* Schmalenbach's assessment of the *Blücher*'s creation is that she was to be an improvement on her predecessors *Scharnhorst* and *Gneisenau,* which themselves were a logical design successor to all prior German armored cruisers. Those two armored cruisers fell victim to the superior speed and firepower of the first British battle cruisers sent to remedy a defeat these ships had inflicted on the older armored cruisers of Read Admiral Christopher Craddock's squadron.

This type was a reply to the standard second line ship of the day a little faster than a battleship, less well armored or carrying slightly lighter guns than battleships. Innovative German gun design had yielded a 21 cm [8.2-inch] weapon which was as capable as the older 24 cm weapon [9.2-inch] carried in older cruisers, so *Blücher* got the new gun.

In the *Blücher,* six twin turrets were emplaced fore and aft with four amidships, with the same arrangement as in the first two classes of German dreadnoughts, the *Nassau* and *Helgoland.* Turbines, which would have made a more economic arrangement of main armament and magazines possible, were not available, so *Blücher* had to have triple expansion coal fired steam engines. The space requirements for the engines and the location of the guns meant: "As there was no space for the magazines for the broadside turrets between the boiler and engine rooms, their magazines were placed in the forecastle next to the fore turret. The ammunition was forwarded through a special connecting walk along the centerline of the ship on the armored deck. Two hoists supplied the four broadside turrets with projectiles and powder, but as she was to be used as a gunnery trial and test ship, this disadvantage was executed to get an opinion of the value of this design."[41] *Blücher's* characteristics and weaknesses thus derived not from the tactics of the battle but because of outside circumstances. Those circumstances also had an influence on the battle in terms of its materiel, and those circumstances also had an impact as derived from decisions made off the battlefield.

In at least one respect, the results of Dogger Bank do go back to the construction of the *Dreadnought* and the impact it had on the plans and ambitions of Grand Admiral von Tirpitz. As Kelly puts it: "Tirpitz was shaken by the news" [of the *Dreadnought's* capabilities.]"[42] The British intention was to anticipate developments in the United States and Japan, not Germany, but what mattered was that Tirpitz thought the British intention was "that the *Dreadnought* and later the *Invincible* battle cruiser type were directed against Germany." Nevertheless, the Germans did make some serious mistakes, which resulted in the *Blücher* being armed with 21 cm [8.2-inch] guns instead of 28 cm or 30.5 cm [11- or 12-inch] weapons as the *Invincible* was. Parenthetically, the 21 cm guns were 45 caliber, and a later model (1906) than those on *Scharnhorst* and *Gneisenau*

which were Blucher's immediate predecessors, thus they did represent
some improvement, albeit at a fatally smaller bore than HMS *Invincible*.
Something else – Tirpitz and the Kaiser seem to have been by no means
as well informed about British naval programs and intentions as were the
British. Tirpitz was getting his information of secret British programs via
the German naval attaché,[43] while the British were being served by none
other than Sidney Reilly, "Ace of Spies."[44]

> As a result of the St Petersburg Flying Week that he organized Reilly obtained
> information on German aircraft developments. By getting the job of sole agent in
> Russia for the German firm of Blohm and Voss of Hamburg, the naval builders,
> he managed to see all the blueprints, plans and specifications of the latest devel-
> opments in German naval construction. All these were passed back to Britain.
> ... The Germans did not know he was a British agent, but they were sufficiently
> suspicious of his name to have him watched day and night, yet he still secured
> copies of the plans.[45]

In January 1905, ten years before the battle, Lord Fisher's Committee on Designs had decided on the capabilities of the *Invincible* class
cruisers, in addition to the *Dreadnought*. The long-range armament was
designed to keep the new classes of ships outside the 6,000 yard range of
torpedoes, allow for a single fire control system, and increased accuracy
in spotting shot when all landed together, as opposed to ships of mixed
armament.[46]

The decision for the critical 12-inch gun armament spelled the death
of three German armored cruisers which were subsequently outranged
and outclassed by their British opponents. The 12-inch caliber was chosen because of the advantages it gave to the British fleet to have a fast
squadron at its head which could engage enemy battleships.[47] Fisher
decided that it would be a good idea to hide this from the Germans, if he
could. Here is what he did:

> As German agents (particularly the Naval Attache) attempted to penetrate the
> secret of the *Invincible*, Lord Fisher was determined to oblige them. He had pre-
> pared a set of plans for the ship which bore every semblance of official origin, but
> which showed the armament to consist of 9.2 inch guns. These drawings were
> put under the nose of a well-known German emissary, who gleefully dispatched
> them to Berlin, and doubtless received a substantial reward. The Germans
> appear to have been taken in, for a few months later; they designed the *Blücher*

as a "reply" to the *Invincible*, and gave her an armament of 8.2-inch [21cm] guns. While these weapons may have been equal in ballistic properties to the British, they were of course hopelessly inferior to our 12" guns, and so it befell that she was outclassed and obsolete even before she was launched.[48]

David Ramsay notes that the agents had provided details on mobilization plans for all dreadnoughts through the *König* class, and that the 28 cm [11-inch] gun would be the armament for Germany's first generation of battle cruiser. Based on this, according to Ramsay, Rear Admiral Jellicoe as Controller of the navy improved the specifications for the *Lion* class.

But Jellicoe may have had more than one other insight. As controller, he had analyzed the German naval estimates and deduced "that the later ships would be vastly more powerful than the earlier ships."[49] Nevertheless, despite the earlier assertions that he should have known more about the German ships, Jellicoe notes in 1905: "It was difficult to ascertain the particulars of the German ships."[50] This appears contrary to what was known elsewhere and to the contents of British Admiralty publication *German Navy CB1181*. It is very likely both sides were well aware of each-others' capabilities and numbers. Wrapped in a very elegant description of the *Goeben* is an introductory paragraph about the arms race which is enlightening:[51]

> Durch Verrat erfuhr auch die britische Admiralität das Geheimnis der deutschen Dreadnoughts. Ein Ingenieur bei einer Privatweerft verkaufte, wie bei der Kontrolle der Zahl der Bauplanne der *Seydlitz* den Englandern und wurde vom Reichsgericht in Leipzig unter Ausschluss der Offientlichkeit verurteilt. Die Admiralitat nutzte aber diese Kenntnis nicht aus, wie man in Reichmarine Reichsmarineamt während des Krieges feststellen konnte als die Plane fur den Schlachtkreuzer *Queen Mary*, Baubeginn 1910, und das Linienshciffe *Orion*, 1909, ebenfalls auf geheimen Wegen nach Berlin gelangten.[52]

A rough translation is that the British Admiralty knew in advance the characteristics of the *Seydlitz* as revealed in the conviction in open court in Leipzig of a German engineer from a private firm who sold the plans of the *Seydlitz* to the British. Moreover, the German Admiralty also obtained and had in its possession during the war plans of the *Queen Mary*, commenced in 1910, and the super-dreadnought *Orion*, begun in 1912. Thus, Jellicoe's analysis would have made him double sure of *Seydlitz*'s characteristics, and he may well have been right in terms of what he

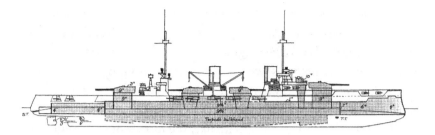

2.8. Oscar Parkes's SMS *Von der Tann.*

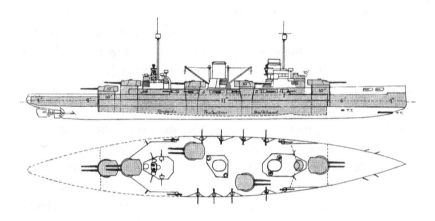

2.9. Oscar Parkes's SMS *Goeben* and *Moltke.*

was actually able to know despite the British Admiralty and intelligence services' bureaucratic entropy. The important thing is that both sides knew more than they let on in their post-war apologia and there was even less excuse for the conflict.

To find out why Hipper took *Blücher*, it is necessary to go to the immediate account of the battle. In fact, some additional studies notably that by Seligman, have shed even more light on this shady aspect of *Blucher*'s and the rest of the battle cruiser program construction.[53] After *Blücher* was built, the next German cruiser, large cruiser, or proper battle cruiser was SMS *Von der Tann.* She appeared in the famous Royal Review at Spithead to starboard of the British battle line, her lighter grey a contrast to the dark warlike grey already worn by the British fleet. She was the first true German battle cruiser, but took no part in the battle because she was in the yards with her engineering spaces torn apart; the wartime wear on new technologies was not anticipated, so a proportion of Hipper's ships were inevitably in the yards. But this was less of a problem for him as he could choose when to strike; Beatty could not.

Next were SMS *Goeben* and *Moltke,* the former of which survived in the Turkish navy until 1972. Although *Goeben* took no part in the Dogger Bank battle, her role in the First World War is illustrative of the diplomatic heft of a battle cruiser. As Kelly lays out the disposition of the German battle fleet on the outbreak of war: "To the south, the presence in an Austrian Adriatic base of the German battle cruiser *Goeben* alarmed the British Mediterranean Command."[54] There is much more to the *Goeben's* story and it has been related in the official histories as well as Arthur J. Marder;[55] in addition there is a well-illustrated story of the ship in *Auf der Spurren der Goeben,* published in 1979 shortly after the ship was scrapped. If indeed *Goeben* rather than *Blücher* had been part of the First Scouting Group, the battle would have been much more even, perhaps even a deadly precursor to Jutland, when a third of the British Battle Cruiser Fleet did not return. *Goeben* was *Cruiser H* in the new German shipbuilding program of 1907. Most of the German battle cruisers were built under this program, including *Goeben, Seydlitz, Derfflinger, Lützow,* and *Hindenburg,* as well as *Mackensen,* which was never completed.[56] The battle cruiser *Goeben* (March 1910 keel laid) and her sister *Moltke* (January 1909 keel laid) were notable as much as for their turbine engines (Parsons Turbines, made either in the UK or under License)[57] as for their superb protection and moreover their improved 28 cm [11-inch], 50 caliber gun. Alleged to be somewhat slower than their British counterparts, this does not appear to have been so in practice – the classified British characteristics books for these ships rated them at 28 knots over the measured mile and 27.25 knots full speed.[58] The German ships' characteristics books have them at 24.75 knots over 6 hour forced draft course.[59] From the German perspective, regardless of the geopolitical outcome of the German Mediterranean squadron's actions, the operation was a success. The British side represented both unambiguous tactical failure and strategic defeat due as much to Admiralty incompetence as locally inadequate interpretations of orders and lack of command initiative.[60] Beatty was concerned about *Goeben* from much earlier and wrote the C-in-C home ports on 8 September 1913, well before hostilities regarding the detached battle cruiser *Indefatigable,* then serving in the Mediterranean. He noted that with the transfer of that ship to the Mediterranean, should the Germans return *Goeben* from the Mediterranean, the two battle cruiser forces would be equal – the *Lion, Princess Royal, Queen Mary,* and *New Zealand* versus the *Moltke, Von der Tann, Seydlitz,* and *Goeben.* He also noted that the equality would only exist until the new *Derfflinger* joined in the summer of 1914, at which point they would be inferior to the Germans.[61]

It turned out *Goeben* did not come home. The manner of her escape into Turkish waters and service on the outbreak of war did not help Beatty's temper. Or his attitude toward higher echelons: "It is inconceivable the mistakes and blunders we have made and are making."[62] Beatty's opposite number at Dogger Bank, Rear Admiral Franz Hipper chronicled the news that "one of the captured British trawler captains reported that the English had lost a ship in the Mediterranean. It must have been an engagement between the *Goeben* off Messina and probably involved an *Invincible. Goeben* should have been in action with two such ships and one of those should have been the ship sunk. That would be a colossal result/outcome."[63] The result was not as favorable as Hipper hoped, but *Goeben* ended up safe under the guns of the fortress at Constantinople and thousands of British and Commonwealth soldiers would die as a result; one of the battle cruisers would be mined and several British and French pre-dreadnoughts would be lost in what would become the Dardanelles Campaign.

The *Goeben's* activity constituted what was "Arguably the Imperial Navy's most significant contribution in the entire war. . . . Instead of heading west for home, likely a suicide mission, Pohl and Tirpitz, without the emperor's knowledge, flummoxed the British and French with an order to Souchon to head for Constantinople. On 11 August Souchon arrived at the Dardanelles with the Royal Navy in pursuit. . . . For the price of two ships, Germany had closed off Russian access to the Mediterranean, added an important ally, and vastly complicated the strategic problems of the entente."[64]

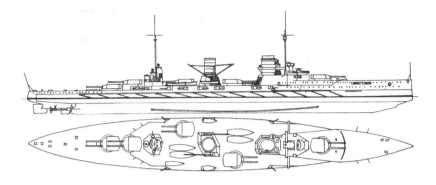

2.10. Preston's SMS *Seydlitz,* from *Battleships of World War I,* used with permission.

There are some other relevant facts to the capabilities of *Moltke* and *Goeben* – Tirpitz made the decision that all battle cruisers would have turbines as opposed to the more technically conservative triple expansion steam engines which would be retained for all eight of Germany's first battleships – the *Nassau* and *Helgoland* classes. Tirpitz also decided the *Moltke* and *Goeben* would have 28 cm [11-inch] guns as opposed to the 30.5 cm [12-inch] allocated to the *Helgoland* class of battleships. The *Moltke* and *Goeben* would be 22,000 tons each and have ten vs. eight 28 cm guns.[65] These decisions made the German ships superior to any of the first six British battle cruisers because there was enough displacement to allow sufficient protection for fighting in the line of battle, and the German 28 cm gun, particularly the 50 caliber weapons, which proved equal to the British 12-inch, 45 caliber in destructive power, and at least as good in rate of fire.[66]

Then there was the famous *Seydlitz;* photographs of it on fire fill the numerous British histories of the Great War. *Seydlitz* is a different story in that she follows the first generation of German battle cruisers as a transitional ship between *Moltke* class and the *Derfflinger* class. *Seydlitz's* displacement was increased from 22,000 tons to 25,000 tons, which enabled her increased protection, and, probably, most importantly, a forecastle deck which was a deck higher than her predecessors, which probably saved her after the severe damage she suffered at the Battle of Jutland, some sixteen months after Dogger Bank.[67] *Seydlitz* resembled

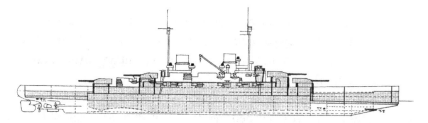

2.11. Oscar Parkes's *Derfflinger*.

Moltke and *Goeben* with five twin turrets deployed one forward on the forecastle deck, two in the waist, en echelon, and two super-firing on the quarterdeck aft. Her 15 cm [5.9-inch] secondary armament of twelve guns was deployed in casemates just under her main deck around the center of the ship. There were additional 12–8.8 cm [3.4-inch] guns built into her superstructure fore and aft, although these were later replaced with 8.8 cm AA guns on the after superstructure. When Admiral Hipper hoisted his flag in her in 1914, he remarked that it was "terrific to have such a fully capable and appropriate flagship."[68] She was faster than her predecessors, reaching 28.1 knots in her measured mile speed on trials.[69] This German battle cruiser was not only an evolutionary improvement on her earlier sisters, but had to be a well-run ship to survive the kinds of trauma suffered at Dogger Bank and Jutland. The following additional descriptions are taken from the *Deutsche Kriegsflotte/Nur fur dienstgebrauch* (*German War Fleet/Only for Service Use*) cited earlier; the authoritative *Schlachtschiffe und Schlachtkreuzer 1905–1970* (*Battleships and Battle Cruisers 1905–1970*),[70] and the author's work *Admiral von Hipper: The Inconvenient Hero*.[71]

Last came *Derfflinger*, *Lützow*, and *Hindenburg*, powerful, modern, and fast. Two other classes of ships were planned – the *Mackensens* and *Ersatz Freya* classes, but only two made it to the water and none were completed during the war.[72] *Derfflinger*, *Lützow* and *Hindernburg* were a reply to the *Lion* class and they mounted a lighter 30.5 cm gun which proved to be very effective in combat with the 13.5-inch British weapons. The wreck of the *Lützow* survives more or less intact where she sunk on the night after Jutland. She is on her side, with some salvage of copper parts undertaken, shells and powder still intact, and probably dangerous after almost a hundred years under water. The *Derfflinger,* nicknamed the "old dog" by the British, was raised and scrapped but not actually taken apart until after the Second World War.[73]

The German light cruisers, destroyers, and U-boats which partici-pated in the action are described with their British opposite numbers in the chapter on order of battle.

3

Prologue to War and Battle

In the final analysis, the single most important technical decision made by either side in the prologue to the war was the decision taken by the British to arm the *Queen Elizabeth* class of super-dreadnoughts with a 15-inch gun. Although not present at Dogger Bank, this weapon and these ships were to nullify any German tactical advantages obtained either by redoubtable construction or tactical proficiency throughout the war. Churchill played a pivotal role in their procurement. As Vice Admiral Sir Peter Gretton put it, citing Roger Keyes: "Churchill's quick brain and vivid imagination were invaluable, and in the majority of cases, his intervention was in the best interests of the service. I believe history supports Keyes."[1] So does the author. The failure to get the *Baden* class into service at the same time as the British 15-inch gunned ships entered service meant that the German navy's battle line and its battle cruiser extension were never quite strong enough. This was a resource issue, and reflected the belief in a short war and a decision that ships' guns were more important supporting the western front than the Baltic coast afloat. The effects of the British blockade on German resource allocation were ultimately telling. There is another embedded point here – the role of the Kaiser. Under the constitution of the Reich, the Kaiser was the commander in chief of the navy and of the Prussian army in peacetime; in wartime he became the C-in-C of all the other States' armies. In practice, this meant that throughout the navy's existence the Kaiser had daily influence on its doings. The navy did not have the Great German General

Staff to manage the Kaiser's naval whims. But the Kaiser and many of the navy's staff were oddly united in being tired of Tirpitz. Compared to that body, the Admiralty Staff, or the *Admiralstab,* despite being set up in practice to reflect the lessons of the ground forces, was a mere shadow of the General Staff in practical or moral authority.

The Kaiser had no adult supervision, other than Tirpitz, and that was by no means balanced or assured, and was more absorbed with the two-front land campaign, upon which German's survival depended. After the outbreak of the war, Tirpitz was effectively marginalized, principally because the key to influence in the wartime Imperial Navy was the right of *Immediatvortrag,* or access to the Kaiser. The other reason was the Kaiser's preoccupation with the existential struggle in Germany's two-front land wars. Immediatvortrag came with the position of a very few officers, only one of whom, the High Seas Fleet Commander, was in the fleet itself. This meant that the German battle fleet, which the Germans referred to as the "Front," had one officer to represent its views to the highest military authority. The phenomenon reflected the degree of militarization of German society and was not present across the Channel. The German battle cruiser commander had to go to his immediate superior should he have any ideas which might affect his own ships' strategic use, as indeed would the British battle cruiser fleet commander to his own C-in-C Grand Fleet. The British monarch would rarely involve himself in the day-to-day doings of the fleet in peacetime, much less in its wartime operations. The king might have an opinion and might referee a difficult issue, but there was simply no parallel.

There were however, some remarkable service parallels, the difference being that instead of commanding a pre-dreadnought battleship as Beatty did as a captain, Hipper commanded the armored cruisers *Gneisenau* and *Yorck.* He notes their losses in his *Nachlass* [private war diary]. Every ship he had ever commanded had been sunk. One final parenthetical – SMS *Blücher,* was a generation more modern that von Spee's armored cruisers when assigned to the scouting forces, compared to any other armored cruiser. She was transferred from front line scouting force duties in 1912 to training with the idea that she would ultimately contribute more as a modern training ship to the fleet's battle readiness. Subsequently, there were only four heavy ships assigned to the scouting forces until the outbreak of war, and with overseas deployments there were as few as three heavy ships in the scouting forces. The decision was made to increase front line numbers by one as it was felt she was strong enough to survive in the line, albeit her offensive power was not as great as the dreadnoughts. She was a big cruiser, capable of surviving most forms of underwater attack, and with the exception of her ammunition distribution system, pretty hard to damage.

On the other side of the North Sea, Hipper's opposite number, David Beatty, worked up to command his forces through a sequence of increasingly responsible commands. He commanded the armored cruisers *Juno* and *Suffolk* and later the pre-dreadnought battleship *Queen*. In the 1912 maneuvers, Beatty was given a squadron of cruisers and hoisted his flag in the ill-fated armored cruiser *Aboukir,* which served as a platform to demonstrate his abilities in command of a squadron of ships in large scale operations. His task was to rehearse the interception and destruction of a German landing force. Having performed to Churchill's satisfaction, Beatty then found himself commanding the battle cruiser squadron with his flag in HMS *Lion,* which he would take into action at Dogger Bank.

Hipper began 1912 as deputy flag officer Scouting Forces in January at the age of 47, having some 20 years in the German navy. He was promoted to Rear Admiral at that time and assumed duties which were an equivalent echelon below those of Beatty. As deputy flag officer, Scouting Forces, his main task was command of all torpedoboats assigned to the High Seas Fleet. He was also responsible for administration and command of the four light cruisers which constituted the Second Scouting Group. His task was to make these ships and men into an instrument which would make German tactical victory or survival highly likely should an engagement be fought on German terms. Like his opposite number, Hipper was always worried about numbers and the relative quality of his materiel. Tirpitz had shorted the light cruiser and torpedo arms of the German navy of major resources in favor of the battle fleet. The German light cruisers carried 10.5 cm [4.1-inch] main armaments, instead of 6-inch for the British, were fewer in number, and marginally slower, due to less expensive coal fired engines. The German destroyers were smaller, less heavily armed, and fewer in number than those the British could deploy against them, until later in the war. These ships however were all well trained, superbly manned, and could be concentrated at a point the Germans wished if they had the tactical initiative.

The German Fleet command recognized the technical inferiority of their smaller ships and was willing to go along with Tirpitz's argument that the core of the battle fleet, the heavy ships had to be funded first. Nevertheless, Tirpitz argued that the German destroyers were actually technically superior. This position did not then, nor does it a century later, hold much water. After the war, when the criticism of this part of the German materiel base was made public, Tirpitz blamed any significant faults on lack of funds and the relatively small size of the torpedoboats, which he himself had encouraged. In 1919, he further asserted that in 1909–10 the fleet and the Torpedoboat Inspectorate had actually asked for smaller boats. Tirpitz was dissembling in the post war political morass. Whatever the truth of the matter, German destroyers were small, mostly powered by coal, and, because they were small, suffered in sea-keeping and endurance as well as in action with better armed British boats. Indeed, Hipper actually commanded the First Torpedo Division from 1908–11 and when he read what Tirpitz had written in his *Memoirs*, he commented to Admiral Adolph von Trotha on 24 December 1919 that "at the beginning of the war, our torpedo boats did not have the firepower that the enemy's destroyers possessed. In this respect his [Tirpitz's] assertions are very misleading." Even worse, at the beginning of the war, the torpedoboats were 40 percent under inventory in torpedoes, for the same fiscal reasons as above.[2] Hipper, unlike Beatty, had no upper echelon experience – the Imperial Navy was too immature to rotate really talented combat commanders through shore echelons like the Royal Navy – this would have occurred had the generation after Hipper succeeded into anything beyond the Lilliputian Reichsmarine. As it was, Erich Raeder, Hipper's chief of staff, became the embodiment of the Kriegsmarine and for all intents and purposes the new Tirpitz for the next war.

Two other snippets deserve mention. The first is Hipper's scouting forces (battle cruisers, light cruisers, destroyers, submarines, and aircraft) were not consolidated to the same home port until 1913, for which Admiral von Ingenhohl must be given credit. The other thing Ingenohl gave the BdA was authority equivalent to a deputy battleship squadron commander, of which there were only six such admirals in the High Seas Fleet – Hipper thus had such authority over all scouting forces – air and U-boats as of 1914. He also had authority to command the High Seas Fleet itself, if combat circumstances dictated. Although the High Seas Fleet Commander actually issued orders to all those participating in a fleet-wide operation, Hipper in theory could do so if the battle was only going to involve scouting forces. Hipper's forces were concentrated and, at least at the tactical level, had unity of command. Beatty was not so lucky.

The battle cruiser, like much of the fleets of which it was part, was new and held a universe of power and possibilities. Both commanders set out to develop these before the war. The reader should keep in mind that the preparations themselves were designed for when the scouting forces of both sides would belong to maturing fleets. They both probably thought about it in terms where each force would be about ten ships – for Hipper ten of the twenty battle cruisers would have been deployed at home, the rest abroad; Beatty might have assumed the same although the heavier *Queen Elizabeth*'s and the new battle cruisers at home with the older out protecting the dominions. Neither Admiral thought he ever had enough ships. The worst enemy was usually one's own bureaucrats in Berlin or London, for Hipper and Beatty in that order. Hipper's final tactical work between 1913 and 1914 involved defining the mission of the battle cruisers. He was a tactical pioneer, somewhat like Beatty but with a much worse geographic and numerical strategic position. Under Hipper, the German battle cruiser force assumed a key role in naval tactics and strategy. The ships represented an unprecedented combination of speed, firepower, size, and relatively heavy armor; the only other nation to have a battle cruiser force at this time was England. Hipper became Germany's battle cruiser commander in October 1913, relieving Admiral Gustav von Bachmann who had initiated the concept of the "battle cruiser charge" during the 1912 fall maneuvers as a cover for the withdrawal of the German battle fleet from possible envelopment. The concept was both sound and dangerous, and Hipper refined the tactic by practicing it several times before it was actually used successfully four years later at the Battle of Jutland. In the circumstances of that action, the well-practiced tactic looked positively brilliant.[3]

The other element of cruiser tactic which the Germans constantly exercised was the offensive one – the "battle cruisers breakthrough," where the fast dreadnought battle cruisers overwhelm enemy screens to ascertain the strength and disposition of the enemy main fleet. In Hipper's private account of the 1914 May fleet exercises, the drill was repeated at Hipper's insistence. It was true that all scouting forces were involved in this maneuver, including torpedoboats, destroyers, light cruisers, and the battle cruisers. All were exposed to underwater attack and, of course, progressively heavier gunfire as the penetration of enemy screens was attempted. Hipper recognized this was basically a slugfest as speed was not going to be much of a defense. He assumed he would be up against the British battle cruiser forces whose speed would be equivalent to his own. German gun crews' predilection to keep magazine doors open and too much ammunition in the open were noted even then, and both were regarded as tactical disadvantages. The problems were mitigated in action by more conservative German designs and ammunition which burned but did not explode. The Germans were also concerned about a torpedo engagement between opposing battle cruisers – this is a weapons included in all the big ships' designs but often ignored by historians because little seems to have come of it. This aspect of the breakthrough maneuver was recognized like all the others as ultimately difficult and dangerous. In fact, should the breakthrough be achieved, and the German scouting forces achieve their objective, they would have done so in the face of heavy and concentrated attack by huge volumes of gunfire and damage from the enemy's light forces. *In fact,* the difficulty and danger of a Fleet engagement was fully recognized. Both principal tactics were recognized as a last resort as serious damage to the battle cruisers was likely to result. That said both sides expected, and often were rewarded with the ability of their ships to absorb tremendous damage and still continue to fight. Or as the British Admiral Lord Chatfield put it: "Ships are built to fight and must be able to take blows as well as to inflict them."[4] But these were also tactically bloody courses without alternatives to the Germans in WWI. They were needed because the other sources of reconnaissance, notably aircraft, Zeppelins, and U-boats were all fraught with difficulties and suffered from nascent development and insufficient funding because of the higher priority dreadnought program. All lacked reliable and secure communications. The U-boat could see little at night and the aircraft and Zeppelin were extremely vulnerable to the adverse weather conditions, particularly headwinds, for which the North Sea was famous.[5]

On the other side of the Channel, Sir David Beatty was experiencing his own challenges and difficulties with the development of his Battle Cruiser Squadron, later to become the Battle Cruiser Fleet. In a humorous and insightful anecdote, Rear Admiral W. S. Chalmers, Beatty's first biographer describes an incident in the end of March 1913. The battle cruisers were to "cut across the enemy's van at high speed," which was analogous to the battle cruiser breakthrough Hipper was so exactingly practicing. Unfortunately for the audience, which included the First Lord Winston Churchill and the Prime Minister of France, a tramp steamer got in the way and Beatty had to abort his high speed dash. Beatty was not perturbed – his comment to the commander in chief being "Well sir, that was unfortunate; the two fleets were much too close to start with and of course the battle cruisers had no room to manoeuvre. . . . I hope the First Lord is not too disappointed."[6] In the time before war broke out Beatty, like Hipper was a careful student of tactics, and sought to understand the characteristics and limitations of the weapons he had been given to wield in a war at sea. Beatty had superb talent at his command: his flag captain was a great sea officer and naval thinker who later achieved the rank of Admiral of the Fleet: Lord A. Chatfield. He made a great riposte to Maurice von Egidy of Hipper's *Seydlitz*.

Chatfield, as captain of HMS *Lion,* makes a valuable witness to the development of the battle cruiser type in British service. Beatty was hand-picked by Churchill as Naval Secretary of the Admiralty in early 1912 when the latter had rejected command of the Atlantic Fleet and was thus ashore without employment, and ironically no fan of Churchill.[7] Having been selected by Churchill on the basis of the strength of his views and clarity of expression, "in the interval [between January 1912 and March 1913] he accompanied Churchill on inspections and conferences which took him to the heart of the discussions which determined the Navy's posture in 1914. . . . He saw his own role as ensuring Churchill was given correct naval advice, in both conversations and written submissions."[8] Further, there is compelling evidence Beatty understood and forecast the likely German courses of action in the event of war in 1914.[9] Beatty concluded (correctly and with much foresight as Hipper's own *Nachlass*) that:

> The possible and probable objects of the German Naval Forces at war with this country are:
> 1) To interrupt and destroy the overseas trade especially food supplies, upon the safe Carrying of which the existence of the nation depends.
> 2) To endeavor by constant attacks by destroyer, submarine and mine-layers so to reduce our fleets that they might reasonably hope for a successful issue when they give battle with their entire available force.
> 3) By such attacks to drive our fleets etc. such a distance out of the North Sea and contain them for sufficient time to enable a large expeditionary force to be launched – i.e. to hold the North Sea for a sufficient time to enable an invasion of the British Isles to take place.[10]

During this peacetime interregnum, Beatty traveled in very high circles, no doubt due to the corollary effects of his wife's wealth and position as well as his own standing a legitimate naval hero as well as from his earlier career and current postings. For example, on 1 June 1912, he wrote his wife that he was attending a working dinner with H. H. Asquith, the Prime Minister, Field Marshall Lord Herbert Kitchener, Prince Louis, and himself.[11] The closest Hipper got to this was dining in the wardroom of the Imperial yacht some years before.

Something neither fleet seems to have anticipated in peacetime was the prospect of engagements only between battle cruisers rather than as part of a fleet engagement.[12] Dogger Bank turned out to be just that, but only because the deputy battle cruiser commander did not press home the action; if Hipper had been pursued the battle could have grown into a major action as we now know. In any case, as Chalmers said: "Beatty thought deeply about the function in war of his speedy and powerful squadron. The latest ships, *Lion, Princess Royal,* and *Queen Mary* could steam at a maximum speed of over twenty-eight knots; the older ships, *Indomitable* and *Indefatigable* could only do twenty-six. Until about 1910, no other heavy ships in the world could attain such speeds, and Beatty knew the Germans had such cruisers in commission. Upon assuming command, Beatty decided his squadron must be trained to maneuver in close order at the highest speed possible. He announced "that the next series of tactical exercises would be carried out at twenty four knots . . . when Beatty was questioned on the wisdom of this he replied, 'Are we going to fight at twenty four knots or not? It is more likely we shall steam at twenty seven knots and leave the lame ducks behind.' which is exactly what happened a year later at Dogger Bank."[13] Indeed, it was so: "Their Lordships frowned and the Inspector or Target Practice was disturbed. But David Beatty was pleased. He clearly saw his tasks in the coming war."[14] More importantly Beatty synthesized the results of the numerous innovative exercises. He ordered and actually enumerated the five functions of the battle cruiser squadron and later fleet in September 1913, and these were duly embodied in the British Grand Fleet Battle Orders. They were as follows:

a. To support a reconnaissance of fast light cruisers
   on the enemy coast at high speed.
b. To support a blockading force.
c. To form support between the cruiser force and the battle fleet when cruising.
d. To support a cruiser force watching the enemy's battle fleet.
e. Finally to form a fast division of the Battle Fleet in general action.

With the exception of supporting a blockading force, all of these were carried out in the Great War.[15] In spite of a reputation for audacity and bravery over consistency and common sense, the British commander "had complete command of himself, his mental faculties, confidence in his judgment, and could under pressure decide rapidly on his next step without hesitation or visible anxiety."[16]

In January 1915, the building programs and fleet development of both sides were much closer than later when the effect on German fleet building capacity of blockade and heavy casualties in the ground war had sapped her potential and allowed Britain's pre-war and early war programs to come to fruition. If we compare the two nations' capital ship programs, an interesting picture emerges. The plans of the pre-war naval race started to come unglued shortly after Dogger Bank. The Germans had four more battleships – the *Baden* class, with 38 cm (15-inch) guns planned through 1915, which were part of their pre-war appropriations. Only *Baden* and *Bayern* joined the fleet in late 1915 and early 1916 respectively. The two remaining ships, *Sachsen* and *Württemburg* were not completed and did not join the fleet because the resources were transferred to the U-boat building program. Further, only the *Lützow* and *Hindenburg* joined Hipper's forces after the war broke out – *Lützow* was almost immediately lost at Jutland and *Hindenburg* joined late in 1917 – these ships carried only 30.5 cm (12-inch guns) and thus represented no improvement over the previous weight in shell for Hipper's ships. However, based on an assessment of damage to *Lion* at Helgoland Bight, this might not have been much of a disadvantage.[17] There is also an interesting anomaly in Tirpitz's *Anhang 6* [Appendix 6] above – he credits *Hindenburg* with 34 cm guns which would have been a significant upgrade in Hipper's capabilities, if true. Nevertheless, the Germans had three ships less before counting to the *Queen Elizabeth* class of five ships, all of which joined before mid-1916.[18]

In terms of Dogger Bank, these ships were not yet available. Looking at the remainder of the British program, there were *Repulse* and *Renown*, very fast 15-inch gunned battle cruisers, variants of the *Royal Sovereign* class; both joined by 1917. Last, there were three *Courageous* class hybrid ships which ultimately became aircraft carriers. Beatty had no kind words for these – neither did Jellicoe.[19] For their part, the Germans had intended four *Mackensen* class battle cruisers and three *Yorck* class battle cruisers. Only two ships, *Mackensen* and *Graf Spee*, were launched in 1916 and 1917 respectively. British intelligence sources in the German Admiralty had either dried up or been rolled up, as by 1918, the British expected these ships would be surrendered as completed units.[20] Little appreciation seems to have been afoot regarding the terrible conditions in the winter of 1917 in Germany under blockade.[21] In addition, three other battle cruisers in the war program had been started but work halted due to both resource constraints – people and material not money. The last seven ships would have been more than a match for the British battle cruiser fleet even if it included the *Queen Elizabeth* (QE) class. But they were not to be. Germany ultimately overreached herself in ambition and hobbled herself with bad organization and hierarchical dysfunction. *Blücher*, the weakest link in Hipper's line at Dogger Bank, was a reflection of these phenomena.

PROLOGUE TO BATTLE: OPERATIONAL AND
TACTICAL BACKGROUND TO DOGGER BANK

The war had been underway for six months and both fleets had suffered losses – the Germans largely from cruiser warfare around the globe, the

British raid on Heligoland Bight, and an occasional torpedoing; the British from underwater attack and surface action.

The operational background to the battle really focuses on the evolution of the war at sea in the principal theater of war: the North Sea. For both sides, the transition from peace to war involved mobilization, deployment, continuous training and equipping of new and old ships, as well as repair and maintenance in support of operational requirements. Much of this was untried ground, with little peacetime planning, and some degree of wishful thinking on both sides as regarded opportunities for action. On orders to mobilize, Beatty told his wife: "I cannot think that such a step would have been taken unless war is inevitable. All I can say is we are ready and will win through though it will be terrifically quick. . . . Once we start I cannot think it will last too long."[22] What Beatty did have in mind was to destroy the pretensions of the German navy and he believed he had the weapon to do it.[23] Nevertheless he also recognized after a few weeks at war that underwater weapons, the mine and torpedo would severely reduce his freedom of action.[24] The same was basically true of Franz Hipper, stuck on the mud banks of the Jade aboard *Seydlitz*.[25] Nevertheless, the first innings would go to the Royal Navy and Beatty on 28 August 1914 in the Battle of Heligoland Bight.[26] The fog of war was literally and operationally present on 28 August. Liddell-Hart's thinking is useful: "Errors of judgment there must be in war, and few would cavil at them, especially those due to the fog of war. But it is different when the fog is self-created by confused thought." Or was it the actual fog itself, attendant high speed action, and actual weather which made the outcome less certain than predicted.[27]

As part of the prologue to Dogger Bank, Heligoland Bight reflects the frustration of both sides' naval commands to do something and stay within the procrustean limits of their respective grand strategies – for the Germans it was the Kaiser's dictum not to risk the heavy ships, except the battle cruisers and for the British, to tolerate risk but only on a razor's edge, again the balance falling on the British battle cruisers. The British planned an offensive action, based on an idea presented to the Admiralty by the commander of submarines, Sir Roger Keyes.[28] The Admiralty approved but then added its own twists followed and additional ideas from the Grand Fleet itself. Keyes' concept was remarkably simple: an exploitation of German dispositions as discovered by his submarines. He said:

> 7. I would submit that a well-organized drive, commencing before dawn from inshore close to the enemy's coast, should inflict considerable loss on these destroyer patrols....
> 8. This of course will require some organization, but a carefully thought out and well executed plan might achieve great success.[29]

This ultimately developed into a much more complex operation, which however successful in attriting German light cruisers did not give Beatty "much confidence in the Admiralty's ability to coordinate complex operations." Frustrations in this line would continue with Admiralty fog covering the loss at Coronel and the Escape of the *Goeben* as well as the tip and run raids in November and December 1914. This activity, and the sometimes unpredictable interplay between the navies in the North Sea, reflected the desire of both sides to get at each other on the tactical level and the application of restraint and calculation to every move by higher authority. Distant blockade for the British and attrition for the Germans were strategic conundrums both sides tried mightily to get around in the first six months of the war.

The initiative was largely up to the Germans who opted for operations which used the battle cruisers as bait. They developed their tactics in such a way as they gradually engaged more and more resources until they risked more than they should have at Dogger Bank.

At sea, two things affect battle, other than the capabilities of the combatants: weather and geography. On the morning of 24 January 1915, the two forces approached each other on what was a relatively calm sea although the wind picked up as the day progressed. The largest ships were the battle cruisers: for example the *Lion* Class, of which *Lion* and *Princess Royal* were present, displaced about 27,000 tons and were 720 feet long and drew about 30 feet of water; crews were about 24 feet above the waterline. The light cruisers of which the *Nottingham* and *Chatham* class were an example, were 5,400 tons displacement, 450 feet long, drew 15.25 feet of water; the lowest exposed guns and crews were about 10 feet off the water. The smallest ships in the British force were the torpedoboats or torpedoboat destroyers, of which 35 were involved ranging from about 500 to 1,500 tons; most were less than 300 feet long and had about 6–10 feet freeboard aft and perhaps 15–20 feet forward. These ships were very wet and uncomfortable. The bigger ships were less affected by weather than their smaller light cruiser and torpedoboat escorts.

The German capital ships ranged from the *Derfflinger* at 28,000 tons down to the armored cruiser *Blücher* at 16,569 tons. The German light cruisers ranged from 4,300 to 4,900 tons and were of similar size and dimensions to their British opposite numbers. The German destroyers were smaller, from 670–537 tons on average, whereas the British were as large as 1,000 tons down to about 650.[30] The German destroyers were coal fired and had less of a radius of action than their British counterparts; their ability to operate over long distance or time in heavy seas was physically limited by the physical endurance of their crews and coal storage. For more details, see the chapter on order of battle.

The log of HMS *Tiger,* which was third in the British battle line and thus in about the middle of the formation, tells us that from 0500 on the morning of 24 January 1915 until about 1230 when the battle was over the weather was overcast and mainly cloudy with periods of passing rain showers during the last hour or so of the engagement. The air temperature was 43–44 degrees Fahrenheit during the action. The humidity was almost 100%. During the action, the barometer was steady at 29.8. The wind was from the east-southeast at force 4 in the early morning and then from the north at force 3–2 during most of the battle.[31] The wind was up to about 16 knots towards daylight and moderated to 7–8 knots during the action. The sea state was 3 moderating to 2 during the latter parts of the action. The sea was moderate during the intercept phase and then nearly calm during the action.[32] This meant that the intercepting force had what was basically a following wind which would blow their smoke in the direction of the enemy who was approaching from the southeast. It also meant a significant wind-chill factor for exposed and frequently wet sailors.

The log of SMS *Moltke,* third in the German battle line, describes the weather as well.[33] For the early morning hours of 24 January, when the First Scouting Group and accompanying forces were proceeding north east into the German Bight towards Dogger Bank, the weather was light clouds, not very dark, lightly overcast; the wind was east by north, sea states 2; as it got lighter, the wind shifted to the north east and the sea state increased to 3. By morning, the wind had shifted to the east north east and it was dark as late as 0600; it was still overcast at daybreak twilight; the seas beginning to raise at sea states 3 to 4.

In sum, the weather for the Battle of the Dogger Bank on Sunday 24 January 1915 was moderate for the North Sea, but the visibility was anything but perfect, especially with intermittent rain showers. In a battle between dreadnoughts, one might think the wind would not matter as much as it would in the days of sail. This was not so, because the position of the enemy was determined by observation – there was no radar – and the ships were largely coal fired, which meant huge clouds of funnel smoke could and did make targeting difficult. The wind direction was from behind the British forces, which meant their smoke obscured them to German gunners much of the time. The Germans made up for this by having their destroyers make smoke so that the British would have to fire at German muzzle flashes, which were exceedingly bright and good aim spots. The most important factor for those in combat was wind-chill, which would be an added stress. A secondary fact was the sea-keeping qualities of the ships involved. British naval architects calculated the design of their ships against sea states and came up with curves of sea-sickness and predicted where it would affect combat effectiveness. Several of the *Blücher*'s casualties died of exposure; her captain ultimately succumbed to pneumonia. All of these things were the consequences of a decision having been made by the High Seas Fleet Commander to conduct a reconnaissance in force in the North Sea in January. The general direction of both forces was determined by geography and propinquity. The specific location was determined by something else – an intercept of German communications and British Admiralty orders to counter the German move. The Admiralty order is contained in both Vice Admiral Beatty's official report on the action and in Sir John Jellicoe's cover report to the Admiralty. Here it is:

From: Admiralty, London
To: Commander-in-Chief, Home Fleets
Date: 23 January 1915
No: 210

Urgent. 4 German Battle Cruisers, 6 light cruisers and 22 destroyers will sail this evening to scout on Dogger Bank probably return tomorrow evening. All available Battle Cruisers, Light Cruisers and Destroyers from Rosyth should proceed to a rendezvous in Lat 55 13 N Long 3 12 E arriving 7.0 am tomorrow morning. Commodore T is to proceed with all available destroyers and light cruisers from Harwich to join Vice Admiral "Lion" at 7.0 am at above rendezvous. If the enemy is sighted by Commodore T while crossing their line of advance they should attack. W/T is not to be used unless absolutely necessary. Acknowledge. Telegram has been sent to C-in-C, VA Lion V.A. 3rd B. S. and Commodore T.[34]

Amplifying and receipt telegrams follow in the record. The readers should know this was not the actual intercept. It was an operational order, not an intelligence order, derived from multiple sources and reflecting the command judgment of the British Admiralty to focus major force on the point of German attack. The most important strategic lesson of the battle was to validate the fundamentals of the intelligence process pulled together by former battle cruiser captain, "Blinker" Hall. That process was flawed, but still worked for the most part. Signals intelligence was the fundamental source of success in the battle, however crudely handled. What mattered most was that first paragraph, for two reasons. First, it was the operational death knell for Hipper's mission, and potentially his force. Second, it represented a breakthrough in the process of using intelligence to serve effectively the objects of war itself. The other technical lessons went beyond the obvious – the damage to *Lion* was not appreciated, whereas the damage to the *Seydlitz* was understood and acted upon. This latter was to keep the doors between magazines shut in action and reduce the number of open charges in areas subject to incoming shellfire. Nevertheless, the lessons learned and applied have limited effect – the vulnerabilities of the British centered on underwater attack and the chemical in stability of British powders. Simply put, British powders would explode and German powders would burn. Several German turrets were put out of action during the war but no ships were lost from internal explosion except the obsolescent *Pommern*. British losses are well known and documented.

It is important to remember, as laid out in the introduction, that time and distance played significant roles in the North Sea theater. The ships involved were generally slower than those we have become accustomed to with fleet speeds usually around 16 knots, although the dreadnoughts might make 18 knots while covering the distances noted in a battle.

The Germans have left posterity with a remarkable little chart [figure A.1] the distance in *Seemeilen,* or nautical miles, (2,000 yards or 6,000 feet instead of 5,280 feet on land) between all the key points on the chart. This enables us to view the problems faced by the combatants, both in time and distance, and perhaps get a better understanding in the difficulty faced by the combatants.

The North Sea is both shallow and treacherous proving a challenge to navigation much less naval warfare. It is hostage to incredibly foul, dangerous weather and low visibility which affected both combatants throughout the war. However, the readers should be aware of some basic numbers.

From the German man naval bases in the Jade River around Cuxhaven, the distances were:

1. To Scapa Flow – @475 nm (the principal
   Grand Fleet base) [26.5 hours]
2. To the Firth of Forth – @440 nm (the normal British battle
   cruiser base, and sometimes the Grand Fleet locus) [24.4 hours]
3. To Hull – @310 nm (and most targets on
   the British east coast) [17.2 hours]
4. To London or the Thames – @340 nm [18.8 hours]
5. To Dover – @340 nm [18.8 hours]
6. To Portsmouth – @445 nm [105 + 340 nm main
   British naval base and repair facility].[35]

Each side had to calculate the amount of coal and oil required for sorties and the likelihood of action with respect to fuel expenditure: "The Grand Fleet used about 100,000 tons of coal a week and the efforts which had to be made to get this amount of coal up to the Orkneys put a tremendous strain on the British railway system. Enormous quantities of rolling stock and a huge numbers of colliers were kept busy simply ferrying coal to Scapa, and the effect on other sectors of the British war effort can be imagined. The strain on officers and men was very great, as each battleship took hours of hard physical labor to coal. The Grand Fleet carried out a large number of sweeps and was always at a high state of readiness, which meant the coaling went on continuously."[36] The British did a lot more of this than the Germans though they did have their share. Here is the captain of HMS *Lion*'s own description:

> Every ten days or so, the battle cruisers would return to Scapa to refuel, provision, water and store. We would remain in port for perhaps thirty-six hours. It was an even more strenuous time than at sea. "Out torpedo nets, prepare to coal," would be signaled with the anchors. The colliers would come alongside and two thousand tons of coal would be dug out of their holds, hoisted in by the seamen and marines, and stowed away in the bunkers by hard-worked stokers. Stores and provisions, mails and official papers, and perhaps a large consignment of gifts from friends and organizations, would be sent for by store-ships daily arriving from the south and would have to be distributed. It was war. No one minded working twenty hours a day. Then off to sea again and the cycle would be repeated.[37]

The Germans could always coal in port, which was the terminus of their rail lines which used interior lines of communications. The principal advantage for the High Seas Fleet was they could choose when to go out, and thus ease their logistics. Nevertheless, shortages were an issue for both sides at one time and another, but notably for the Germans later in the war.[38] The rate of consumption for one of the German battle cruisers, the *Moltke* was roughly 3 tons an hour at 14 knots, which was most economical speed. Thus, the range of the ship was 4,120 nautical miles at 14 knots. At higher speed, much more coal would be consumed. The British *Lion* class was about the same, although she stored 3,000 tons coal at maximum load to the 3,100 tons for the German ship.[39] The British battle cruiser fleet carried a mixture of coal and oil fuel which *Lion* for example, carried 3,700 tons of coal and 1,130 tons of oil. The *Tiger*, the last battle cruiser built before the war, had an even split of 2,450 tons each oil and coal. As the war went on after Dogger Bank, more and more oil fuel was used, on both sides, which allowed more operational freedom, and relief for the crews, but by war's end both fleets still were largely coal fired. The bottom line was the logistics of fuel was critical to both sides and a great physical burden to both countries' crews. As newer construction entered, the fleets' oil was used in increasing quantities and proportion, until post war it became the norm.[40]

In sum, we know how far the ships of both fleets had to steam to get at each other or principal targets, how hard it was to get there, and how much effort it took just to operate, much less fight. To properly set the stage for the battle, the reader needs an appreciation of the evolution of the strategy, tactics, and interim lessons learned to the point of the battle. It boiled down to distant blockade on the part of the British and attempted attrition by the Germans. A review of the documents in the official histories is instructive, however, in that it paints a picture of admirals struggling within procrustean restraints to get at each other in spite of the strategic *Sitzkrieg* imposed by their political masters. The respective battle cruiser forces did promise the opposing fleet commanders some flexibility, and they definitely tried to use it in the first months of the war. That more did not come of these efforts is an accident of fate.

When the war commenced, both sides looked for opportunities to damage the other. This work is about the background to Dogger Bank, so it will concentrate on how the Germans looked to torpedoboats, submarines, and mines. There is a stack of charts and tables which documents this activity in the German official history. The British history is not as complete, and for good reason was more focused on the struggle for the seas beyond the North Sea theater, until all the German overseas combatants had been sunk or neutralized. If you include *Goeben* and *Breslau* in the Mediterranean, this did not happen until 1918. Nevertheless, it is instructive to remember that the balance of dreadnoughts and battle cruisers, to say nothing of pre-dreadnoughts, always overweighed the Germans.

Whatever the technical balance of power, when war commenced, the first action was to deploy to wartime stations and set up the distant blockade. The Grand Fleet steamed to the Orkneys and the Channel Fleet sewed up the straits of Dover. Older British ships were manned and mobilized as the Fleet went to war footing. The Germans did the same, concentrating their dreadnoughts and more capable cruisers, torpedoboats, and submarines in the Jade estuary. Aircraft and Zeppelins were subordinated to the Scouting Forces commander, Rear Admiral Franz Hipper. The two fleets were not equal in experience. The German fleet was still in a build-up mode with the crews of older pre-dreadnought ships manning the newer ones as they came off the ways. The prewar dreadnought building programs were still underway and the fleet did not reach wartime strength until early 1916 after the loss of almost the entire generation of earlier armored cruisers. The German U-boat service was in its infancy and comprised only nineteen boats with four under construction and two deployed. These were deployed between inner and outer patrol lines of destroyers, in a semi-circle based on the German North Sea bases in the Jade estuary. The battle cruisers were assembled inside the Jade River bar, which at that point had not been fully charted,[41] and the battleships behind these, all securing the army's northern flank while it ploughed through Belgium toward Paris.

The German generals did not care if the British Expeditionary Force was intercepted and destroyed while crossing the Channel as they considered it a negligible force. The navy was quite happy to do as much damage with the new undersea weapons as it could. If the German fleet had been used it would have been at risk, but as long as the Grand Fleet was at Scapa when the action started, they would have had some hours to break through the old pre-dreadnoughts guarding the force and attack the transports. Unless the transports were cut off, they would simply have returned to port. When hostilities began, the Germans thought the British had disappeared and the British thought the Germans would come out and challenge them, to break the blockade.

Interestingly enough, a British assumption that the United States would remain neutral turned out to be important enough to enter the German calculus. If the United States objected to the British blockade in terms of "freedom of the seas," then the British might have to count on dealing with the U.S. navy, which was almost as large as the German navy. Fortunately for the British, their assumptions about U.S. attitudes proved correct. The Germans were deluded.

The Germans charted six major incursions into the North Sea by the Grand Fleet up to January 1915. The British conducted a series of sweeps with the Grand Fleet in August. The Germans did consider attacking the British troop transports with the High Seas Fleet. Hipper reported a fleet conference on the flagship *Friedrich der Grosse* on 9 August, where the issue was discussed but rejected – not because of the overwhelming numbers of the Grand Fleet which had seemed to disappear in to the northern North Sea, but rather because the Germans feared the British would sow the waters between them and their base with mines and submarines while the High Seas Fleet was engaging the British second and third fleets and attacking the transports.

In actuality, the British submarine order of battle at the time comprised of 45 *C*, *D*, and *E* class submarines. These ships were believed

deployed with the fleet and a few in coastal defenses.[42] Again, the calculation needed to be made as to how many were operational, how many
could be deployed across the German line of advance, and how effective
they would have been. It is now known the British mine-laying capability
and British mines were less than first rate; British mines were less effective than their German counterparts. There were no British submarine
mine-layers. The British submarines of the day were on average capable
of only 10 knots submerged and thus not capable of keeping fleet speed
while submerged. They were, however, capable of keeping fleet speed
while surfaced, except in the high speed chases – economical speed for
capital ships was around 14–16 knots.[43] The subs' top speed was about
16 knots.

   The German U-boats were slightly better and were soon used by
Admiral Scheer as fleet scouts. Hindsight is always 20/20, but the considered judgment of the German fleet commanders was remarkably
similar to their British colleagues. Both the Germans and the British
deployed their submarines as scouts, a duty for which they were less than
ideal, but to which their capabilities had not yet matured. Nevertheless,
the new talented and aggressive British submarine commander, Roger
Keyes, made the first submarine movement of the war by sending two
submarines into Heligoland Bight in August 1914. More importantly, he
deployed a line of thirteen submarines from North Godwin Sands up
to Ruytingen Shoals to cover the crossing of the British Expeditionary
Force into France.[44] Thus should the High Seas Fleet have actually sor-
tied to attack the British Expeditionary Force, they would have had the
numerous pre-dreadnoughts to deal with in addition to submarines in
their rear. The High Seas Fleet command was right to refrain from attack.
An action in the Channel would have been prolonged and bloody with
the Grand Fleet arriving to snap up survivors.

   At the outbreak of war, the German move was to deploy two lines
of U-boats north:[45] one on the Dogger Bank itself, east to west scouting
north in a line of nine boats, one much further north in the patrol area
where the Grand Fleet was scurrying out one of its first sweeps. The
northern line lost U-13 and U-15. The latter was sunk by HMS *Birmingham*
on 9 August at 0500. The Grand Fleet headed west north west between
the Shetlands and the Orkneys. The German U-boat lines returned
south. U-13 was also missing and later determined lost.[46] Both sides

were confused and frustrated with the absence and apparent inactivity of the other – as David Beatty put it: "Let us hope they will be forced to send their fleet to sea, which I am afraid will be very unlikely until they have caused us considerable losses from the mine and submarine, which has not been very successful up to the present and I think the danger will lessen instead of increase as the war goes on."[47] Meanwhile, the Grand Fleet had conducted its first sortie into the North Sea. Jellicoe on 16 August "went ten miles beyond Horns reef/Flamborough Head. Sighted nothing. Now steering North by West sweeping front 150 Miles broad."[48] The Germans had no clue they were out since Germany was between deployments of their submarines and other scouts. They also had not yet organized their strategic wireless intercept effort, which was later set up at Neumunster. In the flag quarters of SMS *Seydlitz*, Franz Hipper wrote: "16 August. Nothing reported tonight. A flotilla of TBDs [torpedoboats] and two cruisers have made a sweep 120 miles north of Helgoland and nothing is to be seen . . . our U boats have searched as far north as 60 latitude and from there to the South to the entrance of the English channel . . . nothing has been seen of the enemy; except for guard ships and patrol craft there are no English ships to be found in the North sea."[49]

Actually, the enemy was having a bad time. The Grand Fleet was at anchor in 17/18 August with nets out and patrols underway and a false alarm of a submarine was given followed by an accident which resulted in a torpedo being launched by a destroyer in the direction of the battle fleet. The battle cruisers were out at the time and received a signal that a U-boat was in Scapa Flow and an order to rendezvous in the New Hebrides. As Lord Chatfield put it: "Here was a pretty kettle of fish. The Great Fleet was homeless and insecure, like American colonists chased by stealthy Red Indians. We hid in the creeks and bays of the west of the west Scottish coast Beatty called a meeting. . . . Admiralty conferences took place. . . . And so the long study of this new and serious problem for the Navy began in earnest."[50]

Nevertheless, the Grand Fleet Commander Sir John Jellicoe was still determined to *do something* to wit: On 18 August, Jellicoe told the Admiralty: "Am sending by post to day . . . general plan of next movement South which involves cooperation of First and Third Flotillas and Orders to submarines in Heligoland Bight. The general scheme is a sweep in force at dawn to within thirty miles Heligoland, flotillas leading covered by cruisers with battle fleet supporting. If flotillas are available Sunday 23rd, p.m. would be suitable date for them to meet me at a rendezvous to be given later, the actual movement taking place daylight 24th."[51]

On 20 August, the Admiralty forbade a sweep as Jellicoe requested telling him to rest the Fleet, and move *Invincible* and *New Zealand* to the Humber to join Beatty, which they did. The critical role of torpedoboats or destroyers is evident as a reflection of their role as anti-submarine forces. In the event of an action with the High Seas Fleet, Jellicoe correctly assumed that the Germans, if they did come out, would be accompanied by the maximum number of available TBDs, which meant a maximum torpedo threat.[52]

The British subsequently decided at a lower level to do a reconnaissance in force against German patrols in the Heligoland Bight on 28 August 1914. The story had been told in depth by Eric Osborne in his magisterial *Battle of Helgoland Bight*.[53] There are two points which can be added. The first is that the actual involvement of the battle cruisers was the direct result of an on the spot decision by Admiral Beatty, the British BCF commander. Beatty was ordered south to support a British light cruiser raid led by Rear Admiral Reginald Tyrwhitt and the Harwich Force. To this end, the Second Cruiser Squadron went in to support Tyrwhitt and was itself hotly engaged. Beatty was concerned that German capital ships could come out and overwhelm the British light forces. He decided to intervene: "I ought to go and support Tyrwhitt but if I lose one of these valuable ships the country will not forgive me." He did it anyway.[54] The reaction of the British Admiralty to the battle was illuminating:

> An order was issued complaining of the expenditure of ammunition and torpedoes by the Battle cruisers and Harwich force. . . . The expenditure said the Admiralty, was unacceptable and should similar expenditure occur again our reserves of ammunition would be exhausted prematurely. . . . This was an unpleasant and hampering order . . . it showed a target practice rather than a fighting mentality at the Admiralty.[55]

In the lead up to Dogger Bank, therefore, the Germans did lose U-boats, but their efforts went on as did those of the other smaller ships. In perspective, the threat of action in the Bight represented a potential repeat of 28 August and kept the Germans thinking defensively. This was true although they recognized that their light cruisers had advanced too far from their bases without support and that would not happen again. Hipper also thought that an action in the Bight might cost him one of his battle cruisers should a general action develop. Nevertheless, Ingenhohl and Hipper agreed they had to be ready to support a general engagement with heavy forces as a matter of principle.[56] This was justified by British action when they tried another raid on 10 September. But this time the Germans were ready; Hipper had mined the Bight and withdrawn the vulnerable advance patrol lines only on 9 September, and the British presented with no targets and a dangerous minefield, withdrew.[57] As Jellicoe put it:

> the operations in the Heligoland Bight on 10 September were carried out in accordance with the orders laid down. The movements of the battle fleet were hampered by low visibility.... [U]nder these circumstances the superiority of our battle fleet becomes much less marked as the conditions are unfavorable to accurate gunnery, while at the same time the destroyer and submarine menace is greatly increased.[58]

After the 28 August engagement in Heligoland Bight, neither the Germans nor the British gave up. The next German plan was submitted in late September 1914 and called for Hipper to take his three battle cruisers in support of the minelayer *Berlin* to attack the northern blockade line in the North Sea.[59] The operation had the Kaiser's approval, but the battle cruiser sortie was postponed due to machinery troubles and the operation was later cancelled because strong British forces were found to be operating across Hipper's planned course in the waters off Norway.

However, *Berlin* was sent without support on 16 October and evaded Jellicoe's fleet and blockade forces and laid a minefield which sunk HMS *Audacious*, a British super-dreadnought, on 27 October 1914. *Berlin* ended up interned in Trondheim, Norway, with her crew.[60] The loss of *Audacious* underlined British dreadnought vulnerability to underwater attack – she hit a single mine aft flooding the port and partially the center engine room[61] and ultimately sank subsequent to progressive flooding and power loss and then a magazine explosion, probably due to unstable cordite. Jellicoe now commanded a fleet whose characteristics he had helped to form and whose limitations were becoming obvious.[62]

On 24 September 1914, the British held a high-level conference to deal with future naval operations in the light of immediate war experience. The conferees included the First Lord (Churchill), the Chief of the War Staff, the Director of the Intelligence Division, the Naval Secretary, the Private Secretary, the Commander in Chief, the Vice Admirals commanding the First, Second, and Fourth battle squadrons, the Chief of Staff, the Captain of the Fleet, Commodore Submarines, and Commodore Torpedoboats. They decided an attack on Heligoland was out of the question because: it was not worth the expected losses; that Kiel should not be attacked because it would diminish British naval strength by losses to the destroyer and light cruiser strength of the Fleet; that the Heligoland approaches should not be mined under current conditions; and that submarines should be used in anti-submarine role to protect the fleet from German submarines.[63] Finally, defensive strategy should be to protect the east coast and its shipping land and harbors with cruisers and light forces, with deliberate offensive operations into the southern North Sea were made only with four days' notice and with fully coordinated support from the entire main Grand Fleet.[64]

Jellicoe was, however, looking for some activity the first week of October from the German battle cruisers.[65] Churchill did believe that if the High Seas Fleet were to come out, it would have "some definite tactical object, for instance to cover the landing of an invading force [which he considered unlikely], to break the line of blockade to the northward in order to let loose battle cruisers on to the trade routes, or simply for the purpose of obtaining a naval decision by fighting a battle."[66] Churchill was correct. The Germans were looking at fighting a battle cruiser action in the northern North Sea but declined to do so for the reasons stated above. Hipper was wise not to have conducted such an action since supporting the *Berlin* might have led to an ambush by stronger forces; the other option a battle cruiser breakthrough into the Atlantic was indeed under consideration, but it faced huge logistical challenges.[67] Interestingly enough, though this was not actually happening, there was a report of "large ships passing north of Faroe Island and serious possibility confirmed by personal report from trustworthy Danish agent of German intention to send out cruisers into the Atlantic Ocean." The Admiralty considered it imperative to send a battle cruiser to guard North Atlantic sea lanes. Jellicoe rejected the idea on 10 November noting "it is in the highest degree improbable that Germany would send heavy cruisers into the Atlantic."[68] He was right. The Germans had something else in mind.

They held their conference on 3 October aboard *Friedrich der Grosse* with Chief of the Admiralty Staff Hugo von Pohl, High Seas Fleet Commander Friedrich von Ingenhohl, and the commanders of the First, Second, and Third Battle Squadrons. At the meeting, it was decided to continue the defensive *Kleinkrieg* strategy, and not use the fleet to directly seek battle with the Grand Fleet for the present. They had not yet appreciated that a calculus based on the mere existence of ships was a vastly imperfect measure of the enemy's strength. Only much later in the war did the Germans appreciate a more detailed assessment was required. Both the commanders could correctly estimate their own strength, but not the enemy's due to lack of detailed information or analysis. On the British side, amateur estimates of British strength by Churchill compared to more accurate estimates by Jellicoe would lead to some serious disagreements. This was because Churchill had a political view and Jellicoe a professional one, and probably because Admiralty intelligence had matured to the point where it could give either political or professional customers precisely what they needed. This is an area for further research.[69]

The Kaiser concurred and the order was passed to all Admirals the following day. German operational focus shifted to offensive mine laying with strong surface craft support, the twin objectives being both the toll the mines would take in situ and the possible bait the forces would be for the defensively minded British.[70] Ingenohl proposed a major operation off the English coast, noting that fleet morale and readiness would be improved by a sortie under war conditions. The operation was approved by the Admiralstab [Admiralty Staff] in Berlin and the Kaiser in Grand Headquarters. He specified that airship and aircraft scouting were to be used to assure the fleet would not be surprised or cut off. The details of the plan to mine and bombard the British east coast began to take shape on 26 October, when Hipper wrote the first of three drafts of the Operations.[71] War Plan 19 emerged from Hipper's drafts and was basically a mine laying operation by cruisers of the Second Scouting Group. They were to transit to attack under cover of darkness, conduct

the bombardment and lay their mines by daybreak and steam back to
the Jade. Hipper's battle cruisers were to stand by off the coast and out
of sight; their mission was to deal with superior enemy forces, light or
heavy should the mine laying cruisers need support. A division of torpedoboats was to escort the light cruisers and attack shipping should
targets of opportunity arise. At first, Admiral von Ingenhohl objected
to the plan because a hospital was in the direct line of fire of the coastal
batteries and a stray projectile might have terrible consequences.[72] But
this factor was less important because the British had recently captured
a German hospital ship sent out to rescue the survivors of four torpedoboats sunk in the English Channel. The final plan emerged without
escorting torpedoboats because of the danger of fratricide on German
mines and the newly planned bombardment of Great Yarmouth by the
First Scouting Group.

In their official history, the British called this action the Gorleston
Raid. It did not make the Jellicoe papers, but it did increase Beatty's "ap-
prehension that he might have to encounter a future raid with inadequate
force, a fear no doubt reinforced by the news of Rear Admiral Craddock's
defeat at Coronel, the result, as Beatty was convinced, of the Admiralty's
failure to provide him with adequate force."[73]

The British did not have actionable intelligence that the Germans
were in such close proximity to the Thames estuary during the Gorleston
Raid.[74] The British official history concluded that it was "an operation of
no military significance whatever." Admiral von Ingenohl had intended
the raid to raise fleet morale as it was an operation in wartime circumstances. In any case, the High Seas Fleet was out in force in support of
Hipper, albeit about three hours steaming behind him. The German
fleet did get about half way across the English Channel.[75] The British
response was confused and late, and but for the gallant efforts of three
small ships – *Halcyon, Lively,* and *Leopard* – the Germans would have
been completely unhindered. But there were officers in the German navy
who had the same target practice mentality as their Admiralty counterparts: Admiral Paul Behncke, deputy Chief of the Admiralty Staff, questioned expenditure of so many armor piercing shells against non-naval
targets; Admiral Pohl endorsed the criticism and caused a rejoinder from
the Fleet C-in-C von Ingenohl that only 40 armor piercing shells per ship

had been used and most of them against the attacking light ships not land targets. He did however admit that the battle cruisers did not have high explosive ammunition and that it would be a good idea to so equip them. Thus the British were not the only ones with penurious pachyderms.[76, 77] Hipper declined to wear the Iron Cross he had been awarded because the results were so meager.[78] Ultimately, the most important thing about this operation was that the High Seas Fleet had carried out an operation which had never been practiced in peacetime and which involved combined operations of different ship types with different functions; all participants did get appropriate intelligence and operational support. Nothing really went badly from their perspective. So perhaps it was not a bad idea to repeat the operation with more ambitious goals.

The British reaction to the raid was comprehensive. It was only three days before Gorleston that the British First Sea Lord, Prince Louis of Battenberg, had resigned and been replaced by the superannuated Sir Jackie Fisher. This change was on the mind of the British high command and came at a time when the British Navy, admiral to seaman, were frustrated by a lack of decisive action and unwillingness to take any risk. The lack of confidence had spread to the British Prime Minister who had come to believe "the Germans are so much better than we are at sea." This all came about because from the British perspective there had been the escape of the *Goeben* and *Breslau* in August; the loss of the *Aboukir, Hogue,* and *Cressy* to a single U-boat in September; the loss of *Audacious* in October to a mine; and the loss of another cruiser, *Hermes,* to a torpedo the week before. On top of this, there was now the Gorlesdon raid. The Germans had no idea how badly spooked the British were.[79] On the day of the attack, Jellicoe was at Lough Swilly with the Grand Fleet. The First and Second Battle Cruiser Squadrons were directed to proceed toward Heligoland to cut off Hipper whose presence had been reported in the Gorleston Raid. But the orders were cancelled when it "became apparent our ships would arrive too late to intercept the enemy." The Germans did lose the armored cruiser *Yorck* on a mine returning to port.[80] The other news was that the British had been defeated at Coronel by Admiral von Spee. Jellicoe was deprived of two of his battle cruisers, *Inflexible* and *Invincible,* which were sent to sink the German East Asia Cruiser Squadron, which they did off the

Falklands, performing one of the tasks for which they were designed. The British response to Gorleston was not just military. The raid resulted in a proclamation to neutrals which declared the mining of the North Sea a violation of the Hague convention and appealed for support from neutral powers. In addition, the British moved the Third Battle Squadron from the Grand Fleet to Rosyth along with the Third Cruiser Squadron. They did not get there until 20 November.[81] They wanted a naval force farther south than Scapa immediately available instead of the relatively modern pre-dreadnought squadron then on the east coast. The British also suspected something bigger. So they decided to probe despite the risk and send their available forces deep into the Bight.[82] This action took place but without any contact with the Germans. For their part, the Germans deployed six U-boats into Grand Fleet operating areas. Subsequent to the action, frustration on not achieving larger goals drove the Germans to again consider an Atlantic raid by battle cruisers referenced earlier, but common sense prevailed.[83]

As we examine this series of operations on both sides, it appears there was a building series of events which would eventually result in a major engagement. What both sides had in common was the propinquity of forces, the intent to take risks to achieve tactical and strategic objectives, and a greater willingness to risk battle cruiser forces rather than core battle squadrons.

There were three more incidents between the Great Yarmouth Raid and Dogger Bank which offered possible action. One of them came very close to a major engagement between fleets and nearly to an outcome very detrimental to the British. The two occasions on which nothing happened were the sweep of 5–15 November 1914 and the bigger effort 17–23 November. The first action was a battle cruiser sweep by Beatty's command which covered a box in the northern North Sea, leaving and returning to the Firth of Forth when the orders to proceed were cancelled as cited above. Beatty was accompanied by half a destroyer flotilla and the First Light Cruiser Squadron. He crossed the track of U-24, which was sighted by a British light cruiser on the 10th, but no engagement occurred.[84] The next action was a sweep of the Grand Fleet from 17 to 23 November 1914 and the subsequent penetration by the Grand Fleet into the German Bight to less than 50 nautical miles west of Helgoland. These two operations were connected and occurred in the context of intensive U-boat activity. During the earlier period, there were no less than six U-boats hunting British capital ships in what were Grand Fleet operating areas. The Grand Fleet itself had proceeded well into the southern North Sea and, in addition, there was U-boat activity in and around the Dutch and Belgian coasts, but it did not interfere significantly with the transport of the British Expeditionary Force. Movement of the High Seas Fleet was the true measure of willingness to take strategic risk, as was that of the Grand Fleet. The bottom line is that there was a tremendous amount of movement without major contact and it was sequential – in other words, there was activity on the part of both major fleets from 3 November 1914 onward; from the Grand Fleet almost from the start of the war. There was no *Sitzkrieg* in the North Sea.

The Grand fleet operation from 17–23 November is an interesting if little reported event. The Grand Fleet and the battle cruisers returned to Scapa and Rosyth, coaled and resupplied, and proceeded to rendezvous at a point near the center of the North Sea on 23 November. From here, the British force proceeded south to a point northwest of Heligoland and turned about heading North and home. If Hipper is to be believed, both sides got very close before turning around:

> 24 November. 1000. A signal comes in from Helgoland that 4 enemy destroyers are off the island. Then additional reports come in indicating the sighting of enemy warships; the last one I saw indicated 5 battle cruisers, 3 light cruisers and some destroyers in the vicinity of the island; at 1200 the Island [which was fortified with several 30.5 cm gun turrets, among other heavy weapons] opened fire. At 1210, the enemy warships turned to the Northwest, and the destroyers headed west. An aircraft later reported that the enemy force was 45 nm from Helgoland headed NW. They included 5 large cruisers of the *Devonshire* class, 12 light cruisers and 8 destroyers. He dropped 5 bombs and hit one of the *Bristol* class with a bomb [sic].[85]

It was during this operation that one of many very severe storms occurred. The reason for the sortie was to intercept a suspected German battle cruiser breakout into the Atlantic.[86] Jellicoe also notes that during this time "reports of German submarines being sighted were very numerous" but that searches for them were fruitless. Indeed there were six U-boats hunting in the Grand Fleet operating areas at the time. Lack of success may be put down to the extremely poor weather, and for the

larger surface operation, the fact that the Germans decided not to risk
their entire battle cruiser force at this time, although with three British
battle cruisers detached it would have been a good time to do so. Both
sides had holes in their intelligence as well as [confusingly] elongated
decision-making processes.[87] This may mean the British were seeking
a way to avenge Gorleston but were discouraged by mines, aircraft, and
possibly U-boats at the last moment.

WAR OPERATION 20. SCARBOROUGH AND HARTLEPOOL

On 15 and 16 December 1914, another operation which involved the entire High Seas Fleet, both German and British Fleets and ultimately the
entire Grand Fleet occurred. Scarborough and Hartlepool, two British east coast towns, were bombarded by the First Scouting Group. A
pattern had by now emerged – both sides were conducting probes with
battle cruiser forces supported by the main fleets, in spite of reluctance
and risk aversion by higher authority. A level of disconnect and lack of
willingness by peacetime admirals on both sides to fight in this engagement led to even more frustration in both fleets. The strategic purpose
for War Operation 20 was to entice the British Grand Fleet, or part of
it, from its base at Scapa Flow to within range of German underwater weapons and/or an overwhelming engagement with the High Seas
Fleet. The objective of the operation was to attack the British east coast,
which would precipitate an outcry from the populace for more protection and which in turn would lead to a re-positioning of British forces,
designed to break up the concentration achieved by the establishment
of the Grand Fleet. The plan also involved laying mines off Scarborough
and Hartlepool designed to interfere with British coastal shipping. From
the German perspective, the operation was designed to attack two larger
and more important targets. Hartlepool had a reasonably large harbor
and some coastal defense works and Scarborough had coast guard station and light coastal artillery. War Operation 20 called for German fleet
commander von Ingenohl to steam out to the middle of the Dogger Bank
and stay there until Hipper finished the bombardment of Scarborough
and Hartlepool and the mining of the offshore waters. Hipper carried
out the bombardment and mining despite the gallant opposition of local

forces, which he dispersed with a few well-placed broadsides. *Blücher*, however, was hit several times and suffered six killed.

The British Admiralty knew Hipper was coming because of a combination of signals analysis, code-breaking, and probably human intelligence, and issued both alert messages and warning orders to Jellicoe and Beatty on the 14th. Beatty's first biographer says Jellicoe knew as early as 11 December that a German sortie was likely.[88] The British Naval Intelligence Division (NID) "also knew this [five battle cruisers, including *Moltke, von der Tann, Seydlitz, Derfflinger,* and *Blucher,* and light cruisers and destroyers] force would leave the Jade early the next morning of the 15th and would return on the evening of the 16th."[89] The Admiralty did not have evidence of a High Seas Fleet movement, so they tailored the intercept force to deal just with Hipper and his escorts.[90] Meanwhile, until the 14th the weather was terrible, with a full gale blowing and operations limited accordingly. The fleet returned to Scapa for some shelter and repairs.[91] Beatty gives a generic description of the gales they now faced:

> We have been having a most poisonous time. Blowing very bad sea . . . Sunday night and Monday morning it was a full gale and it was not pleasant. I haven't a dry spot in my cabin. The decks leak like a sieve and it's like living under a perpetual shower bath . . . we lost a topgallant mast with the wireless and a gun went overboard . . . this is the fourth day which we have practically hove to.

And this was in the Admiral's quarters in the new battle cruiser *Lion* some 35 feet above the waterline. Imagine the rest of the fleet. Beatty at the time described the seas as not unlike those described in Joseph Conrad's *Typhoon*.[92] Notice that the wireless went overboard.

Beatty getting actionable intelligence as soon as the 11th is remarkable, considering Hipper had just finished the operations order on 25 November. His observation:

> I submitted the plan worked out today for the bombardment of Hartlepool and Scarborough. A damned dangerous thing, that one does not know where the English have laid mines or where their submarines are waiting, to say nothing of enemy warships which can be encountered either on the way our or more important across our course on the way back. The Fleet will support the operation, about 20 nautical miles behind me so that the decisive battle can be fought if we run into them. With the help of God can we succeed? I write this in case I don't come back. The plan is really that of the Fleet Commander and his chief of staff. The responsibility is theirs. It could cost us a pair of battle cruisers without

producing much. Don't put up a damn memorial for me unless I have done something.[93]

Beatty's thoughts at the time were that he was happier having been rebased at Rosyth as the chances of getting at the Germans were better from there,[94] and by 15 December he was in receipt of orders to set up an ambush or a German sortie. His own view was: "It is really splendid to think that the naval power of Germany has ceased to exist outside the Kiel Canal and its own ports, and please God even there it will be destroyed before long."[95] However, it had been a long six months and just before he got the orders for the ambush he wrote: "There is very little for me to write about . . . but it to the supreme test that we must apply for any certainty, and when it will be, who knows, if at all which I fear it will never be. Well we mustn't think too much about it but just go on."[96] The next thing we get is his report of the action.[97]

For his part, Hipper carried out the bombardment, evaded British intercepting forces, and returned with his force safely to the Jade. On returning home, Hipper discovered von Ingenhohl had turned the fleet around two hours early and more or less left him to his own devices. This did not sit well with Hipper. Hipper's danger was extreme – four battle cruisers and six dreadnoughts stood between him and his bases. The combination of circumstances that allowed Hipper to escape were very bad weather and extremely poor British communications, as well as a focus on the objective by British Admirals which involved obedience over initiative. As Tirptiz opined correctly: "On December 16th Ingenohl had the fate of Germany in the palm of his hand. I boil with inward emotion whenever I think of it."[98]

What transpired in the subsequent series of confused actions is a monument to the command and control difficulties which develop when higher headquarters, specifically the Admiralty, suffering from command personality disorders and partial information, try to control an action from a distance against weather, fog, and the normal confusion of war. One very interesting incident occurred as Hipper's force returned from their bombardment:

As the Germans headed back toward their base in the Jade River at Wilhelms-haven on December 16 after the bombardment, the weather thickened and heavy squalls reduced visibility. But the Admiralty intelligence had placed the light cruiser *Southampton* so precisely in the path of the German vessels that by 1030 Commodore Goodenough saw their shapes driving through the fog. He could not be sure that they were not British ships on station, however, so he flashed his recognition signal at them. They failed to reply; he opened fire, but soon lost contact. Two hours later, the heavy British forces sighted the enemy. But when the commander of the German light cruisers in SMS *Stralsund,* saw the giant forms of the British battleships looming up through the drizzle, he, with great presence of mind blinked the recognition signal that Goodenough had made to him shortly before. Then he turned away and escaped behind the curtains of mist before the deception could be discovered and the 13.5-inch guns could blow him out of the water.[99]

Hipper's final comment on examining the rest of the action was he only escaped because "some British Admiral made a very big mistake. Thank god."[100] The same communications difficulties were again to be obvious at Dogger Bank. What the reader needs to remember is that wireless telegraphy and its subsequent reverse engineering in intelligence, as well as the other modern command and control methods, were in their infancy.[101]

The remainder of the time between the turn of the year and the Dogger Bank was not empty. The British lost the pre-dreadnought battleship *Formidable* to the *U-24*. She belonged to the Fifth Battle Squadron of the Channel Fleet. Hipper was not amused that the commanding officers of all battleships, and five officers from each, had been given Iron Crosses. His own staff was last in line with eight. The battleships had not fired a shot or been fired at; his own Iron Cross First Class was to be delayed for another time by order of the Kaiser. Von Pohl got one just for approving of the sortie from Berlin. Hipper's mood improved when he was told that another pair of sorties were planned, this time against the Humber, possibly as soon as 11 or 12 January with the second planned on 16 or 17 January for the new moon. Little can be said of the British fleet before Dogger Bank itself, except the battle cruiser fleet had formally shifted its base to Rosyth on the Firth of Forth instead of the bogs of Scapa Flow. What did happen was that the intelligence system which had been developed under Rear Admiral Henry F. Oliver and taken over by Rear Admiral Blinker Hall had matured by the end of 1914 to a sufficient extent that the British were able to get a more reliable picture of German movements so that the Grand Fleet did not have to spend time constantly at sea in anticipation of enemy movements.[102] The Grand Fleet was out training, both west of the Orkneys and in the northern North Sea 10–13 January. The British were setting in place broad training and education processes designed to maintain the fleet for a long war. The Germans do not seem to have done much that was comparable – they did their training by Squadron not by individual ship.[103]

Meanwhile the British got the *Princess Royal* back from overseas and the *King George V* back from the shipyards. *Tiger* had joined Beatty's force in November but that was less than a perfect addition, though few were aware of it.

North Sea gales came on the first, sixth, thirteenth, and nineteenth of January. On 15 January, the Battle Cruiser Fleet was formed from the Battle Cruiser Squadron and constituted under Beatty with 1st Battle Cruiser Squadron (BCS) having the *Lion, Queen Mary, Princess Royal, Tiger,* and the Second BCS being headed by Rear Admiral Archibald Moore, in *New Zealand, Indomitable,* and *Invincible. Indefatigable, Inflexible,* and *Australia* were still on detached foreign service. This arrangement was less than successful and was to have an impact on the battle. Three major issues arose. The first was the lack of operational homogeneity of the fleet – slower vs. faster units; the second the matter of *Tiger's* operational readiness; and the third the question of Admiral Archibald Moore's compatibility and fitness for command.

The first problem was the designed speed of the earlier battle cruisers was 25 knots, and the *Lions* were 28 knots, and the *Tiger* was marginally faster still. The force also had a mix of main armaments – 12-inch guns in the earlier ships and 13.5-inch from *Lion* onwards. Dividing the fleet into two squadrons made operational sense, and recognized that the second Squadron would always be slower than the first, especially in the chase, which is what happened at Dogger Bank.

The operational readiness of *Tiger* is another issue. Coming out of John Brown's Clydebank shipyard on 3 October 1914, she provisioned and sailed for trials and work up in Bantry Bay off Ireland. She arrived at Scapa Flow to join the First Battle Cruiser Squadron on 6 November.[104] The main issue was she had only nine days of shooting in Bantry Bay and she had had ten days of stormy weather at Scapa Flow and scant opportunity to train there either. Moreover, the "main difficulty lay in the

fact that she had a very mixed ship's company, with a large number of
deserters. It had been an uphill task for her Captain to pull them together
in wartime."[105] Someone at the Admiralty had decided to put all recovered deserters in one ship – the *Tiger*. That decision may be put ultimately
at the feet of the flag officer in charge of personnel or Second Sea Lord.
Beatty knew this and had therefore to give any man put in charge of such
a crew considerable latitude in forming the ship's company and make
further allowances for the ships company's performance, which was not
likely to be good. To place such a burden on a man in Beatty's position
was to hand Hipper an extra battle cruiser. But he could not know it. The
Second Sea Lord until the outbreak of war was Sir John Jellicoe, and he
was replaced by Vice Admiral Sir Frederick Hamilton, who would have
made the decision.

The second problem with *Tiger* was the difficulty in working up her
fire control system, which was new. The British naval inventor and gunnery pioneer Sir Percy Scott had concluded that the tremendous difficulties of funnel smoke and gunfire could only be overcome by placing
"the controlling sight for the main armament . . . high up on the mast.
He called the new system director firing and took out a Patent to cover
it in 1907 . . . the fitting of Director Firing proceeded extraordinarily
slowly, and by the outbreak of war, only eight ships had received it and
for their main armaments only. The first of Beatty's ships to be fitted
was the *Tiger*, which did not join his squadron until October 1914 and
then needed a long period to work up efficiency."[106] Winston Churchill
sent Beatty a letter clearly expressing the self-justificatory political view
that ". . . the Navy is as far ahead of the German Navy ship for ship as
the Army has proven itself man for man." Roskill noted: "One wonders
from what source the First Lord can have derived such sublime and ex-
cessive confidence, and so great an underestimate of the enemy – at any
rate as regards materiel. Beatty was far from satisfied with the conduct
of the Fleet's operations as well as with the Admiralty's direction of the
navy."[107] More to the point Beatty characterized the First Lord as "unbal-
anced." Churchill also asserted that Beatty must "for the present put a
bold face on it. The *Derfflinger* is new as well as the *Tiger* and of the two I
have little doubt the *Tiger* would win."[108] The truth (and Churchill knew

it) was *Tiger* had serious problems – as Beatty put it.[109] The third problem with *Tiger* was the selection of her captain – Beatty did not have a free hand in getting Pelly, which was not a good thing. He wrote:

> The *Tiger* is not yet an efficient unit. I took her firing last week and after first salvo her guns refused to go off, all electrical communications had broken down, troubles incidental to a new ship commissioned in a hurry, and in no circumstances can she be considered to have attained the same efficiency as the other 3 cats for at least 6 months. . . . What disturbs me therefore is not doubt whether my unit could defeat its German "opposite number" but whether we can be reasonably certain of annihilating it, without which I should feel we had failed. . . . Nothing will convince me that it is sound strategy to gamble on individual superiority with possible mischance from mine and submarine] when we have at our disposal a numerical superiority which would ensure the desired result, if only we had it in the decisive area.[110]

Not only was Beatty worried about the combat readiness of his force, he was also concerned about his captains. Concerning A. E. Chatfield (who was later to become Admiral of the Fleet and First Sea Lord), Beatty vented: "he is an outstandingly obstinate human being and is inclined to be narrow-minded and tries me very highly. . . . He always sees the bad side of things and never the good . . . it does add to my worries as I can unfortunately see the bad side of things myself quite clearly & like to put them out of sight when I have considered them." The reader must keep in mind that it was the flag captain's duty always to tell truth to authority. In war the truth was often a life and death matter. Of his other captains, he was worried about the *Queen Mary* who had lost the stellar Reginald Hall to promotion and higher service at the Admiralty. Hall had been replaced by Captain Cecil Prowse, who Beatty thought "is not quite the man required for a battle cruiser, too slow in the brain, ponderous, and I fear the ship will deteriorate in consequence."[111] Captain H. B. Pelly of the *Tiger* was a concern, though his initial impression was of a "very efficient officer"[112] Pelly remained in command, but there was more. He had been overruled and lost Captain Rudolph Bentnick to the dreadnought battleship *Superb*, but got him back after Dogger Bank. Bentnick eventually served as Beatty's chief of staff. The *Tiger* was still having engineering problems which merited that Beatty send in the squadron senior engineer, Captain E. Taylor, in addition to Assistant

Constructor Stephens, to the *Tiger* at the end of December, as her material condition merited the most attention of any ship in the squadron.[113]

On top of that, he was also happy to see Commander Henry Parker, Executive officer of *Lion* leave. Apparently, the Commander had been there too long, was out of fresh ideas, and had turned into a bully, which Beatty thought was bad for the war effort.[114] As to that war effort, Beatty felt the weight of it, concluding that in four months since the war started, the weather had done nothing but gone from very bad to horrible, and in the time since the war started "thousands of lives have been hurled into eternity, and we are not much, if any the better for it."[115] Nevertheless, Beatty understood what Chatfield had to do and why and kept him around for years. A contemporary of Chatfield put it this way: "He had a character of flawless integrity and a high sense of honour . . . he had an even sturdy outlook on life . . . and a strong well balanced intelligence . . . his feet were always firmly planted on the ground and his mind firmly in control of actions."[116] He was a very good flag captain to Beatty.[117]

Then there was Rear Admiral Archibald Moore, who Beatty on 21 November characterized as "the only fly in the ointment is Moore, and it is an awful nuisance having him planted in my midst as he is of no use to me and is only a stumbling block. Poor Halsey [Captain of the *Princess Royal*] is the worst off as he has to house him and this is a sore trial. But is only a temporary measure and he will move away shortly to another squadron, and I hope to be shot of him altogether.[118] Archibald Moore ended his career in command of a squadron of elderly cruisers off Africa.[119] As Marder puts it, the British "flag and captains lists at the outbreak of the war contained relatively few officers of exceptional ability."[120] That was not true of their admirals, particularly Beatty. There are some very good appraisals of the British protagonist at Dogger Bank. As Admiral Sir William Goodenough put it: "I have often been asked what it was that made him so preeminent. It was not his great brains. . . . I don't know that it was professional knowledge, certainly not expert knowledge of gun or torpedo. It was his spirit, distinguishing between essentials and not wasting time on non-essentials. . . . The spirit of the resolute, at times it would seem almost careless, advance, (I don't mean without taking care, I mean without care of consequences) was foremost in his mind on every occasion."[121] Beatty fought in colonial wars, as did many of his ranking contemporaries in the Royal and Imperial German navies. In those wars, Beatty was early selected for Commander after having distinguished himself against Dervishes in command of a gunboat on the Nile, and shortly thereafter was one of six Commanders on the China Station when he was involved in the siege of the Taku Forts and relief of Peking legations. His first biographer, Rear Admiral W. S. Chalmers said: "It is sufficient to note that his bravery and energy were conspicuous and that he won the respect or the admiration or the devotion of all those with whom he came into contact."[122] His second biographer, Captain Stephen Roskill, said he was the last naval hero.[123]

The story on the other side of the North Sea was somewhat different. Hipper had problems of his own, including the loyalty of some ambitious captains and the slowness of German battle cruiser construction due to army demands on the work forces for their two front war.

Hipper's flag captain was Maurice von Egidy, captain of the *Seydlitz*. He was both a sailor and yachtsman whose sailor wife was known to critique his ship-handling skills when he entered harbor with *Seydlitz*.[124] Von Egidy was a seaman, not an officer concerned with strategy or greater things. He did not aspire too much else after *Seydlitz*. He would leave such ambitions to Erich Raeder and the small coterie of Admiralty Staff officers around Hipper.

Erich Raeder would rise to lead the German navy under Adolf Hitler. Hipper had great regard for his talents, however ultimately misdirected they might have been. Raeder had already served in Berlin in the public affairs department of Tirpitz's Reichsmarineamt, and as an Admiralty Staff officer had a good appreciation of the political dynamics behind fleet operations. Hipper's first biographer, Commander Waldeyer-Hartz, includes a description of both the role of the staff and its key members. The scouting forces were not a squadron or a fleet as Beatty's command became, but rather like a second-rank battle squadron, about half the size (four or five capital ships versus eight in a German BS). As Waldeyer Hartz put it, the position of the First Admiralty staff officer "which in the course of the War was broadened to that of Chief of Staff, had been held since 1913 by Commander Raeder." Raeder was number one in his class in 1894, and had performed accordingly throughout his career. Like

Hipper, he had served on the *Hohenzollern,* the Imperial yacht. More important, he had the reputation as a "highly competent officer." Hipper's own view of his chief of staff was "my most loyal helper and adviser, not only during the battle [of Jutland] but doing the whole war . . . you can say with pride that you too had your part in this work, and that thanks to your un-resting activity and clear-sightedness that the battle cruisers reached such a high standard of efficiency and were able to come through the trial by fire with such success. I must always give thanks for the fate which set you at my side and for the privilege which was granted to no other Admiral of having you with me right through the war."[125] Raeder's role was indeed critical. Raeder characterized his experience with the battle cruisers as thorough and effective preparation for the combat to come. In particular, he notes one of his responsibilities was as the Squadron communications officer responsible for the "transmissions of battle signals from the battle signal stations . . . which received particular attention during the maneuvers of 1913."[126] Raeder's insights show how the Germans prepared for their engagements at sea. Raeder also gives a picture of the German battle cruisers' evolution from an armored cruiser force; little faster than the main fleet, to a fast division of capital ships. Mirror-imaging Beatty's high-speed maneuvers and target practice, Raeder notes that in the spring of 1914: "All of our intensive efforts paid off when inspection of the Scouting Forces was held in the spring of 1914. With the Commander in Chief of the Fleet, Admiral von Ingenohl, observing from the bridge, Admiral Hipper took the battle cruisers through complicated maneuvers at high speed, executing battle signals promptly with or without the aid of radio. Even simulated 'action damages' decreased the Forces efficiency little or none." Von Ingenohl, not known for public recognition of good deeds, signaled the fleet: "Well done the battle cruisers."[127] Hipper and Raeder's relationship and mutual impact on naval strategy is further developed in Keith Bird's work *Erich Raeder Admiral of the Third Reich,* as well as the author's earlier work on Hipper. Perhaps most intriguing is the role of both in the historiography of German naval strategy. Despite Raeder's public resistance to any criticism of Tirpitz, some of which lasts to this day, the issue was not whether Tirpitz's building program and Hipper's battle cruisers had been the right ones for the Reich, rather the difficulty in admitting that the resources allocated to them were appropriate to the fleet to which the Kaiser and certainly the German navy aspired.[128] There were other officers on Hipper's staff, but none rose to the eminence of Raeder, who headed the German Navy from 1928 to 1943, and oversaw its second rise to global naval power, and finally to its destruction, for much the same resource reasons as Tirpitz's fleet. Raeder was to spend much of the last part of his life as a convicted war criminal in Spandau Prison in an allied occupied Berlin.

Later history aside, it is almost refreshing to return to an examination of the other key officers in the First Scouting Group as it entered the First World War and prepared for battle. Like Beatty's force, the Germans had been developing battle cruiser tactics since about 1911, and the captains of the battle cruisers *Seydlitz, Moltke, Derfflinger,* and *von der Tann* had been in place for some time. *Blücher* had been mobilized from training back into a front line unit and was commanded by a lower ranking commander who died of pneumonia after Dogger Bank. The German captains were Maurice von Egidy (*Seydlitz*), Magnus von Levetzow (*Moltke*), Ludwig von Reuter (*Derfflinger*), and Max Hahn (*von der Tann*). Von Egidy, a great seaman but not a strategic thinker, left the *Seydlitz* 29 November 1917 and subsequently retired.

Magnus von Levetzow of the *Moltke* served as her commanding officer from 9 January 1913 to 26 January 1916. He arrived about the same time as Hipper became commander of the scouting forces, and left the *Moltke* before Jutland. Von Levetzow rose to the rank of Rear Admiral, and was a very active political Admiral and monarchist. In terms of Hipper and the scouting forces, he brought *Moltke* to a high level of operational readiness like the rest of the force, but was constantly intriguing against his chief, whom he thought insufficiently aggressive. Hipper left himself exposed to various political admirals, but in the end they had no effect on his career.[129] Three weeks after the completion of War Plan 20 (the Bombardment of Scarborough and Hartlepool) Hipper confided to Levetzow, who was then captain of the battle cruiser *Moltke*, that "he [Hipper] felt overburdened with responsibility." Hipper's confidence triggered a campaign by Levetzow to have Hipper retired on the basis of alleged ill health. It was actual fleet policy for the BdA (Flag Officer Scouting Forces) to develop a tight bond with all his captains, which was obviously misused in this instance. Levetzow's motive however, appears to have been a combination of ambition and professional differences between himself and Hipper concerning use of the High Seas Fleet. Levetzow favored a more aggressive use of the fleet, whatever the price, than Hipper would countenance.[130] Levetzow's activities are documented in his own *Nachlass*, which is massive and comprehensive. It includes his letters asserting Hipper's weakness but no supporting letters or evidence from Hipper's other captains at that time. Actually, the reverse was true – when Levetzow attempted to get Hipper relieved in 1916, he got a letter from von Egidy, which concluded: "Hipper is perfectly satisfactory to me once he gets underway."[131] The intrigue by Levetzow came to naught. In fact, Admiral Henning von Holtzendorff, Chief of the Admiralty Staff at the time, responded to Levetzow's letter of 15 January after the battle of Dogger Bank that the letter had aged him ten years. He reminded Levetzow that von Pohl, the newly appointed Chief of the High Seas Fleet, thought highly of Hipper. Levetzow's ploy for Hipper's removal was thus ignored.[132] Hipper's ignorance of Levetzow's real nature was reflected in a comment in his *Nachlass* which records that in January 1916, that he was losing one of his best commanding officers to the fleet staff.[133]

The last captain with Hipper at Dogger Bank was Ludwig von Reuter of the *Derfflinger*. Unlike *Tiger, Derfflinger* was fully worked up by the time war broke out, and joined the First Scouting Group in November 1914. Hipper was enthusiastic about her arrival in early October, and followed her arrival in the fleet from commissioning to her joining the First Scouting Group. As soon as she arrived, he took *Seydlitz, Moltke,* and *Derfflinger* on exercises into the North Sea which involved both torpedo firings and high speed runs. He practically chortled at the speed *Derfflinger* showed on her first Fleet sortie.[134] *Derfflinger's* nick-name was "the Old Dog," which turned out to have a terrible bite at Jutland. Her captain was Ludwig von Reuter, who was later to head the Second Scouting Group. Von Reuter was to be made a Rear Admiral. He had subsequent fleet assignments and led the German Fleet into internment and scuttling after the 1918 armistice, but from all intents and purposes was a very good captain of that ship as she was brought into service. He was no Pelly. *Derfflinger* was not full of deserters either.

Max Hahn of *von der Tann* was not at Dogger Bank as his ship was in the yards, with condenser problems, and was in any case due for a badly needed two week yard maintenance period. *Blücher,* not equipped with turbines had actually passed her in the return home from the operation in December, an event which was put down to "bad coal."

Hipper's worst strategic problem was the slowness of German battle cruiser construction and army demands on the shipbuilding work forces for Germany's two-front war.[135] *Baden* and *Bayern,* the German equivalents to the *Queen Elizabeth* class were both delayed because of material and workers shortages. These ships' capabilities made them candidates for interim replacement of damaged battle cruisers after Jutland. This last fact meant that replacements for lost ships would be few in coming and it was uncertain that new ships would arrive in time to maintain the precarious ratio which was high enough to deter a British attack and low enough to deny the Germans a chance at victory. Hipper's position was more precarious than he thought.[136] For example, *Lützow* was begun in 1912, delivered in 1916; *Hindenburg* 1913, delivered in 1917; *Mackensen* 1914, never delivered; *Graf Spee* 1915, never delivered; five additional ships to begin in 1915 and three were in 1916 were never delivered.[137] Another pre-war issue which was to bedevil the German fleet in wartime was the draftee nature of the High Seas Fleet crews with a full replacement of the men taking place every year and almost 56 percent regular turnover. However, with the mobilization of wartime, there was no shortage of trained sailors as many previous crewmembers were recalled to the colors and complements filled out quickly.[138] What happened later as a result of wooden personnel practices is another story.

Two final thoughts before the battle – both commands seem to have suffered from "Battle Squadron disease." That is, in the first part of the war the battle cruisers of both sides were considered more expendable than battleships and their commanders treated as junior to battle squadron commanders. The British solved this with deft personnel moves and reorganization in 1915. The Germans recognized that fast battleships belonged with the battle cruisers and when *Baden* and *Bayern* were first delivered in 1916, the first work they found was with the battle cruisers. In fact, the crew of the *Lützow,* which had largely survived her sinking, was transferred to the *Baden* along with her commanding officer. But all that was after Dogger Bank. Then battle cruiser commanders were glorified cruiser commanders and the battle cruiser forces were the bait for the battleships of both fleets.

The second and final issue arising before the battle is the state of intelligence on both sides. Intelligence can be divided into two functional categories, approximating modern usage: order of battle – how many ships there were and of what kind; and operations – how well did these ships work, what were they doing, and where were they?

Of the first, there appears to have been good analysis done and distributed, but the British fleet commanders seem to have thought the Germans had more ships and heavier guns than they did. What seems to have been lacking is a definitive knowledge, at least in the beginning of the war, of the German shipbuilding situation and resources dedicated to the navy, as well as an understanding of German naval mobilization. That said, there was pretty good understanding of operational movements but not of the actual quality of the German fleet. We have a good understanding of German operational intelligence. We know what they did know about British naval construction but we don't know what they knew about British operational proficiency, if anything. They seem to have been profoundly ignorant of the day to day operations of the British fleet and based their decisions on pre-war assumptions. They did not know where was the British fleet was or what was it doing, at least in the first six months of the war.

In 1914, there were basically three sources of intelligence: old fashioned spies, signals intelligence, and rudimentary derived intelligence or analysis. All played roles in the battle. There were spies in both capitals, but no one has written a definitive wartime history of that element of the game or anything like the magnum opus *British Intelligence in World War II*.[139] In any case, Dogger Bank resulted from one of the most noteworthy intercepts and decryptions of all time which was accomplished by the British. The issue of analysis rises to the fore – there were no all-source analysts per-se on either side. An all-source analyst would have been a staff officer who took reports from spies, diplomats, press, wireless intercept and decryption, previously known operational histories and biographies of key enemy officers and commanders, and put it all together in context for his respective commander as information from which informed operational decisions could be made. Knowledge was power and Churchill preferred secrecy over information superiority over the enemy. So the fusion of all that was known was left not to intelligence professionals but to shore-bound admirals and staff officers and the commanders themselves. Distribution was on a need-to-know basis reflecting Churchill's paranoia about loss of the source and desire to retain as much of its immense potential power to himself. The British story is told by David Ramsay in *"Blinker" Hall Spymaster: The Man who Brought America into World War I.*[140] There was by January 1915 a good solid organization[141] in place to analyze German signals, both traffic and content. Based on a direction finding system completed in the first few months of the war, the British could tell if a German unit was underway and where it was in near real time. The problem was getting this information to the fleet after it had gone through the Admiralty maw. The Germans had direction finding stations in several places and an intercept cryptanalysis unit at Neumunster as well as transmitting facilities at Norddeich. The problem was they lacked the same kind of analysis capability as the British. It turns out both sides had copies of each other's codes, but the British were actually better at radio discipline than the Germans.

What this all meant was that in the case of Dogger Bank, the British had an intelligence advantage, acted on their information, and profited by that information. Nevertheless, as John Keegan puts it: "In peacetime intelligence services may merely tick over. In war, they are supposed to bring victory."[142]

Did the Churchill's signals intelligence coup actually do this? Like many things in history, the answer is complicated. It can be said it involved the interface and working of thousands of working parts, most of which were new to the game: human, technical, and organizational. To begin with, the Germans suffered not one but three losses of codes and cyphers in the first six months of the war. The story of the *Magdeburg* and the loss of her codebooks as told by Churchill is less than definitive. Yes, indeed the codebooks were recovered by the Russians and given by hand to Churchill. Although Germany was largely forced to use wireless, even so the advantage was not immediate and the results were not certain. A good early example was despite the fact of intercept of Tirpitz and Pohl's orders to the *Goeben* and all that their successful execution meant to the German cause, the British could not read the content of the messages at that time.[143] The British had already cut the German cables to the outside world as their first offensive act in the war. This forced use of wireless or communications on British cables represented huge risks for the German cause. This issue must be examined to understand what happened at Dogger Bank.

Five events contributed to the British tactical supremacy on 24 January. The first was the British battle cruiser construction program and fleet buildup discussed above, with all its problems. The second was the setting up of an integrated signals intelligence operation with a talented staff and the support of Churchill and Fisher and the employment of serendipitously talented people including Sir Alfred Ewing. This involved the setting up of fourteen and later fifty wireless intercept stations targeted on German naval operations.[144] The third was the recovery of the codebook (*Signalbuch der Kaiserlichen Marine*) of the cruiser *Magdeburg* on 23 August 1914. The Russians recovered the code and signal books of the *Magdeburg*, although the Germans thought they had successfully sunk them. Churchill's assertions that these were priceless documents were correct,[145] but they were only part of the story. As Kahn puts it, "even the astounding windfall of the *Magdeburg* codebook – perhaps the luckiest in the whole history of cryptography – did not enable Ewing's team to read the German naval messages, for the four-letter code words in that book did not appear in the dispatches. Moreover, the cipher book, despite the confusion surrounding the loss of the *Magdeburg*, was never found."[146] The British had one part of what needed and were working on the problem, but by the end of October they got the second part of the puzzle which were the code books and ciphers from the *Hobart*.[147] This recovery of the Imperial German Navy *Handelsschiffsverkehrbuch* by the Royal Australian Navy occurred in a boarding operation of the German merchant ship *Hobart*. The book was used by the German Admiralty both to communicate with the Merchant fleet and its combatants.[148]

The last of the fortuitous cribs occurred in late November, when a British trawler brought up the *Verkehrsbuch*, naval codebooks from the older German destroyers, *S-115*, *S-117*, *S-118*, and *S-119* which were sunk by a British force lead by the cruiser HMS *Undaunted* on 18 October 1914.[149] No evidence on the German side arose that the codebooks had been recovered. In fact, the British made deliberate and persistent efforts to recover codebooks throughout the conflict, with considerable success. Allowing for all of these insights, it still took time for the British to get their entire apparatus working. The distinguished historian of codes and ciphers, David Kahn labels Admiral Sir Arthur Wilson as the man charged by Churchill with advising top war officials of the sum and substance of intelligence from all sources about the enemy.[150] Wilson was working alongside a very taciturn and micro managing Sir Henry Oliver, whose task it was to see the operational side of the British navy got the intelligence they needed. What we do know is Admiral Oliver was largely responsible for getting Blinker Hall his job as Director of Naval Intelligence. Whatever else Oliver did or did not do, this action not only saved Hall's life (he was in danger of a coronary or stroke at the end of his *Queen Mary* service), but may have saved the British Empire's fortunes in the conflict as Hall had later a pivotal role in ensuring America entered World War I on the side of the Entente.[151] One final point must include the effectiveness of the other British Secret Intelligence Services[152] and their ability to provide good technical information on the High Seas Fleet. Some good sources allege that in the run-up to the First World War, British penetration of the German and Austro-Hungarian Admiralties was almost total.[153] The blow-by-blow description of British spies in Berlin remains to be written, as does its German opposite number in the First World War. What is obvious is that the Germans did not have an Oliver, a Hall, or a Churchill, and thus were at a disadvantage. Two intelligence disciplines were critical on the way to Dogger Bank – human intelligence and signals intelligence, and finally the need on both sides which was not really recognized before 1918, that is, "to strike the right balance between the impracticability of centralization and the dangers and drawbacks of independence and sub-division." [154] There is no doubt Churchill and his successors opted for centralization. Their use of the new SIGINT provided something revolutionary but the intelligence was often, but not always, sufficiently timely and potentially accurate enough to impact operations. The use of the other, older discipline of human intelligence, "which involved the recruitment of spies through bribery blackmail and harassment," has still not been adequately documented.[155] If the same was true in the case of the Germans, little evidence and few claims have surfaced about it. This particular subject suggests itself as an issue for examination by future historians, as most documents should be available a hundred years after the event. There is the issue of how much faith the British naval leadership placed in these reports and agents in places and of course in the wireless intercepts. Chatfield was perhaps more sanguine than Jellicoe, who wrote letters to the Admiralty on opposing strengths which gave the Germans more ships and heavier guns than the ever possessed.[156] Stephen Roskill's assessment of Churchill's choices may be the best retrospective analysis:

> The events of 24th January 1915, coming so soon after the muddles which had occurred during the Scarborough raid . . . inevitably raise the question whether the advantages of possessing excellent intelligence is best reaped by a centralized operational authority, such as the Admiralty adopted or whether the intelligence should be given to sea-going commanders and ordering of movements and dispositions left in their hands. Though the arguments in favor of both systems are evenly balanced it seems to me that confusion is less likely if the delegated system is followed.[157]

There was lots of confusion at Dogger Bank. On the other side, the Germans did not have as much national or technical intelligence talent as the British. The Admiralstab did have a responsible section for its own codes and ciphers, the Chiffrierbureau [codes and cyphers]. It was under the Zentralabteilung [central department] of the Admiralty Staff. From 1911, the organization was under the Central Department of the Admiralty Staff.[158] There was another department, under Commander William Michaelis, called the Department for Tactics and Admiralty [S] [sicherheit – security] which included wireless and communication developments – mostly the blue side service intercepts per-se Michaelis' service in the Admiralty Staff was from September 1910 to September 1913. This officer went on to command the dreadnought battleship *Thüringen* from October 1913 until February 1915, when he took over from the disgraced Rear Admiral R. Eckerman as fleet chief of staff for Admiral Von Pohl. The significance of this is that attention was paid to the key elements of wireless and communications developments for the High Seas Fleet during its buildup. It meant that H S F wireless officers were aware of and good at reading the other side's communications and analyzing communications patterns. Michaelis can be credited with a great deal more. In fact, if it were not for some shortsighted penurious Reichmarineamt functionaries, he might have given Germany the predecessor to the Enigma.[159]

There were three other Admiralty Staff departments, two with geographic responsibility – one for Europe (no mention of England) and one for the rest of the world; lastly, there was a Nachrichten-Abteilung (intelligence division) under Kapitän zur See Arthur Tapken. Alas, the records indicate more of a collection of attaché reports and newspapers from abroad, rather than a thorough all source analysis or even a collection effort. There was a thorough reorganization in April 1915, too late to help with *Blücher*, but which consolidated under the Nachrichten-Abteilung almost all intelligence functions. In addition, there was an entire Abteilung department dedicated to *Chiffrierdienst* (code and cipher service).[160] The effectiveness of this has not yet been evaluated, but would appear to have made some difference in the ability of the Germans to carry out operations, particularly U-boat operations, and battle fleet operations as well.

Another aspect of what was known and when and how such knowledge might affect battles at sea includes the definitive history of the activities of British spies and agents of influence in Berlin in World War I which remains to be written; as does its opposite number of German spies and agents of influence in the First World War. What is obvious is that the Germans did not have an Oliver, a Hall, or a Churchill, and thus were at a disadvantage. Two intelligence disciplines were critical on the way to Dogger Bank – human intelligence and signals intelligence, and finally the need on both sides not really recognized before 1918, "to strike the right balance between the impracticability of centralization and the dangers and drawbacks of independence and sub-division." To some extent, the problem became more difficult for the British, especially in anti-submarine warfare.

Churchill's verbal painting of Dogger Bank is striking: "The Germans staggered into port, flames leaping above their funnels, their decks cumbered with wreckage and crowded with the wounded and the dead, not to stir again for more than a year."[161] This is great prose, but the

deeper truth is, alas, much more prosaic. The Germans had a mixed record in recognizing their weaknesses. First the *Magdeburg*, although the
admiral commanding the task force reported the encryption key had not
been destroyed with certainty, the Admiralty Staff concluded there had
been no compromise. "They refused to believe that their codes had been
jeopardized and their communications compromised. Neither direct
evidence nor circumstantial persuaded [the authorities in Berlin at the
Admiralstab] that they had a problem."[162] One does wonder if the British
had an agent in place to make sure this happened. David Ramsay noted
that, although Prince Heinrich of Prussia, the naval station flag officer in
charge, conducted an investigation into *Magdeburg*'s loss and concluded
her codebooks could well have been compromised, the fact the ship
went aground in shallow water alone should have given rise to concerns
about the safe sinking of the codebooks. "Heinrich proposed that a new
codebook and even urged mechanical enciphering . . . the Naval Staff
ignored it [all evidence of the loss of the main naval code itself]."[163] They
did conclude the *Handelsschiffsverkehrsbuch* had been lost when the hospital ship *Ophelia* was captured – it was sent out to rescue any survivors
of the four sunken destroyers. The German Admiralty Staff refused to
believe the code had been compromised, but did conclude their super-
encryption had been, so they engaged in what Kahn called bureaucratic
tokenism and put in place new super-encryption codes after the loss of
Ophelia on 20 October and just before Dogger Bank on 20 January and
later on 20 March.

Kahn's explanation of this behavior is instructive. First, one "probable reason was that few beliefs are as widespread or as firmly held as the
belief in the un-breakability of one's own codes." Second, the Naval Staff
may have wanted to avoid the consequences [to them] of the enemy's possession of the codes. The staff would have to tell fellow officers that they
had failed and would be transferred. Plans would have to be changed.
Tactics and organizations would have to be revised. New codes, a costly
labor intensive and complex task would have to be issued. Third, the naval staff might not have understood the consequences of their breaking
the enemy code or of the enemy their breaking your codes.[164]

Indeed, all of this was reasonable for the Admiralty Staff officers in
Berlin.[165] For the fleet it would have meant operational changes, learning

new procedures quickly in time of war and recognizing they had to fix a problem. Nonetheless, willingness to confront authority was common in German naval officers of the day – some of it clandestine, some of it quite open. In fact, it got to the point where the Kaiser had to issue an edict demanding obedience of his officers. The unhappiness with inaction in the fleet regularly assailed the ears and inboxes of the Admiralty Staff.

The ability of the German navy to intercept and decrypt British signals was established and developed following developments in the German army communications stations established behind the western front. The navy-specific German signals analysis effort was established at Neumunster and led by *Leutnant zur See* Martin Braune, Imperial German Navy.[166] We do have some insight into the operational side of wireless intercept, as all signals are recorded for most actions in the German official history *Der Krieg zur See*. More interestingly there are a number of references in the *Nachlass* of the German commander at Dogger Bank. They are cryptic, and less definitive than a particular appendix to one of the battle cruiser *Moltke*'s action reports authored by Levetzow.[167] Levetzow, who may be taken as typical of Hipper's captains in his approach to intelligence, said in an extensive war diary entry on F/T (*Funktentelegraphie* – wireless telegraphy), that "during the entire return trip [of the December bombardment of Yarmouth and Scarborough] no enemy wireless traffic was heard." Levetzow also reported that the closer one got the English coast, the stronger the signals and greater the volume of the traffic. He noted that the very first mention of the German operation at sea was at 0611 and it consisted of a signal which was transmitted in groups of three letters (trinomes) and that this particular signal was repeated three times. Levetzow noted further traffic analysis by his wireless staff on the *Moltke* to the effect that there was a long signal at 0705 from station "SW." This signal was sent to the British destroyers *T-80*, *T-85*, *T-87*, and *T-90* which had engaged the German battles cruisers off Yarmouth. *Moltke* was able to confirm the exchange of further wireless traffic between the boats but not decipher it. In addition, after a final signal from T-90 at 0950, nothing was heard from other stations. Levetzow concluded it was likely the signals from and to the British destroyers were in the clear, but there was no way to prove it. Lastly, he observed that the ships which had been called in the morning were also heard from later in the evening. He thought that "al" was the wireless name of the *Lion*. Last, he observed that the name *T-90* was heard from fifteen stations on the evening of the 16th.[168]

Levetzow's observations reveal an appreciation of the importance of wireless intercept, but betray no suspicions the German code had been thoroughly compromised. Moreover, they do not explain continued functioning of the German navy against an enemy who can reasonably be assumed to have their ciphers and codes, the knowledge of which was readily available to them. U-boats were continuously unable to find targets because of weather, whereas the reality was the targets were often routed around their positions, and their height of eye was limited due to low freeboard and length of periscope masts. This issue needs another detailed look by historians to parallel the works produced about the Second World War. Beyond F. H. Hinsley and Richard Deacon, it can be said is that the works about the later period, particularly the series led by Hinsley, *British Intelligence in the Second World War,* and Stephen Dorril's *MI-6* provide retrospectives which are of some use. Jock Haswell's *British Military Intelligence* reminds readers that time, fire, and war can be very destructive to history, especially when added to administrative fiat.

The Germans placed increasing use of operational deception in World War I, but not before Dogger Bank.

Buried in all the correspondence about the battle in the German archives there is an interesting paper from the much maligned Ingenohl, dated 19 January 1915. It objects to the Kaiser's limitations on the action of the High Seas Fleet. We do not know if Hipper or the captains of his ships or the fleet's officers who were all bleating about their frustration at inaction knew about this.

Admiral von Ingenohl's paper to the Admiralty Staff wanders all over the strategic landscape. It is as if the British have put him in a box. He rejects cruiser warfare as strategically insufficient to solve Germany's problems. He does not think sending a single fast light cruiser loaded with mines will justify the risk. He does not think that the High Seas Fleet can make a difference in a decisive battle sufficient to justify expected losses. This thinking explains his premature turn around in the December bombardment operations. Further, if a battle was fought, the absolute requirement was to fight it as close to home waters as possible so damaged ships could be saved. What we see here is an admiral already defeated by British naval strategy. His view was that the only way out of the strategic dilemma was to strike at British trade and seaborne commerce and the only way to effectively do that was to conduct unrestricted submarine warfare. The date on the paper is 19 January 1915. That he ordered Hipper out five days later without sufficient support, and in the face of total ignorance of British dispositions, codes or no codes, defies logic and reveals a man either still brave enough to take risks for his country in the context of continuous cabals against him or a man on the edge of his wits.[169]

4

The Order of Battle

A large hole in a ship below the waterline is obviously far
more likely to make her sink than a hole above the waterline.
Thus when the torpedo came into service it soon posed
a much more serious threat to our battle fleet in the days
before World War I than the shells of the biggest guns.

Admiral of the Fleet Earl Mountbatten of Burma

THE "ORDER OF BATTLE" WHICH WAS DEPLOYED BY EACH SIDE
represented the sum and substances of their bureaucratic processes,
which must be remembered as competing not complementary – that is,
not mirror images of each other. The British decisions for larger displacement and heavier guns and to be able to fight at longer ranges with more
ships at hand were the result of long ago decisions made and resources
committed. The German decisions to build defensively in numbers of
ships, weight of guns and shell, and robustness of construction were dictated by other strategic considerations than the British. The fight when
met was almost even but for numbers. The decision to conduct a reconnaissance in force was dictated not just by current potential numbers, but
by numbers and actions since the outbreak of the war, which had been
going since the previous August. In light of a century's hindsight, it does
make Hipper look overanxious to get at the enemy, even at the price of
numerical risk. The competing British and German battle cruiser programs evolved differently. The British *Invincible* type was a cruiser cousin

of the *Dreadnought,* and the brainchild of Admiral Sir John Fisher, First
Sea Lord of the British Admiralty when the *Dreadnought* was conceived
and built. His opposite number responsible for the construction of the
German fleet was Grand Admiral Alfred von Tirpitz.

The British Empire and the Royal Navy and its leadership started
from different strategic assumptions than the German Empire and the
German fleet. Both fleets had started anew with the *Dreadnought* and the
Nassau, but the British assumptions were more likely to lead to victory
than the German. It was not just competing assumptions, however. Both
fleets were evolving and changing rapidly in the pre-war years and even
more so in the first six months of the war. In terms of the order of battle
of both fleets, capital ships would only be added sparingly after 1915.
Both fleets had problems with real estate and safe training grounds. Both
fleets had people problems, ammunition reliability issues, and problems
integrating newer and much larger ships and large new subordinate organizations into effective war fighting entities. These to a lesser or greater
extent effected the outcome of the first battle between dreadnoughts.

The term order of battle is an enumeration and measure of the ag-
gregate fighting units available to both sides in January 1915. The details
of many of these ships and some of the same data are covered elsewhere.
It is helpful to understand what each side had and how well it worked
so the resources available in toto can be understood. Almost all general
works of the times, including the German and British fleet commanders
present something of this in their analyses.

Both nations were reaping the benefits of decades of efforts, of which
only the last ten years focused against each other. What is important is
that both the German Imperial Navy and the British Royal Navy had
been absorbing large numbers of new, highly technical ships whose capabilities were not really known until the war. Dogger Bank established
the parameters of twentieth century naval engagements – ships fought at
unprecedented ranges, damage could be unpredictable, lethal, and not
necessarily understood, command and control was rudimentary, and
intelligence of the enemy was subject to personalities, vagaries of technology, and national characteristics. Luck was still present. The order
of battle of both sides nevertheless represented the product of national
resource allocation against national political needs and priorities, as well

as the strategic situation. From 1912 onward, the German naval challenge to the British had to take into account the needs of recapitalizing the German army against a two-front threat.

THE GERMAN HIGH SEAS FLEET OF 1915

Displacement, speed, and guns (English measures provided in brackets for comparison, e.g., 17 cm [6.7-inch] weapons). All German dreadnoughts had a heavy secondary armament of 15 cm [5.9-inch] guns; predreadnoughts had even heavier 17 cm. The German fleet was thoroughly exercised in night fighting and had excellent searchlight control. All German capital ships carried torpedoes, as did their British contemporaries.

First Battle Squadron

Ostfriesland, Thuringen, Helgoland, Oldenburg (dreadnoughts, 22,500 tons; twelve 30.5 cm guns [12-inch]; 20.5 knots, reciprocating engines coal fired; in service 1911 onwards).

Posen, Nassau, Rheinland, Westfalen (dreadnoughts, 18,600 tons; twelve 28 cm guns [11-inch]; 20.6 knots, reciprocating engines coal fired; in service 1909 onwards).

Second Battle Squadron

Preussen, Schlesien, Hessen, Lothringen, Hannover, Schleswig Holstein, Pommern Deutschland (pre-dreadnoughts, 13,000 tons; four 28 cm [11-inch], 18 knots, reciprocating engines coal fired; in service 1904 onwards).

Third Battle Squadron

Third Battle Squadron was working up in the Baltic and unavailable at the time of Dogger Bank.

Kaiser, Kaiserin, König Albert, Prinz Regent Luitpold, Friedrich der Grosse (dreadnoughts, 24,700 tons, ten 30.5 cm [12-inch] guns, fourteen 15 cm [5.9-inch] guns; 22.4 knots, steam turbines, mix of oil and coal fired engines; in service 1912–13).

König, Grosser Kurfurst, Markgraf, Kronprinz (dreadnoughts, 25,700 tons, ten 30.5 cm [12-inch] guns, fourteen 15 cm [5.9-inch] guns; 22.5 knots, steam turbines mix of oil and coal fired engines; in service August, July, October, and November 1914 respectively).

Four other super-dreadnoughts were under construction during the war, but *Baden* and *Bayern* would not join until 1916; two, *Sachsen* and *Wurttemburg*, were never completed.

There were three additional squadrons of pre-dreadnoughts including the *Wittlesbach,* older *Kaiser* class, and *Siegfried* class which were useful only for coastal defense and terribly vulnerable to underwater attack and modern shellfire.

The Scouting Forces

On the outbreak of war, all large, armored and light cruisers, destroyers, torpedoboats, U-boats, aircraft, and Zeppelins were assigned to the Scouting Forces. The overseas cruiser squadrons included the battle cruiser *Goeben* (sister to *Moltke*) and light cruiser *Breslau* in the Mediterranean, the armored cruisers *Scharnhorst* and *Gneisenau,* and light cruisers *Leipzig, Emden, Königsberg, and Dresden. Goeben* and *Breslau* survived to serve under the Turkish flag. The remainder was destroyed overseas.

The First Scouting Group was the principal subject of the German side of this story. Like their battleship cousins, German battle cruisers had a heavy secondary armament of 15 cm [5.9-inch guns] and torpedo tubes.

Derfflinger (fast dreadnought, 26,600 tons, eight 30.5 cm [12-inch guns], fourteen 15 cm [5.9-inch guns]; coal and oil fired steam turbines, 27 knots; in service November 1914). Sisters *Lützow* and *Hindenburg* would not join until 1916 and 1917 respectively. Seven other battle cruisers were either under construction or planned, but never joined during the war due to shortages of men and materiel.

Seydlitz (fast dreadnought, 25,000 tons, ten 28 cm [11-inch guns], twelve 15 cm [5.9-inch] guns; coal and oil fired steam turbines, 27 knots; in service May 1913). Flagship of scouting forces.

Moltke (fast dreadnought, 23,000 tons, ten 28 cm [11-inch guns], twelve 15 cm [5.9-inch] guns; coal and oil fired stream turbines, 27 knots, in service September 1911).

Von der Tann (fast dreadnought, 19,300 tons, eight 28 cm [11-inch guns], ten 15 cm [5.9-inch] guns; coal fired steam turbines, 25 knots attained 27.75; in service September 1910).

Blücher (hybrid, classed as large cruiser, assigned to Scouting Forces after the war broke out – see below, 15,842 tons, twelve 21 cm [8.2-inch] guns, six 15 cm [5.9-inch] guns; coal fired reciprocating engines, 24.5 knots; in service 1909, major refit/reconstruction 1913/14 Kaiserliche Werft Kiel). See both above and below for more details.

The Second and Fourth Scouting Groups comprised the light cruisers available to the High Seas Fleet; the Third Scouting Group comprised an older armored cruiser force.

The ships present at the battle from the Second Scouting Group were: SMS *Graudenz, Rostock, Stralsund,* and *Kolberg.* These ships represented construction years 1913, 1912, 1911, and 1908 respectively. They were as modern collectively as any cruisers in the High Seas Fleet, and could be considered the representative best of the light cruiser forces. They all carried only 105 mm (4.1-inch) main armament.

The *Graudenz* was built at the Imperial Naval Dockyard Kiel, and launched 25 November 1913. She was assigned to the Second Scouting Group almost from the beginning and survived the war to be surrendered as the Italian *Arcona* until 1944. Like all German light cruisers, pre-WWI she was armed with the 4.1-inch (105 mm) gun and two submerged torpedo tubes. This gun threw a small weight of shell – about 54 pounds – and was inferior in range and destructive power to the standard 6-inch main armament of the British light cruiser listed below. The *Graudenz* and her sisters were steam turbine driven and used a combination of coal and oil fuel. After the battle *Graudenz* was refitted with seven 5.9-inch guns and an additional two deck mounted torpedo tubes. She and her sister were also fitted to fit to carry 120 mines. This was after the battle, and in the face of yet further opposition from Tirpitz on financial grounds. *Graudenz'* other data was as follows: length about 139 meters; displacement, 4,900 tons; speed about 29 knots; armament twelve 4.1-inch, two underwater torpedo tubes, complement 373. She had a ¾-inch deck and a 2.5-inch armor belt.

The *Rostock,* was built at Howaldswerke commercial shipyard Kiel, and launched 12 November 1912. She was sunk at Jutland in May 1916. Armed with twelve 4.1-inch guns and two submerged torpedo tubes.

They were identical to the *Graudenz* guns. *Rostock* used a combination of coal and oil fired boilers which drove steam turbines on two shafts. Rostock's other data was a follows: she was 139 meters long; displacement 4900 tons; speed about 27.3 knots; armament as noted above and complement 373. She had 2.5-inch main belt and a ¾-inch deck.

The *Stralsund* was built at the A. G. Weser Bremen and launched on 4 November 1911. This class included the ill-fated *Magdeburg,* whose loss included that of the German navy's codebooks; the *Breslau,* which survived into 1918 until lost on several mines. *Strasburg* was the last large German ship to get home prior to the war. This class was initially bad seaboats and had to be refitted with larger bilge keels. They were rearmed with 15 cm [5.9-inch] guns but too late for Dogger Bank. *Stralsund* actually survived as the French *Mulhouse* until 1935 when she was scrapped at Brest. Other data as follows: she was 136 meters long; displacement was 4550 tons; speed was 28.3 knots on three shafts; armament at the battle was twelve 10.5 cm guns and two 20 cm underwater torpedo tubes. She had a 2.75-inch main belt and a ½-inch deck.

The *Kolberg* was the oldest and smallest light cruiser present in the Second Scouting Group at Dogger Bank. Her sisters *Mainz* and *Köln* had been sunk at Heligoland Bight. Her other sister *Augsburg* was a torpedo and gunnery training ship. *Kolberg* was built at the Imperial Naval Dockyard Kiel and launched on 10 July 1909. She was 130 meters long, and displaced 4,350 tons. She was coal fired and could achieve a speed of 25–27.5 knots on four shafts. Like her sister ships, she had twelve 10.5 cm [4.1-inch] guns and two underwater torpedo tubes.

The German light cruiser and destroyer program was the result of different national priorities that that of the British. These ships were built to provide a tactically effective if minimal scouting capability for the German battle fleet and as overseas cruisers to protect a growing merchant fleet and a much smaller collection of colonies from lesser powers. The Germans built a total of thirty-eight light cruisers from 1895 through 1918, compared to sixty-four for the British. The British started arming light cruisers with 15.2 cm [6-inch] guns in 1908; the Germans, due mostly to penury, did not fix the problem until 1915, when they engaged in a significant up-gunning from 10.5 cm (4.1-inch) to 15 cm (5.9-inch).

The German destroyers present at Dogger bank were there functioning as a underwater attack capability which would allow Hipper and his big ships a counter to larger British numbers and provide cover for escape, as the perennial lesser force. The "torpedoboat crew" alumni association included most of the upper echelons of the German navy, but surprisingly when they got there they did not always provide for more powerful or more expensive and thus more effective German destroyers. Hipper's destroyer escort forces included the Ninth, Tenth, Fifteenth, and Eighteenth Half Flotillas. These included the V-1, G-7, V-181, and S-33 classes; the chart for the battle in the German official history includes this list, while the text account says Fifth torpedoboat Flotilla V (nine vessels) and Fifteenth and Eighteenth Half Flotillas (10 vessels) were actually present. For the sake of completeness, all the types mentioned in the chart will be covered. There were in addition U-21, in the outer German gulf, which was closest to the action, followed by U-19. Other U-boats were assembling, but would only be in a position to attack crippled British ships in the inner gulf, should they appear. On average, half of the German U-boat forces were in overhaul in early 1915. Data on U-19 and U-21 is also included as real or imagined U-boat threats did affect the course of the battle.

Because the German destroyers were largely coal fired, their engines required regular maintenance and only five and half flotillas of the eight assigned to the High Seas Fleet were normally ready for action at any one time. Beyond this, there were serious readiness problems. The German official history noted: "The longer the war lasted, the more difficult it became to pick the right moment for opening offensive operations."[1] And even worse: "The monotony of reconnaissance work without frequent encounters with the enemy quickly lowered the high level of training at the outbreak of the war. From the beginning of the war up to January 1915, neither the First or Third battle squadrons nor the destroyer flotillas (with the exception of the ninth and a few individual vessels) had any opportunity to engage in torpedo practice. There were several new ships which never had any trials of their torpedo equipment. The same is said to be true of day and night artillery practice with wartime munitions."[2]

So Hipper's escorts were less than fully trained and tactically rusty, but led by experienced officers and full of talented crews. Here are the particulars for the destroyers he had along: *V-1, G-1, V-187, S-33* classes.

V-1 class was built by A. G. Vulcan Stettin. They were 235.5 feet long, displaced 569 tons, and were capable of 32/33 knots on twin turbine powered shafts, driven by coal fired boilers. They carried two 10.5 cm [4.1-inch] guns, four above water torpedo tubes and could be fitted with 18 mines. Their complement was 73.

The *G-1* class was built at Germaniawerft from 1908 onwards and displaced about 650 tons. They carried four torpedo tubes and two mines and were equipped with two 10.5 cm guns like the *V-1* class. They were coal fired and capable of 32.5 knots.

The *V-187* class was built by Vulcanwerft and displaced about 600 tons, were armed with two 88 mm [3.5-inch] guns and four torpedo tubes – two single trainable mounts and one amidships twin trainable mount. They were capable of 32.5 knots.

The *S-33* class was built at the Schichauwerke in Danzig and displaced about 750 tons. They were armed with two 88 mm [3.5-inch] guns carried eight 20-inch torpedo tubes, in four twin mounts. They were coal fired turbine driven and capable of 32.5 knots.[3]

Aircraft and U-boats

Two other types of military unit matter for the Germans at Dogger Bank – aircraft and U-boats. The aircraft include Zeppelins, which were scouting for Hipper and one of which, *L-5* allegedly dropped bombs on *Blücher*'s rescuers, and an aircraft from Helgoland which did drop bombs on the battle scene. In addition, there were several U-boats alerted to assist Hipper's forces returning but none in the battle area. *L-5* was actually present throughout the engagement and followed the First Scouting Group home, making sure of no further British pursuit.[4] The aircraft were from Borkum and Helgoland and were aircraft number 25 and aircraft number 83.

The closest U-boat was *U-33*, in the German Bight; *U-17* and *U-14; U-34* had a casualty and was headed for Helgoland harbor. The first three were headed northwest at 1320, to support Hipper.[5] These ships, small and primitive, were extremely dangerous to British surface ships, especially older ones. The *U-9* had sunk the armored cruisers *Aboukir, Hogue,* and *Cressy* in the fall of 1914.

U-14: displacement 514/644 tons; length 190 feet; heavy oil/electric motors 14.8/10–7 knots; 4–18 inch torpedo tubes; complement 29. *U-14* was rammed and sunk by the trawler *Hawk* after being disabled by gunfire off Peterhead 5 June 1915.[6]

U-17: displacement 564/691 tons; length 204.25 feet; heavy oil/electric motors 15.4/9.5 knots; 4–18-inch torpedo tubes; complement 29. She survived the war and was broken up in Germany.[7]

U-33: displacement 685/878 tons; heavy oil/electric motors 16.7/9.7 knots; 4–20-inch torpedo tubes; 2–3.4-inch guns; complement 35. She survived the war and was scrapped at Blyth after surrendering.[8]

THE BRITISH ORDER OF BATTLE JANUARY 1915

This section includes the Grand Fleet as it was in December 1914, as a comparison to the High Seas Fleet shown above. The British fleet worked up to wartime conditions, recognized a need for training and set up schedules for doing it beginning in October 1914, when it began to appear there was less and less prospect of the war ending quickly.

The British fleet was composed of the dreadnought battle fleet of three dreadnought battle squadrons and the Third Battle Squadron (pre-dreadnoughts) and two battle cruiser squadrons, with associated cruisers and destroyers.

The British Grand Fleet was composed of three battle squadrons of seven ships each with the fleet flagship *Iron Duke*. The squadrons were not as homogeneous as the Germans as ships of different classes ended up in each.

Divided by class there were:

Iron Duke, Marlborough, Benbow, and *Emperor of India,* at 25,800 tons displacement, with ten 13.5-inch guns, coal and oil fired steam turbines, speed 21 knots, 1911 program.

King George V, Centurion, Ajax (*Audacious* was lost on a mine in 1914), at 25,700 tons, with ten 13.5-inch guns, coal and oil fired stream turbines, speed 21 knots, 1910 program.

Orion, Monarch, Thunderer (*Conqueror* in dockyard hands repairing from a collision), at 22,500 tons displacement, ten 13.5-inch guns, coal and oil fired steam turbines, speed 21 knots, 1909 program.

St Vincent, Collingwood, Colossus, Hercules, Neptune, Vanguard (*Superb* in dockyard hands), *Bellerophon, Dreadnought*, 17,000–20,000 tons displacement, ten 12-inch guns, coal and oil fired, 21 knots, 1908, 1907, 1906, and 1905 programs.

Erin (ex-Turkish), 22,780 tons displacement; ten 13.5-inch guns, coal and oil fired steam turbines, speed 21 knots, 1914 war acquisition.

Agincourt (ex-Turkish), 27, 500 tons displacement; fourteen 12-inch guns, coal and oil fired steam turbines, 22 knots, 1914 war acquisition.

Of these *Benbow, Emperor of India, Erin,* and *Agincourt* could not be considered fully combat ready.

The Grand Fleet mattered for 24 January 1915 because it was only three hours steaming behind the battle cruiser engagement (see Corbett map for strategic disposition). Attached to the Grand Fleet were four light cruisers *Sappho, Bellona, Boadicea,* and *Blonde* and the destroyer *Oak.* In addition, there were the First, Sixth, and Seventh Cruiser Squadrons totaling nine armored cruisers and the four light cruisers of the Second Light Cruiser Squadron. There was also integral to the fleet the Second Destroyer Flotilla of twenty ships led by the light cruiser *Galatea* and the destroyer leader *Broke.*

These ships took no part in the Dogger Bank action itself, but would have engaged should a general action with the High Seas Fleet developed.

In close support of Admiral Beatty's force, there was also the Third Battle Squadron based in Rosyth, composed of six pre-dreadnoughts of the *King Edward VII* class. These were the *Dominion, Hibernia, Africa, Britannia, Hindustan,* and *Zealandia. King Edward VII* and *Commonwealth* were refitting and not present for the action. The Third Cruiser Squadron of four armored cruisers supported this battle squadron. Three armored cruisers of the four were available. The *King Edward VII* class were the latest large class of pre dreadnought and displaced 15,600 tons, were armed with four 12-inch and four 9.2-inch guns; they were powered by coal and oil fired triple expansion steam engines giving a speed of 18 knots. These ships were meant as a blocking force should Hipper have attempted to escape toward the east, or as a support force, should Beatty need additional assistance.

The British forces actually engaged in the Dogger Bank battle included the First and Second Battle Cruiser Squadrons, including the *Lion, Tiger, Princess Royal, New Zealand,* and *Indomitable,* and the First Light Cruiser Squadron, including *Southampton, Birmingham, Nottingham,* and *Lowestoft.* The Harwich flotillas also participated on the British side and they included light cruisers *Arethusa Undaunted,* and 35 destroyers.[9]

Lion: displacement 27,000 tons, eight 13.5-inch guns, coal and oil fired steam turbines, 27 knots, 1909 program.

Princess Royal: displacement 27,000 tons, eight 13.5-inch guns, coal and oil fired turbines, 27 knots, 1909 program.

Tiger: displacement 28,430 tons, eight 13.5-inch guns, coal and oil fired turbines, 29 knots, 1911 program.

New Zealand: displacement 18,500 tons, eight 12-inch guns, coal and oil fired turbines, 25 knots, gift of the government of New Zealand 1910.

Indomitable: displacement 17,410 tons, eight 12-inch guns, coal and oil fired turbines, 25 knots, 1905 program.[10]

The light cruisers involved in the Battle of the Dogger Bank were remarkably similar to their German contemporaries except in the matter of main armament.

Birmingham, Nottingham, and *Lowestoft* were a three ship class launched in April, May, and April respectively, in 1913. They displaced 5,400 tons, were 430 feet long, and were armed with nine 6-inch guns and two 21-inch underwater torpedo tubes. They were coal and oil fired turbine driven ships, designed for 24.75 knots. *Nottingham* was built at Pembroke dockyard. *Birmingham* was built at Elswick and *Lowestoft* at Chatham dockyard. All three were completed in 1914.

Southampton, the Commodore's ship, was of a slightly earlier class also of three ships. She displaced 5,400 tons, was 430 feet long, and was armed with eight 6-inch guns and two 21-inch underwater torpedo tubes. She was built on the Clydebank and had an American pattern Curtis turbine and two screws which could drive her at 25 knots. She was coal and oil fired.

Arethusa and *Undaunted* came from the latest class of Royal Navy
light cruisers to enter service on the outbreak of war. They displaced
3,520 tons, were more lightly armed with two 6-inch and six 4-inch guns.
Like the other cruisers in Beatty's packs they were 450 feet long, and
turbine powered, but were all oil fired. *Arethusa* was built at Chatham
and *Undaunted* at Fairfield. They were designed for 30 knots. The entire
cruiser element of Beatty's force was new ships and led by fine officers
such as Commodores Goodenough and Tyrwhitt.

The destroyer of the Royal Navy in 1915 was the result of as much
if not more technical and operational effort as expended in the German navy. The ships were more numerous and larger, and like their light
cruiser cousins, more heavily armed than their German contemporaries.
The British destroyers which concern this work include the Second
Flotilla, which escorted the dreadnought battle fleet with 16 ships; the
Fourth Flotilla of seventeen ships, which was assigned to the battle cruisers; and the Harwich flotilla of twenty ships, which could be used as the
Admiralty saw fit to employ in support of their objectives. Peacetime and
initial wartime organization for British destroyer flotillas was twenty
ships, divided into five divisions of four boats each. Each flotilla was led
by a captain in a light cruiser or a specially designed flotilla leader later
in the war. One division was always in maintenance, while the others
were on notice of one, two, or three hours' steaming. There were several
classes of destroyer involved in the Dogger Bank on the British side,
including:[11]

(14) *I* class: displacement 767 tons; length 246 feet; armament: two
4-inch, two 12pdrs, two single tubes with total of four 21-inch torpedoes
carried; speed 27–32 knots depending on builder of where built; Yarrow,
Thorneycroft, or Parsons. The engines were oil fired steam turbines. They
were from the 1910–11 building program. Oil was very important because
it decreased the strain on crew, required half the number size engine
room ratings, and took up less of the displacement.[12]

(7) *M* class: displacement 1,154 tons; length 273feet; armament: three
4-inch; two pom-pom; two pairs of double tubes and four 21-inch advanced whitehead torpedoes carried. The engines were oil fired steam
turbines with a radius of action of 2500–3000 nm.[13]

(12) *L* class: displacement 1,000 tons; length 269 feet; armament three 4-inch guns, one machine gun, two sets of double tubes, four 21-inch torpedoes carried, four mines; speed 29 knots. The engines were oil fired steam turbines; these ships had a 2,800 nm radius of action without refueling. The builders were included in the 1912–13 program.[14]

There were an extraordinary number of variables which underlie the outcome of this initial battle between dreadnoughts. First and foremost, there were the realities of the vulnerabilities to underwater attack of this kind of ship, especially on the British side. Next, there are the contrasting capabilities and limitations of each side's ships, after that, the men who manned and led them, and finally, the overarching physical environment in which both sides had to function. Pre-eminent values for the British in their order of battle construction were superiority in numbers, firepower, and speed. For the Germans, from dreadnought down to destroyer, pre-eminent values were cost-effectiveness and either tactical or technical counters to British numbers and firepower. Ultimately, the political constraints on Tirpitz dictated many of the characteristics of von Ingenohl's and von Hipper's order of battle. For the British, their political leadership in Churchill almost guaranteed any technical or tactical innovations by the Germans would not matter.

Nevertheless, in this first battle the German 21 cm [8.2-inch] gun on *Blücher* proved a check on British destroyers at key points in the battle, yet also proved unable to seriously damage British battle cruisers either. The lighter 28 cm [11-inch] and 30.5 cm [12-inch] guns carried in the rest of the German force did prove deadly to the more lightly protected British ships; nevertheless, the destructive power of the 34 cm [13.5-inch] gun proved decisive in the destruction of the *Blücher* and the near loss of the *Seydlitz*. The mere existence of the German U-boats and destroyers listed above proved effective in blunting the British tactical advantage achieved in the chase. The role of the leadership in the action was also critical, in terms of the decision to break off the fight with the German battle cruisers and concentrate on the destruction of the *Blücher*. The impact of admirals' mistakes on order of battle, no matter how carefully built and trained, cannot be underestimated.

5

Chase and Intercept

THE OUTCOMES OF BATTLES ARE ALWAYS DRIVEN BY A MIX OF deliberate decisions off and on the battlefield, echelons of mistakes in both places, and fortune or luck. They are frightening, exhausting, and deadly. They are a reflection of a determination to impose will by force. Dogger Bank 1915 was all of these.

The essential facts of the engagement are not at issue. The Germans had the role of tactical initiator, as they could decide when to come out, and the British in their role as distant blockader would respond. Knowledge of the German plans, as revealed within twenty-four hours by radio intercept and decryption of operations orders made the British task easier. If something were to go wrong on the German side, it was because those who deployed the forces underestimated the risk in facing the strength and timeliness of the enemy response. If anything could go wrong on the British side, it was the responsibility of those who deployed the counter forces and those who operated them.

The German orders went out over wireless from the flagship *Deutschland,* the pre-dreadnought lying in the Jade, serving in place of the *Friedrich der Grosse,* the normal dreadnought fleet flagship, which was in the Baltic on exercises with the rest of the Third Battle Squadron, the most powerful in the High Seas Fleet.[1] This meant that only the First and Second Battle Squadrons, comprised of eight early but powerful dreadnoughts of the *Helgoland* and *Nassau* classes and eight pre-dreadnought of the *Deutschland* and *Braunschweig* classes, were available to support any sortie by the battle cruisers. The German objective was to roll up any British trawlers on their line of advance and sink any stray warships in their line of advance, which was a sortie in the direction of the Dogger Bank. There was no evidence of any target worthy of the coal expenditure of the battle cruisers. It was as if they were being sent out as bait, but without a trap attached.

The German First Scouting Group was comprised of the battle cruisers *Seydlitz, Moltke,* and *Derfflinger,* and the armored cruiser *Blücher.* These ships have been described in detail earlier, but some salient points need to be reviewed for this part of the narrative.

It is important to remember three things: the first three ships carried 28 cm and 30.5 cm guns and the *Blücher* only 21 cm [8.2-inch]. All were fully worked up and combat ready. *Blücher*'s other main difference was that she was driven by reciprocating engines as opposed to the turbine drives of the other ships; she was smaller and slower. The question is often asked why Hipper took her along. There were three reasons. The first was she had been assigned as a member of the First Scouting Group[2] because of her size and strength. She was bigger and faster than any of the previous generation of armored cruisers. Moreover, she had modern fire control and her 21 cm [8.2-inch] guns actually had greater range than the larger weapons of the dreadnoughts – 19,100 meters range at 30 degrees elevation, which was also greater than the 13.5 degree and 18,100 meters range for *Moltke*'s larger 28 cm [11-inch] guns.[3] The second reason was that she had functioned effectively as a member of the group during the two previous operations off Scarborough and Hartlepool. Third, it was the consensus and order of the fleet commander that she belonged with the First Scouting Group. Her official speed was 24.5 knots on 32,000 IHP under forced draft. Hipper still thought her a 23 knot ship. *Moltke* and *Seydlitz* were 25–26 knots and *Derfflinger* at least 27.[4] The possible problem would be her value in a stern chase; brutally put, if she were at the end of the line, she would not slow the others' escape and would naturally absorb the attention of those enemy ships closest to the formation. The one drawback was her ammunition distribution arrangement, which was unique and vulnerable. In essence, the concentration of fire, intended or accidental, would have done serious damage to any ship at the rear of Hipper's line, dreadnought or armored cruiser. Taking her along was probably a good idea. She was for all intents and purposes an armored cruiser version of the *Nassau* class dreadnoughts.

Early in any action German fire control did have an advantage: the
length, weight, and location of its range-finders throughout the group
and on individual ships. These things were important to initial accuracy
of fire. As damage accumulated, the effectiveness of local control of main
and secondary armaments became vital. To some extent, this focus on
fire control redundancy explains the ability of *Blücher* to sustain her resistance to overwhelming firepower so long and valiantly. Peter Padfield
explains:

> The Germans had turret-mounted range-finders, manufactured by Carl Zeiss,
> which were nearly 20 feet long for 28 cm [11-inch] turrets and up to 27 feet for
> 30.5 cm [12-inch] turrets. As accuracy is directly proportional to base length,
> these were naturally far more effective instruments, and usually gave better
> opening images in the unexpectedly long-range encounters which occurred
> during the war.[5]

Since she was the fleet gunnery training ship, *Blücher* was equipped with
the latest versions of these range-finders and had multiple ones throughout the ship.

The German flagship *Seydlitz* left the Jade at the head of the First
Scouting Group and passed wartime *Lightship A* at 7 PM on 23 January.[6]
The weather was light haze, not very dark and lightly overcast. The wind
was east by north, force 2. The formation proceeded toward the Dogger
Bank according to the operations plan. An hour and a half later, they
passed the Norderney lighthouse at about 2.3 miles. Shortly thereafter,
the wind came up for about force 3. About 0500 in the morning of the
24th, *Seydlitz* and her cohorts passed through a mass of fishing boats on
both sides of the formation. SMS *Graudenz*, a light cruiser of the Second
Scouting Group acting as reconnaissance signaled flashing light that
there were vessels to the north of them which turned out to be more fishing steamers. They were of undetermined nationality as it was dark, and
their flags could not be made out. At 0557, the formation altered course
to northwest by west; at 0600, the wind shifted to east northeast and the
weather turned dark. The formation steered northeast and then northwest by ½ west and increased speed to 15 knots at 0700. Throughout
the night there was no hint of a British trap, at least aboard *Seydlitz*. The
Germans continued proceeding another 21 miles or so into the Dogger
Bank. After dawn the sky became cloudy. At that point the first gunfire

was heard towards the west and a signal followed from the light cruiser *Kolberg* that she had a light cruiser and many destroyers in sight to the southwest and behind them heavy smoke to the west southwest. *Seydlitz* and her formation turned west and increased speed. Full daylight occurred at 0829 and at 0835 Hipper turned the German formation to the south east and increased to maximum speed, which was 23 knots. He suspected a trap. A few minutes later the big ships slowed to allow the cruisers and destroyers of the escort to pass to their disengaged side and assemble on the formation's port bow. By then, the German flagship had sighted four *Arethusa* class light cruisers on the formation's starboard quarter and heavy smoke behind them. The *Arethusa*'s were deployed in a line on bearing, northeast to southwest. SMS *Kolberg* signaled two *Arethusa* class and two *Birmingham* class and behind them eight big ships.

The reader should refer to the four charts provided, two German and two British. (They are reproduced from the British and German official histories.)

At 0843, the German formation, which was in line of bearing, went to 20 knots and the German light cruisers assumed positions ahead of the big ships. By 0917, the entire formation had gone to 23 knots. At 0925, the range to the nearest British battle cruiser was 160 hm (16,000 meters). Hipper told *Blücher* to open fire.[7] The British squadron was under fire from 21 cm [8.2-inch] guns for almost three hours. *Blücher* scored some hits on the British big ships, but they were not decisive – the shells did not hit vital areas heavily enough to do serious damage to Beatty's ships. But when smaller British ships tried to close to torpedo range, they were driven off. The *Blücher* was in action for almost four hours and expended hundreds of 8.2-inch rounds. As Chatfield put it, these ships were intended to fight and survive damage from the enemy. To what extent determined the course and outcome of the action.

Meanwhile, on the British flagship HMS *Lion,* which had been at action stations since 0700, as had the rest of the squadron,[8] Beatty wrote that the cruiser "*Aurora* reported she was in action with the enemy... followed by a report that four enemy battle cruisers had been sighted bearing east South East from HMS *Southampton*." A journalist named Filson Young had unique access to this scene. Beatty and his staff were not in the conning tower. In fact: "Beatty, Chatfield, the Flag Commander,

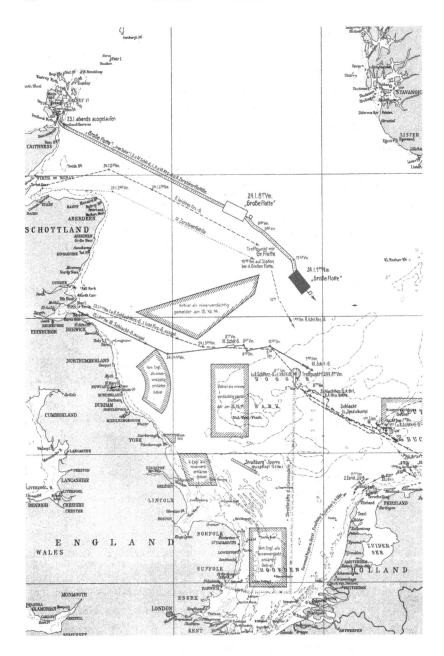

5.1. *Karte 17 Die Unternehmungen vom 23. Bis 24. Januar mittags 1915 Strategische übersichtskarte* [The Operations of 23 to 24 January 1915, Strategic Overview chart from *Der Krieg zur See*, III].

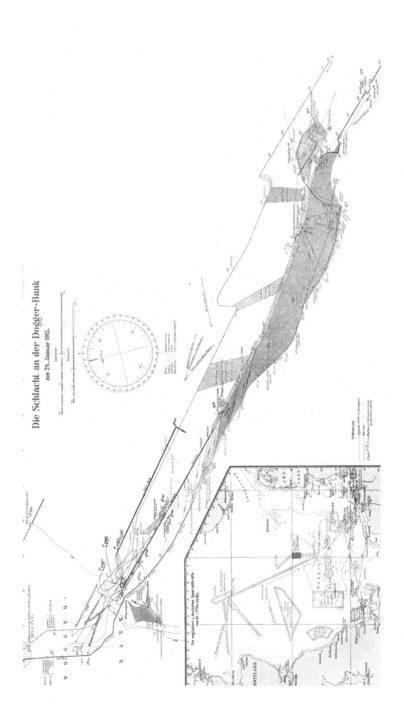

5.2. *Karte 18 Die Schlacht an der Dogger-Bank am 24 Januar 1915* [The Battle on the Dogger Bank on 24 January 1915, chart from *Der Krieg zur See*, III].

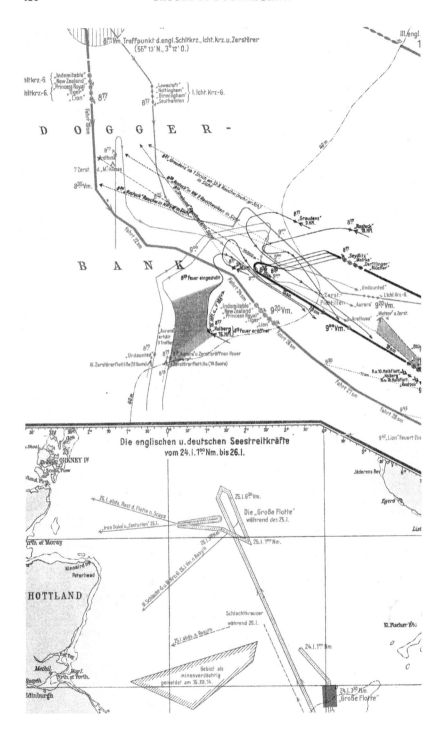

Die englischen u. deutschen Seestreitkräfte
vom 24.1.1⁰⁰ Nm. bis 26.1.

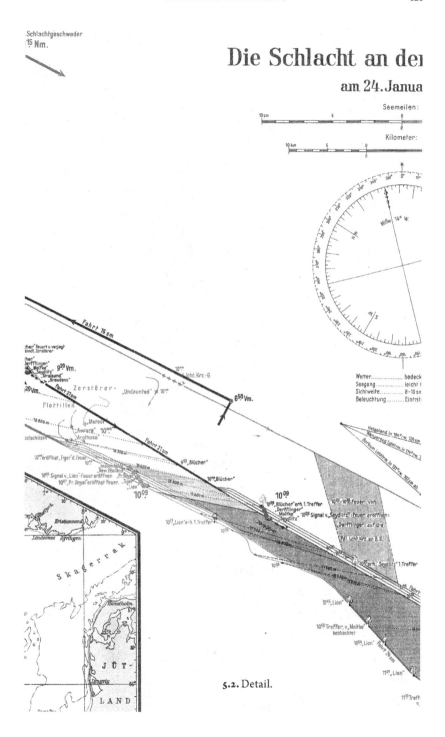

Schlachtgeschwader
15 Nm.

Die Schlacht an dei

am 24. Janua

Seemeilen:

10 sm   5   0

Kilometer:

10 km   5   0

Mißw. 14° W.

Wetter.................. bedeck
Seegang................. leicht t
Sichtweite............. 8–10 sm
Beleuchtung.......... Eintrit

Fahrt 15 sm

9²⁰ Vm.

6⁵⁰ Vm.

10⁰⁰ lcht. Krz.-6.

Zerstörer- „Undaunted" 10⁰⁰

Fahrt 21 sm

Flottillen

Helgoland in 100° w. 134 sm
Wangeroog Lehtrm. in 114° rw. 1
Borkum Lehtrm. in 119° rw. 162 sm ah

18800 m

„Aurora", 10⁰⁰
„Arethusa"

Fahrt 21 sm

9⁵² „Blücher"

10⁰⁰ „Blücher"

10⁰⁰ eröffnet „Tiger" d. Feuer

18 300 m

18 500 m

New Zealand

10⁰⁵ Signal v. „Lion" Feuer eröffnen

„Pr. Royal"

10⁰⁷ Pr. Royal eröffnet Feuer. „Tiger"

„Lion"

10⁰⁹

18800 m

10⁰⁹

10⁰⁹ „Blücher" erh. 1. Treffer
„Derfflinger"
„Moltke"
„Seydlitz"

10⁰⁹ Signal v. „Seydlitz" Feuer eröffnen

10⁰⁹–10⁰⁹ Feuer von
„Derfflinger" auf die

Fdl. Lcht. Krz. an B. B.

Kristiansund

Lindesnes Ryvrlhgen

10²¹ „Lion" erh. 1. Treffer

S k a g e r r a k

10⁰⁵ erh. „Seydlitz" 1. Treffer

Fahrt

Hansholm

10⁴⁵ „Lion"

J Ü T -

10⁵⁰ Treffer v. „Moltke"
beobachtet

10⁵⁴ „Lion" Fahrt 24 sm

L A N D

11⁰¹ „Lion"

5.2. Detail.

11¹⁰ Treffi
v.

5.2. Detail.

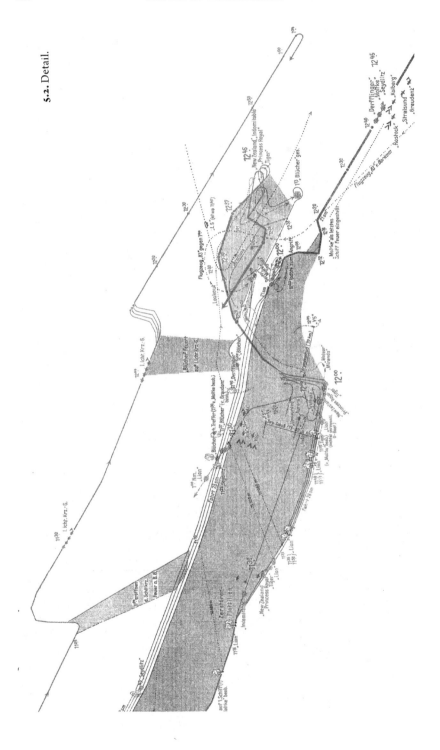

the Secretary, two Flag Lieutenants and myself [Young] were all on the compass platform, enjoying the sensation and prospects of the chase in that clear North sea air ... *Lion* being the leading ship there was nothing before me but the horizon ... the four black smudges on the port bow that only through binoculars were identifiable as big ships."[9] (See figure 5.3.)

The platform on the bridge had the best view, but was very exposed. Filson Young eventually went to the crow's nest, while Beatty conducted the battle from the conning tower and admiral's bridge below the signal bridge. At this point, admirals' bridges were primitive, unarmored, and generally uncovered. Later in the war, flagships were much better equipped with double bridges, improved redundant communications, and the like.

The German ships were on a course headed southeast; the British battle cruiser squadrons headed toward the enemy, first increasing speed to 22 knots. At about 0745, the enemy battle cruisers were sighted, and the British formation increased to full speed. The British heavy ships were on a line of bearing from east south east to west north west and the formation gradually stretched out as the slower *New Zealand* and *Indomitable* were outdistanced by the speedier *Lion, Princess Royal,* and *Tiger.* The British formation at this time was comprised of HMS *Lion* (lead and flagship), HMS *Tiger,* HMS *Princess Royal,* HMS *New Zealand,* and HMS *Indomitable.* The maximum rated speed of the formation by ship was *Lion* at 27.62 knots, *Tiger* 29.07 knots, *Princess Royal* 27.97 knots, *New Zealand* 26.3 knots, and *Indomitable* 26 knots.[10] These were maximum speeds achieved under ideal conditions years before when the ships were new. It is clear that the British had a speed advantage on paper, especially as *Blücher* could only do 23 knots. But it was more than that – when the battle opened it was not only a race of ships but of men. The two slowest ships, *New Zealand* and *Indomitable,* were about to turn in record performances due to their stokers and engineering staff. Beatty's report includes a mention in dispatches for fourteen officers and ratings from *New Zealand,* who ranked from stoker to commander, in recognition of her 27 knots speed achieved in the action; and for *Indomitable,* he said: "Engineer Lieutenant Albert Knoth, who is principally responsible for the good steaming of the ship, she having made ... half a knot in excess of any record before made in the ship, even in her lightened condition

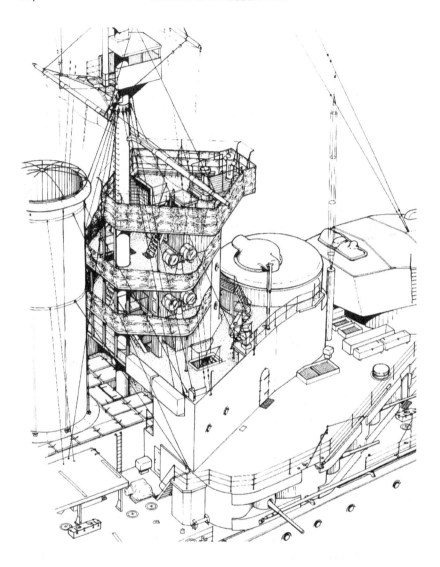

5.3. Close-up sketch of HMS *Lion*'s bridge from John Roberts' *Battle Cruisers*. The top deck containing the compass platform is where Admiral Beatty and his staff were for much of the battle. Hipper's position on *Seydlitz* was inside the command tower using the Admiral's command reviscope.

on trials."[11] Similar levels of effort were reported by the commanding officers of the three surviving German ships, and several individuals were singled out. On *Blücher* it would have been the captain and first officer; on *Seydlitz* it was four individuals – the first officer, the senior engineer, and two senior petty officers, for one of whom a class of destroyers was named in World War II: Wilhelm Heidkamp.

As the first shots echoed across the churning North Sea, both sides strove for position so they could steam, see, and shoot to advantage – and win. *Blücher* was first and foremost a gunnery training and experiments ships before the war, and the crew carried the experience gained from that work into her last battle. She had been in service since 1909 and been gradually fitted with director fire controls, first for port and starboard secondary batteries, and literally the day before the battle the installation of director fire control was fitted for her main armament, though it had not yet been tested. It was a Siemens product, which culminated work underway since 1912 when *Blücher* conducted gunnery trials off the Faeroe Island in heavy weather. She had the tripod foremast to enable a stereoscopic optical range-finder to be carried. Her Siemens technicians did not accompany her to sea, lucky for them. Unfortunately for him, Commander Erdmann had convinced the powers that be – including both Admirals Ingenohl and Prince Heinrich – that his ship should go to war in accordance with her capabilities, so they sailed with the untested equipment.[12]

It was shortly after the light cruisers of both sides, HMS *Aurora* and SMS *Kolberg,* skirmished that *Blücher* opened fire and drove the British light ships and destroyers away from the German formation. She could do nothing about HMS *Lion,* however, which was on the southwestern end of the British battle line and opened fire at 0852 with a ranging shot from one of her B turret forward, super-firing 13.5-inch guns at 20,000 yards.[13] It fell short, but the Germans noted the extreme range at which the fight began. Filson Young noted that "the enemy appeared on the eastern horizon in the form of four separate wedges . . . of smoke. Suddenly from the rearmost of these wedges came a stab of white flame." It was *Blücher* opening fire. Young also reported what hits looked like: "this dull glowing and fading glare which signified the bursting of one of our shells."[14] British light forces included seven light cruisers and nineteen

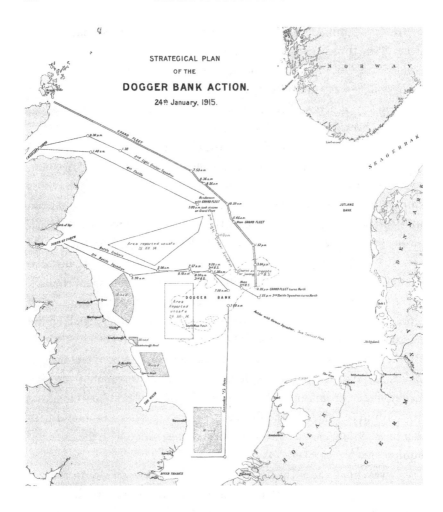

5.4. "Strategical Overview Battle of the Dogger Bank January 24th.1915" from *History of the Great War*, Julian S. Corbett, *Naval Operations, Vol. II*, (London: Longmanns Green and Company, 1920). Inside Book. Prepared by the Historical Section of the Committee of Imperial Defense.

destroyers from two different commands: the Harwich Force, and the First Light Cruiser Squadron escorting Beatty. SMS *Kolberg*, a German light cruiser of the Second Scouting Group was slightly damaged in the first exchange and reported the contact back to Hipper, who also steered toward the sound of the guns and *Kolberg*, turning away on his approach

5.4. Detail.

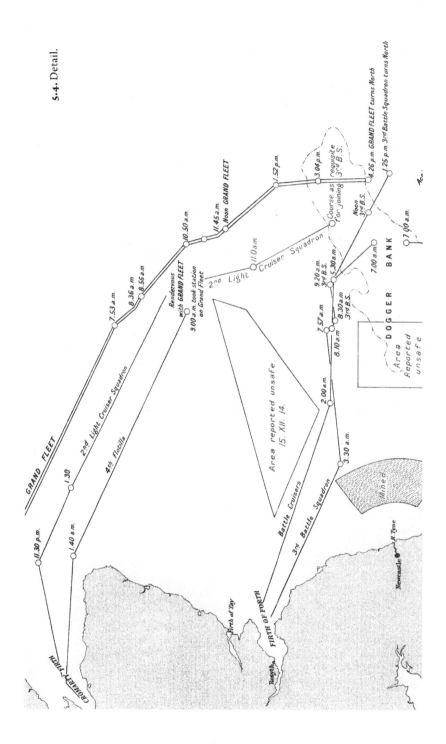

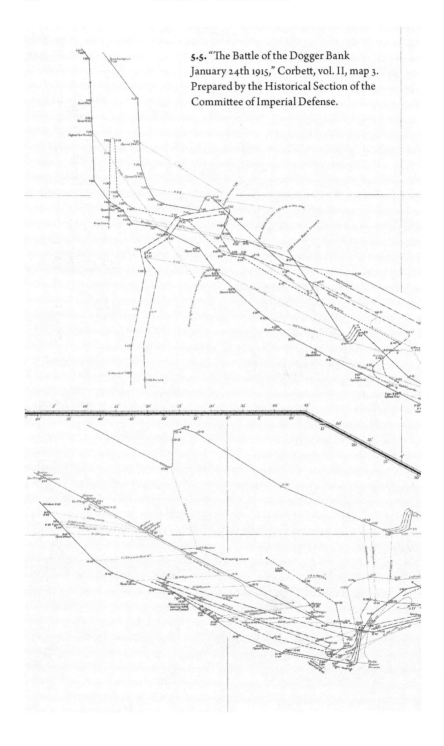

5.5. "The Battle of the Dogger Bank January 24th 1915," Corbett, vol. II, map 3. Prepared by the Historical Section of the Committee of Imperial Defense.

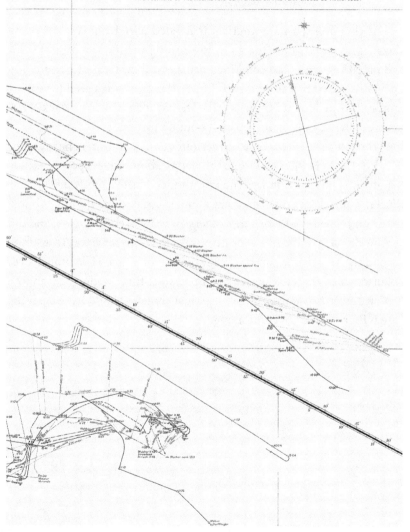

BATTLE of DOGGER BANK
JANUARY 24TH 1915.

TRACKS OF

LION & 1ST & IIND BATTLE CRUISER SQUADRON	1ST & 3RD FLOTILLAS
LEADING SHIP	ARETHUSA
LION	AURORA
TIGER	UNDAUNTED
PRINCESS ROYAL	INDIVIDUAL DESTROYERS
NEW ZEALAND	
INDOMITABLE	

1ST LIGHT CRUISER SQUADRON

SOUTHAMPTON	ENEMY MAIN FORCE
BIRMINGHAM	" LIGHT CRUISERS
NOTTINGHAM	" DESTROYERS
LOWESTOFT	

BEARINGS
LINES OF FIRE
THE POSITIONS OF THE MOLTKE AND DERFFLINGER ON THIS PLAN SHOULD BE TRANSPOSED.

to gain an appreciation of the enemy force and its dispositions.[15] At this point, *Blücher* was closest to the enemy. The scene on the bridge of *Blücher* is described by the ship's communications officer:

> With the naked eye only an interminable throng stood to port aft . . . with glasses . . . their number increased with each new count. All involved in the count were of a cheerful disposition . . . finally the Commander laughed and came to a decision on what I should encipher and send to *Seydlitz* [The signal read:] . . . *Blücher* to BdA [flag officer scouting forces]: "9.19 morning: *Blücher* to *Seydlitz:* to BdA: in sight aft 7 enemy light cruisers and now 26 destroyers. Further smoke clouds behind.[end transmission] *Blücher*.[16]

At this point, a parenthetical is needed about the two opposing sides' light ships. These forces were running behind the capital ships and on either flank. The combined cruiser and destroyer force coming up against Hipper was a powerful one – the destroyers could launch a hundred torpedoes at Hipper's force should they make an attack; Hipper's smaller vessels could muster about 60 torpedoes. Nevertheless, it took only one such weapon to do serious damage to British heavy ships of the day, and Hipper was none too happy about such exposure either. An obvious observation was the importance of the effectiveness of the *Blücher*'s anti destroyer armament of ten 15 cm [5.9-inch] guns. Almost to the end they kept British destroyers away from their targets, and did serious damage to the heavy destroyer *Meteor*. The same was true of the secondary armaments on the bigger German ships. Heavy destroyer defenses worked. Also the fact that there were four "wedges" meant the British had to fire at four targets, not just three as would have been the case if *Blücher* had not come along.

6

The Engagement

AS *BLÜCHER* OPENED FIRE, HER EARLIER RANGING SHOTS FELL among the chasing British light cruisers and destroyers, sufficient to drive them off, but she soon had to shift fire to the British heavy ships. As the engagement developed, the German ships slipped into a single line ahead with *Seydlitz* in the lead followed by *Derfflinger,* and *Moltke,* and, of course, *Blücher.* At first, Captain Ludwig von Reuter had swung *Derfflinger* out of line contemplating a hunt for British light cruisers, but thought better of it as he too spotted the huge pillars of smoke which signaled the presence of British heavy ships. Hipper managed to get the Second Scouting Group of four light cruisers ahead of him and his destroyers on his starboard side as the chase developed. The level and type of wireless traffic indicated to the Germans that there was a probable battle squadron nearby.[1] In fact, Admiral Jellicoe and the Grand Fleet were 150 nautical miles, about nine hours steaming, to the north northwest. The High Seas Fleet was still stirring at anchor in Sunday routine in the Jade and Wilhelmshaven, with its most powerful units in the Baltic. A critical strategic factor for the German fleet was the ability to transit quickly and safely from the North Sea ports and the Jade River to the large arsenal and ports in the Baltic, via the Kiel Canal, which had just been completed and widened. This passage was 61.75 miles long and sixteen battleships could pass in an emergency in six hours.[2]

The British would conduct the battle by deliberate fire from as long a range as possible, taking advantage of their superiority wherever possible to inflict and avoid damage. It is probable that the German sights were better adapted to the shaking of the ships while shooting, but the second British shot from *Lion* at *Blücher,* which was at 20,200 yards, was over the target and created a mountainous waterspout on *Blücher*'s port quarter. As Peter Padfield described it: "the British instruments which were operated on a coincidence principle, in which two horizontal sections of the target had to be exactly lined up so the vertical lines formed exact continuations, the German ones were stereoscopic, which meant that there was no lining up of the images, but simply a subjective comparison of two complete images, one entering each eye . . . in any case the decisive advantage the Germans enjoyed was in the opening ranges; after that 'spotting' [the observation of fall of shot] played an increasingly important part." Moreover, once the German range-finder personnel were shaken by incoming fire or extreme vibration, accuracy suffered. Lastly, the ranges engaged in were over 21,000 yards and were double the standard practice range of either side. Hits were obtained nevertheless.[3] In fact, the second British shot from *Lion* at *Blücher* was at 20,200 yards and was over the target. The Germans observed the fall of shot 1,000 yards astern and cheerily went to battle stations.[4]

Between 0815 and 0845, *Lion* had closed the distance to the Germans by 5,000 yards. At 0854, "slow deliberate fire from *Lion*'s forward turrets commenced at *Blücher*." At 0909, *Lion* hit *Blücher* with her first 13.5-inch shell. From the British side, gunfire from the Germans looked like bright white flashes and hits appeared yellowish, and persisted as flames resulted.[5] The view from the German side was similar, although smoke from the German funnels made it harder to see the British. Hipper chronicles the action and says around 0930 German time *Blücher* drove off a British destroyer with gunfire.

Maurice von Egidy did not feel the need to clear ship for battle until 0955. This was probably because *Seydlitz* was the head of the line and therefore would not be in range of the enemy for a while longer. Von Egidy noted there were five large warships with tripod masts bearing on the formation's starboard quarter, and "the foremost one opened fire, firing deliberately . . . at 0958, *Blücher* signaled the flagship '5 enemy battle cruisers.'" Given the speed and the amount of smoke emitted by the Germans, Chatfield, the British flag captain, von Egidy's opposite number, noted that "it was impossible to distinguish hits at the time, but *New*

Zealand reported that *Lion* commenced hitting *Blücher* at 0909." On the German side, the *Derfflinger* opened fire at 1008 and *Seydlitz* increased speed again to 23 knots as soon as the cruisers settled down ahead; *Seydlitz* reported opening fire at 1019, and *Lion* reported enemy incoming at 1014. This was probably *Derfflinger,* which opened fire at 1011 and continued shooting at the first ship from the left (*Lion*) until 1023 with all 8 main battery 30.5 cm (12-inch) guns. *Seydlitz* was also shooting at *Lion* 1010 to at least 1030. Von Egidy noted that "the enemy was covered in smoke and we are in a clear position, bad for artillery shooting." By 1016, the British could not be seen at all in the smoke. At the same time, the British went to two-shot salvo fire. At 1023, *Seydlitz's* bow shook and careened to port, as she had been hit forward by a shot from the enemy at 15,000 meters.

Meanwhile *Tiger* opened fire on the *Blücher* at 0922,[6] and at 0924, the *Lion* shifted fire to the *Moltke,*[7] which had herself opened fire at *Tiger* from 1020 onwards. The range varied from 16,000 to 19,000 meters. The German Third Admiralty Staff officer on *Moltke* reported a hit on the middle smokestack of *Tiger,* and there were two other hits, one with undetermined results and one forward at 1115.[8] As of 1018, *Blücher* was still not seriously damaged and as a result of smoke *Seydlitz, Moltke,* and *Derfflinger* were all shooting at the *Lion.*[9] At 0935, all sorts of things happened. Beatty, sensing confusion amongst the squadron's fire distribution, signaled: "Fire on your opposite number." Chatfield thought it was *Derfflinger.* It didn't matter, as at the same instant "a heavy shell hit the [*Lion's*] waterline abaft the stoker's bathrooms, penetrating into the bunkers. This was speedily shored up with hammocks and mess stools."[10] There were additional shots, also from *Derfflinger,* which fell short. But even short shells were very dangerous as they created mountains of waters which crashed down on the fire control instruments and control towers drenching everything and everybody; their explosive force, though mitigated by water and distance, could still do extensive damage.

By about 0950, both German ships had been hit. *Derfflinger* took a shell amidships near her mainmast and the British thought her on fire at the time.[11] *Lion,* however, had a gun jammed and cleared at the time and at about 0954 (British time) at about 15,000 yards *Lion's* A turret was struck by a 30.5 cm [12-inch] shell, killing, and wounding some of the people in the turret and knocking out one gun. The left gun continued to fire.[12] At 1030 British time, 1130 German, *Blücher*, which was still in the line and firing at more targets than she had a right to, was hit amidships and there was a serious fire. She lost control of her steering and made a complete circle; her speed dropped to 17 knots.[13] Seeing this, Beatty ordered *Indomitable* to "attack the enemy breaking away to the North," but as *Blücher* regained her original course the order was not followed.[14] *Blücher* sent a signal to Hipper, as the conning tower was being hit by heavy shell, that the engines had lost steam and could only make 17 knots and that her gunfire control had been knocked out.[15] *Blücher* endured many hits from *Lion, Tiger, Princess Royal, New Zealand,* and *Indomitable.* But it was a single 12-inch hit from *New Zealand* which sealed her fate. As Schmalembach tells it:

> The most fateful hit of the day, fired by HMS *New Zealand,* hit *Blücher* at 1030 hours at her most sensitive place: the horizontal ammunition trunk under the armored deck used for the ammunition supply of the two forward most broadside turrets. The British shell (12-inch) ignited about thirty-five cartridges hanging in the special service rail. As the trunk was also used for protection for the most important internal communications, the rudder gear, the engine telegraphs, and fire control system were all interrupted. Steam pipes to the foremost boiler room were destroyed the speed dropped to 17 knots.[16]

Thus damaged, *Blücher* "became a wounded and doomed antagonist. The British noticed that after the hit, *Blücher,* whose fire control system had worked superbly, was suffering from a falling off in her broadsides with shells falling short and with a very large spread."[17] This meant she could no longer deal with overmatched guns of adversaries which assailed her from all quarters. A remarkable description from inside the *Blücher* at this time has surfaced:

> A journey through the ship showed the devastation that was already directed [occurred] in the interior of the ship. Boiler room III [had] made much water, and had to be abandoned. In the middle gangway two men lay whimpering in a great pool of blood. One had both his legs severed off, the other had his back broken. They were taken to the main dressing room by stretcher, cushioned in hammocks. The dressing station was packed with laid out badly wounded men. The physician dealt calmly with these poor men cutting and bandaging working energetically to reduce the pain and agony. I proceeded further through the *Zwischendeck* [middle deck]. Boiler Room V had fallen out. It represented a

horrifying picture there were corpses, severed limbs, shell splinters and boiler parts lying amongst one another.[18]

Moltke's log entry sheds a bit more light on her position consistent with the above, as being hit in the "paternoster" compartment as reported above.[19]

Blücher's fight deserves more attention, and the evidence comes from the British ships who engaged her. *Princess Royal* took *Blücher* under fire about 0907, and after several deliberate rounds, hit her once at a range of about 19,800 yards with a 13.5-inch shell. The Siemens installation nevertheless worked well and resulted in *Princess Royal* being straddled numerous times. The *Blücher*'s guns were fired at a high elevation (30 degrees) and some of the overs actually landed on the disengaged side of the *Princess Royal*.[20] At 1022, *Tiger* reported hitting *Blücher* causing a fierce fire.[21] At 1120, *Tiger* was again engaged with *Blücher*, who hit *Tiger* with a 21 cm [8.2-inch] shell on the water line which did not penetrate. *Blücher* then fired a torpedo at *Tiger* which missed. *Tiger* fired a torpedo at *Blücher* at 6,400 yards which hit at 1144. A 20.5 cm shell passed through *Tiger*'s after funnel at 1150; a second torpedo from *Tiger* missed.

From 1140 to noon, all *Tiger*'s starboard 6-inch guns were engaged with *Blücher* at ranges as short as 4,500 yards. Charles G. Taylor, the engineer captain Beatty sent over to get things right, was killed in the action. At noon, *Blücher* was on fire from stem to stern and *Tiger* ceased fire.[22] Meanwhile, about 1130, *Princess Royal* found herself in range of the *Blücher*, opened fire, and hit her from 12,000–16,000 yards, "one shell blowing away her bridge and another setting her forecastle turret on fire, which burned furiously for about ten minutes. Both her boat cranes were knocked down . . . *Blücher* sank at 1215."[23]

New Zealand, which had claimed no hits on *Blücher*, came upon what Captain Lionel Halsey described as a "shambles" with "guns pointing in all directions, fore turret burning fiercely, the whole ship beneath decks in flames from one end to the other, tripod foremast leaning forward, foretop shot away, and all hands remain[ing] alive were on deck and abandoning ship." Captain T. W. B. Kennedy noted *Blücher*'s crew fought most gallantly. Smaller British ships also had some observations. Commodore Goodenough, Commander First Light Cruiser Squadron, noted that *Blücher*'s fire against the British light cruisers had been very accurate and only by luck were hits avoided at 14,000 yards.[24] At 1005, *Southampton* came under fire from the *Blücher* at 16,000 yards. At 1027, she again engaged *Blücher* but was driven off by heavy shell; she was again driven off at 1105; from 1120–1130 she engaged *Blücher* and finally made several hits with 6-inch guns. HMS *Nottingham* engaged between 1130 and 1145 when *Blücher* was little more than a floating target. Some hits were scored.[25] HMS *Birmingham* also engaged *Blücher* but no hits were made; her gunnery was thrown off by the high speeds of the chase.[26] HMS *Lowestoft* engaged *Blücher* early on and was straddled by an 8.2-inch salvo, and thought to be hulled. It was a near miss, although parts of the German round bounced off *Lowestoft*'s after funnel.[27]

Blücher's survivors were rescued by British destroyers and light cruisers until a Zeppelin approached the scene and dropped bombs on the rescuers. The culprit was allegedly Zeppelin *L-5*.[28] It turns out the actual bomb dropper was a seaplane from Borkum. Nevertheless, bombs were dropped.[29] Even the *Blücher* survivors thought it was *L-5*. The survivors who were rescued by British forces were interrogated aboard the battleship *King Edward VII*, and were well treated and consequently spoke freely.[30] The senior surviving officer other than Commander Erdmann (who was wounded and unable to talk) was Korvetten Kapitän (LCDR) John Ross, the ship's executive officer or First Lieutenant. He was responsible for the ship below the waterline. He came topside when the fumes made staying below untenable and proceeded to navigate the ship from after steering as the forward bridge was gone. Although Ross thought the High Seas Fleet would come out soon, some of the other surviving officers believed they did not give the Scouting Forces enough support, and if they did come out it was only in response to urgent pleas. An interesting note was that *Blücher*'s gyrocompass still worked right up until the ship capsized. The main conning tower and steering gear also remained intact to the end. And indeed *Blücher* was finally sunk by opening Kingston valves and scuttling her. However, further resistance was hopeless and all gun turrets had been put out of action by gunfire. Fire from burning paint and fumes associated with it caused many casualties. One of the seamen described the critical hit; again, this is consistent with other accounts: "Fourth salvo did enormous damage, both the personnel and materiel. Carried away after superstructure, completely disabled two turrets aft and disabled a very large number of men."

The *Blücher* was believed to have hauled down her colors 10 minutes before she sank. John Campbell, whose research on World War I naval engagements is without parallel, believed *Blücher* made one hit on the *Indomitable* and one hit on the *Tiger,* and put the destroyer *Meteor* out of action.[31] Fregatten Kapitän Erdmann, commanding officer of *Blücher,* died of pneumonia and other effects of his wounds while in British captivity. Twenty-three of twenty-nine officers and 724 of 999 petty officers seamen and stokers died. The survivors became prisoners of war.

All this while, the major part of the engagement was still being fought. At 1043 (German time), a 34 cm [13.5-inch] shell from *Lion* penetrated the barbette armor between the two after turrets of *Seydlitz*.[32] The laconic entry by von Egidy read: "Major fire in the ship aft. Turrets C and D do not answer calls. After steering must be abandoned." It got worse. The access tunnels had to be abandoned, as their ventilation systems were non-operable. On the *Seydlitz* by 1104, the magazines for both after turrets and the torpedo magazine were flooded. *Seydlitz's* after rudder controls were not accessible so she was steering using her screws. If her rudders were jammed they were close to amidships, which was lucky. Four members of *Seydlitz's* complement deserve special mention – the Senior Gunnery Officer, Korvetten Kapitän Richard Foerster, ordered rapid fire for the *Seydlitz's* remaining turrets, which resulted in a salvo every ten seconds for some minutes and massive incoming fire targeted on the *Lion*. Foerster thought that the ship was going to blow up so it was best to go down shooting. The other officers were the First Officer, Korvetten Kapitän (LCDR) Hagedorn, *Obermachinstenmaat* (senior petty officer officer) Wilhelm Heidkamp and *Feuerwerker* (Fireman) Muller. The party went aft through the smoke, found the right valve, which was red hot, and shut it with bare hands. They saved the ship.[33]

At 1125, *Seydlitz* was hit once more by a heavy shell amidships, but it apparently did little damage. But at 1149 (German time), *Seydlitz* also observed the *Lion's* predicament, noting that the "the lead *Lion* appeared to have turned ... the lead English ship has been heavily hit on her beam."[34] *Moltke,* which had been following *Seydlitz,* observed a major hit amidships on *Tiger* followed by a large fire, after which the fire from the enemy dropped from broadside fire to single to double rounds and petered off.[35] The hit reported was on *Tiger*'s amidships turret, which was hit and knocked out at 1050.[36] Back on the *Lion*, at 1001, a 28 cm [11-inch] shell from the *Seydlitz* pierced the armor in the engineer's workshop causing a power loss to secondary anti-torpedoboat armament and knocking out two of the three dynamos, endangering her power. Damage control efforts failed.

As Chatfield put it: "by 1018 the effects of the enemy's concentration on *Lion* began to be felt. Their salvos were rapid and shots fell well together. At 1018 a salvo of two 12-inch shells from the *Derfflinger* hit the ship. The shock was very great, and was thought at the time to be due to a torpedo." The two shells hit at different places. The first hit the torpedo body room and flooded that space, the port cable locker, the torpedo flat itself, and spaces above up to the main deck. The second stove in several armored plates below the water line, opening up a section of the foremost port coal bunkers to the sea. But it wasn't over. Another shell hit the lobby of A turret (the foremost twin 13.5-inch main armament) and caused a fire which was put out, but not before there was a report of a fire in the magazine, which Chatfield ordered flooded. Turned out there was no fire and the order was countermanded. Flooding the magazine meant the *Lion* lost her forward turrets as the ammunition was soaked and useless, like *Seydlitz*'s after turrets. The damage was not as bad – the crews had survived, but the guns could not fire ammunition they no longer had. Suffering from a forest of shell hits and near misses, Chatfield zig-zagged to port and then to starboard to break the German squadron's fire control solution. While he was doing this, dozens of shells from *Seydlitz*, *Moltke*, and *Derfflinger* continued to bracket *Lion*.

Tiger, next in line, could not seem to hit anything according to Commodore Goodenough, who was in a position to observe the action. This was all in the space of four minutes between 1049 and 1051. On *Lion*, there were several 28 cm or 30.5 cm [11- or 12-inch] shell hits, the last of which hit abreast *Lion*'s F boiler room and shook the ship heavily. The port engine room was damaged, and worse, the last ship's dynamo went off line causing complete loss of power. One of the other shells that hit the ship further damaged the port engine room, reducing the ship's speed to 15 knots. *Lion* was out of the fight and listing 10 degrees to starboard, so she pulled out of line and headed northeast.[37]

At almost the same time, Beatty saw what he thought was a U-boat and ordered a general turn eight points to port to a course north by east, almost at right angles to the enemy's course, which Hipper used to rapidly increase the range between the two forces.[38] Beatty said he "personally observed the wash of periscope 2 points on our starboard bow. I immediately ordered 'Turn 8 points to port together.'" This was done at 1100. Beatty was concerned not only with the submarines but also with the risk of crossing the track of the enemy light forces, which he thought were likely to be carrying mines which they would drop in his path.[39] In fact, the nearest U-boat was hours away proceeding north to help Hipper. Beatty may have actually had that information on his flagship, but battle damage and staff performance probably kept him in the dark. Beatty was lucky as Hipper's forces had no mines loaded in either destroyers or cruisers on this sortie, although they could have done so as indicated in chapter 4.

Another data point is provided by *Indomitable*, which reported a torpedo crossing in front of her by only 40 yards just after passing the *Blücher*.[40] It's likely this was launched by the *Blücher* herself, as the nearest submarines were still just beyond the Jade bar on their way to support Hipper but not there in time to have anything to do with the battle.[41]

At this point things were happening minute by minute on the British flagship, which had just turned almost 180 degrees, was on fire, listing, and otherwise not in good nick. Beatty had just endured being the target of hundreds of heavy shells several of which had struck the ship on which he stood; the weather was still overcast and, for the action, wind was force 2–3.[42] It was likely he was cold and drenched but, because he was who he was, the adrenaline was up and he still intended to win.[43]

He thought Hipper would turn around and support the *Blücher* so he ordered a course which would cut Hipper off from her. But at 1103, Beatty concluded that "the injury to *Lion* was incapable of immediate repair . . . and . . . semaphored to Commodore T to close and detail destroyers as a submarine screen as *Lion* shaped course NW." At almost the same moment, Beatty spotted what he thought was a submarine and ordered the formation to turn 90 degrees to port as the *Lion's* speed was falling to 15 knots. At 1105, Beatty hoisted the signal "attack the enemy's rear," hauled down the course signal, and hoisted the signal "keep nearer to the enemy."[44] Beatty had no wireless available, as it had been lost in the cannonade, and was using two remaining signal halyards abaft the *Lion's* bridge. He left the *Lion* at 1135 in the destroyer *Attack* – a cross-deck transfer in force 2–3 seas – and Rear Admiral Moore, second in command in HMS *New Zealand,* took over the fight. Beatty reached HMS *Princess Royal* at 1230. By that time, the distance between Hipper and Beatty had widened such that reengagement was impossible; Beatty could not catch the fleeing Germans. The cause of this was Rear Admiral Archibald Moore, who had mistakenly read the signals and the situation to mean he should concentrate his force on the already damaged *Blücher* and let the rest of the German force get away: "certain signals were made by *Lion* which were either wrongly received in *New Zealand* or other ships, or not received at all . . . this resulted in your intentions being wrongly interpreted."[45] One can imagine Beatty's reaction to this. Chalmers concludes Beatty made one last attempt to get "the hounds back on the scent" with a signal: "Keep nearer the enemy." Rear Admiral Moore, who took over, is treated kindly for not knowing Beatty well enough to have interpreted all the signals in effect to seek and destroy Hipper's remaining ships.[46]

In any case, *Lion's* situation worsened and she needed to be towed home to Rosyth by HMS *Indomitable.* Beatty's comments were telling. It took from about 1530 to 1730 for the *Indomitable* to get the *Lion* under tow, and Beatty was not stinting in his praise: "The Greatest credit is due to the captains of the *Lion* and *Indomitable* for the seamanlike manner in which the *Lion* was taken in tow under difficult circumstances and brought safely to port."[47]

Moltke had been supporting *Seydlitz* as had *Derfflinger* in their cannonade on the *Lion* which in about 20 minutes had been the target of upwards of 200 heavy shell. That cannonade was serious – we know the *Seydlitz, Derfflinger,* and *Moltke* fired 390, 276, and 310 heavy shells respectively, most of which were aimed at *Lion. Blücher* was rated at 840 21 cm rounds aboard,[48] and probably fired about a third before her fatal hit from *New Zealand.*

Cannonade aside, in these same minutes Hipper decided he must leave *Blücher* to her fate. He did think about closing with the enemy and trying to save her, but he decided that he had a flagship on fire with half her armament, including sixty-five and twenty-six heavy rounds from her surviving turrets respectively.[49] Hipper would have had to fight British light forces and their deadly torpedoes as well as four healthy British battle cruisers while shot of ammunition. His own destroyers were badly tactically placed and short of fuel for a full engagement. There was the real prospect of losing all his "expensive" battle cruisers, of which there were only two and a half left![50] Hipper did not satisfy Beatty's expectations. He was about preserving his force. The Germans had less distance to cover. Hipper and his formation proceeded in good order, getting most fires out as they reached the Jade.

Hipper's signals to the High Seas Fleet on the way home provide a reasonable record of his progress. It is well to remember he had made his first request for battle squadron support and additional torpedoboats at 1035, once he knew he was in action with the battle cruiser squadron of five ships, and again asked for support at 1050 when *Seydlitz*'s damage had become apparent. He had some reason to hope for support as at 1103 von Ingenohl said the main fleet and flotillas would come as soon as possible. The German fleet dispositions were horrible. Most of the fleet which was available was inside the Jade bar at 1030, and the picture is of second line light cruisers and available destroyers hurrying to get into a position from which they might screen the hastily assembled battle squadrons. The Second Battle Squadron of pre-dreadnoughts (less fleet flagship at the time, the *Deutschland*) was to head out at 1210. The First Battle Squadron of *Nassau* and *Ostfriesland* class dreadnoughts did not get steam up until 1210.

Admiral Wilhelm von Lans, First Battle Squadron commander, commanded the relief force, not von Ingenohl who stayed behind in *Deutschland*. Von Ingenohl's performance when he turned the whole High Seas Fleet around early and left Hipper in the lurch in December 1914 contrary to plan, might indicate this time a degree of insouciance. Hipper seems to have thought so as did the men on the *Blücher*.

By 1219, the *Preussen*, another pre-dreadnought, signaled the battle fleet to get underway at 1219.[51] *Ostfriesland*, with von Lans in command, signaled *Deutschland* Hipper's position and speed at 1225. *T-101*, flying the pennant of acting senior officer U-boats, signaled Hipper where a hastily assembled line of U-boats were at 1304, at which point Hipper confirmed *Blücher* was lost. As of 1346, Hipper reported the enemy was out of sight.

The radio intercept operators on *Ostfriesland* now began an interesting day. They were able to deduce the British 1300 position and had the British steering SE; they requested U-boats be told; *Seydlitz* confirmed battle discontinued at 1305. Hipper was given a rendezvous position by the First Battle Squadron commander for 1530. He also informed High Seas Fleet that his destroyers could not be used in a night attack as they did not have enough fuel left. Zeppelin *L-5* told Hipper and the HSF that *Blücher* had capsized at 1305 and the British were retreating toward the northwest. *Seydlitz* asked *L-5* at 1500 how many enemy battle cruisers he saw. The response came back at 1507 as four. British Hipper asked von Lans for his position again and it was updated at 1513. *L-5* actually reported losing sight of the British at 1320 and reported at last sighting they were still steaming at high speed toward home. *Deutschland* asked *Seydlitz* how many enemy battle cruisers he had engaged and the answer was five. Hipper was informed by U-boat commanders of the location of the German boats: about a half dozen boats laid across a possible British line of advance should the British have chosen to chase Hipper to his bases. Pursuing British battle cruisers, pre-dreadnoughts or later Jellicoe's dreadnoughts would have had a gauntlet to run through.

Once the fires in *Seydlitz* were out, the issue was whether the force would have to deal with a reinforced British formation, or whether the British would give up the fight and if or when at all the German High Seas Fleet were to come out. It turned out Hipper rendezvoused with the High Seas Fleet at 1530, noting: "As always, too late." The three cheers Ingenohl ordered for the returning battle cruisers must have been hollow to the officers and men of the returning force. The reality of the situation would have been clearer to the fleet command once Hipper told Ingenohl that he "must enter dry dock tonight and land about 110 dead." And *Derfflinger* needed to proceed to Wilhelmshaven Roads for urgent repairs. When asked the extent of her damage, *Derfflinger* reported leakage due to under water hits; protective passage and bunkers in port boiler-rooms were full of water; the armor plate was bent; the starboard outer shaft tunnel had two leaks and small damage to torpedo nets, cables, search-lights and vent ducts. But there had been no loss of life.[52]

The British thought they had sunk or nearly sunk *Derfflinger*. This was because in the first exchanges *Derfflinger* was probably initially mis-taken for the first ship which was actually *Seydlitz*, and the hits abaft her mainmast taken for nearly fatal as her after turrets didn't shoot for some time, during which only two shot salvos were fired. Also, throughout the battle, it was very hard to see as the German smoke from their engines and guns was being blown down on the British ships.[53] True, *Derfflinger* was on fire aft for a while but did not burn long. The *Lion*'s gunnery of-ficer said, "The general feeling when *Derfflinger* was on fire and only using two turrets was that we had her . . . this proved to be an error."[54]

The lightly damaged British ships preceded to Rosyth without dif-ficulty, but not so the flagship *Lion*. *Tiger* had been knocked about, and more by dint of sheer good luck had avoided disaster when her mid-ships turret had been hit. *Tiger* was actually hit, or so she thought, by fire from all five enemy ships at 1105, at which time Engineer Captain Taylor, who was acting as recorder and timekeeper and was in an exposed position, was killed.[55] It was a 28 cm [11-inch] shell which blew through the gun house and wrecked enough machinery inside to make the middle tur-ret inoperable. There was no fire.[56] *Tiger* aside, as told by Beatty's first biographer: "Getting *Lion* home was now his chief anxiety."[57] The tow used two hawsers between the battle cruisers. The *Lion* was indeed a dead ship with no power, with considerable free water in the ship and no lights or ventilation. It took until the morning of 26 January to get the ship to the dockyard at Rosyth. More than that, the damage below the waterline was so severe as to merit a cofferdam being placed over the collapsed armor and ship's side where *Derfflinger*'s shells had struck. Because the ship was so deep in the water, she could not go into the River Tyne and up to the shipyards and a cofferdam had to be built around her in situ. Stephen Roskill also reminds us that the British Admiralty, and especially Churchill, wished the actual extent of her damage concealed from the enemy.[58] Rosyth did not yet have a dry dock sufficient to take her. So *Lion* had to be repaired in situ using cofferdams and patches. The actual cofferdam and patch required 117 tons of concrete. Nonetheless, the work was completed by 28 March. As Roskill tells it: "close inspection of the damage revealed all too clearly that her 5 and 6-inch armour was inadequate against 11-inch armour piercing shells, and in April Beatty drew the Admiralty's attention to the failure and asked what could be done about it."[59] David Brown, in his book *The Grand Fleet,* describes what happened to *Lion* and the constructor's autopsy is even worse than the battle reports cited above: "At Dogger Bank *Lion* was hit by sixteen 11- or 12-inch (mostly 11-inch) and one 8.3-inch with four hits below the normal waterline on the port side, and one to starboard, damaging a total of 1500 sq. of bottom plating." Brown goes on to note two factors peculiar to Dogger Bank – the fall of shot was for *Lion* mostly oblique so the hits were flatter and not the deadly plunging fire at Jutland; the other factor was the effect of fighting in shallow water "in which the height of the wave pattern generated by the ship is exaggerated with a high bow crest and trough amidships falling below the bottom of the belt."[60] What this meant was that the ship was deprived of the attenuating presence of water and its armor was exposed to direct impacts. Lastly, the inboard edge of the armor plate had a very sharp corner which damaged the ship's structure when hit. This lack of attention to detail did not affect the German ships, and will be discussed further as part of the echelons of mistakes revealed at Dogger Bank.

7

The Aftermath

There is a thin line between mistakes and lessons learned. At Dogger Bank, there were three levels of issues, which in today's parlance fall out to strategic, operational, and tactical. To some extent fortune played a part in all of these, and to some extent they all played a part in the future conduct of the war, the oceans of ink that were subsequently spilled on them, and action taken or not.

The political and strategic fallout was telling but not critical. There was of course, the World War I version of "spin." *Blücher's* loss and the photo of her capsizing was an unequivocal morale and propaganda victory for Britain and the Royal Navy throughout the ages. The photograph appears in almost every history of note, including this one. The damage to *Seydlitz* and *Lion* is less iconic. The political impact was also positive for Churchill and the British government of the day. Again, Churchill:

> The victory of the Dogger Bank brought for the time being abruptly to an end the adverse movement against my administration of the Admiralty, which had begun to gather. Congratulations flowed in from every side, and we enjoyed once again an adequate measure of prestige. The sinking of the *Blücher* and the flight, after heavy injuries of the other German ships was accepted as a solid and indisputable result.[1]

Well, not exactly. To some extent, the residual desire for an offensive strategy after the two raids on the British coast was slaked. There was a deadlock on land as well and alternatives were being sought. At first the

British looked at the islands of Borkum or Sylt in the North Sea, which if taken would enable a close blockade of the High Seas Fleet in the Jade. It was felt that the Channel Fleet's overwhelming gunfire could subdue the island and three brigades of infantry then take it. At the same time, Churchill envisioned the deployment of the Grand Fleet to support the operation. The actual invasion and occupation of Borkum had been dismissed by 3 January 1915, although a bombardment of Sylt was considered a workable plan so long as it had the objective of bringing out the HSF over a field of waiting submarines and mines.[2] Herbert Richmond, later Admiral of the Fleet and a key Admiralty Staff officer at the time, labeled the proposed operations as "quite mad . . . the reasons for capturing it the possibilities about the same. . . . It remains with the Army who I hope will refuse to throw away 12000 troops in this manner for the self-glorification of an ignorant and impulsive man."[3] The Baltic idea was even worse. It could not be done without taking Borkum and going to a close blockade of the Bight.[4] The strategic objective was enabling a landing of a large Russian army on the Pomeranian coast ninety miles from Berlin. The doom of all of these ideas was the concept of underwater weapons as well as the high probability of high casualties and losses to British sea power.[5] The part Dogger Bank played in all this thinking at the Admiralty and War Office is outlined by Churchill, who said: "This action gives us a good line for judging the results of a general battle. It may roughly be said that we should probably fight six to four at the worst, whereas today was five to four." Although Churchill was, as usual, mobilizing his language and deploying it for war, he admitted to Jellicoe that "it would be bad management on our part if your superiority was not much nearer six to four than five to four even under the worst circumstances."[6]

Because Dogger Bank might have led to a fleet engagement early in the war, the stakes for both sides need reprising. In a fleet engagement, the issues became the same as they were at Jutland some seventeen months later. It is perhaps fortunate for the sailors on both sides that Moore did not follow Hipper back into the Bight. At the same time, propinquity of other heavy British forces needs to be noted, most importantly the Third Battle Squadron, which was only twenty sea miles away when the *Blücher* was sunk, and which actually had the British battle cruisers in sight at

1400, an hour later.[7] Jellicoe had his nineteen serviceable dreadnoughts at latitude 56 N, longitude 3.33 E at 1200, about two hours steaming north of the Third Battle Squadron, which Jellicoe told to form up on him as soon as he rendezvoused with the battle cruiser force at 1630.[8]

If the four British battle cruisers had proceeded south, they would have been supported an hour later by the Third Battle Squadron, which was only about twenty nautical miles behind them at the rendezvous. The Grand Fleet was itself about two and a half to three hours behind the Third Battle Squadron. The Germans would have rendezvoused with the two available squadrons of the High Seas Fleet at about 1530 their time, and then been in action with Beatty and his supporting light forces. An hour after that, the Third Battle Squadron, composed of the *Edward VII* class, nicknamed the "wobbly eight" because of their less than stellar sea-keeping, would have arrived on the scene. There were at least U-boats athwart the potential British line of advance.

There is one more unknown, which is to say that Jellicoe probably knew the German Third Battle Squadron was at Kiel, courtesy of the Admiralty or even his Russian staff officer, and so he was in position to impose overwhelming force on the HSF. Moore's mistake is magnified – or, had Jellicoe chosen not to support his other units (BCS and 3rd BS) which would no doubt have had a hot time by around 1730 or later, Moore's mistake would become a stroke of genius which preserved the British from serious losses. Another thought – the later it got the darker, and the British were not trained in night fighting but the Germans were. While we are in a scenario, the *Edward VII* class was 15,700 tons displacement and armed with four 12-inch, 40 caliber guns, four 9.2-inch, 45 caliber guns, and ten 6-inch, 50 caliber guns. They were the last pure pre-dreadnoughts built for the Royal Navy and contemporaries to the *Deutschland* class of the Second Battle Squadron. Of the class, *King Edward VII, Africa, Commonwealth, Dominion, Hibernia, Hindustan,* and *Zealandia* were all available on the 24th.[9] Meanwhile the German Third Battle Squadron was in the Baltic, too far from the action to help, unless it became a reprise of the Four Days Battle of the Anglo-Dutch wars. The advantage was with the British; although the early engagement might have cost them Beatty and their remaining battle cruisers. The British had Beatty, HMS *Princess Royal, Tiger, Indomitable,* and *New Zealand.*

Tiger had damage to half her main armament; the others had the same weaknesses revealed at Jutland. Hipper's three remaining ships had vital damage only to *Seydlitz*. The British pre-dreadnoughts were capable of fire out to 12,000 yards; the German Second Battle Squadron could shoot at a range of 18,850 meters. A battle between these two squadrons would have been a slugfest between equals. Hipper's survival is problematical, but so was Beatty's. The arrival of Jellicoe three hours later would have turned the tide, but not without serious cost. Scheer's arrival from the Baltic might well have been too late, but by that time it would have been a night action, at which the Germans excelled.

Churchill, with characteristic talent for drama and hyperbole, asserted that if the Germans won, "the trade and food supply of the British islands would have been paralyzed; our armies on the continent would have been cut off from their base by superior naval force. All the transportation of the Allies would have been jeopardized and hampered. The United States could not have intervened in the war. Starvation and invasion would have descended on the British people. Ruin utter and final would have overwhelmed the allied cause."[10]

If the British won, and eliminated a significant part of the German battle fleet, the U-boats would have been hard pressed to maintain their base of operations; they would have lost their principal supply of officers; the British might have been able to intervene in the Baltic to keep the Russians from losing the war. What else might have happened is conjecture, but a Russian victory in the Baltic early in the war might have shortened the conflict with all that such an outcome would entrain.

A third possibility would have been a draw where both sides suffered significant losses which might have made either side consider a negotiated peace, albeit after considering the position of the armies in France and Belgium. Whatever might have happened, naval battles in the First World War involved huge stakes, which is why both sides were so reluctant to engage in decisive naval combat.

On the British side, the operational results were clear, as Sir Julian Corbett's *Official History of the War* states: "The effect of the action was to demonstrate the efficacy of the new distribution for improving our hold on the North Sea, and materially to reduce the chances of the enemy being tempted to hazard a military raid on our coasts." Corbett went on to say the need to maintain large numbers of troops for home defense was also less, giving more leeway for operational deployments elsewhere.[11] It may be that Churchill now felt much more secure in bleeding the Grand Fleet of resources. His Dardanelles fiasco cost several pre-dreadnoughts as well as took battle cruisers and the new super-dreadnought *Queen Elizabeth* away from Beatty for some months in 1915.There was something else. The maturation, of British intelligence of enemy fleet dispositions and movements, no matter how flawed and limited by significant operational problems at Dogger Bank, was critical in allowing the Admiralty to allocate resources in other theaters.[12] Indeed, the relative weakness of the British battle cruiser fleet was eased in time by the return from overseas of high value units including *Invincible* and *Queen Mary*.[13] But the evolving strategic situation was more complex; in fact, the Grand Fleet was for the time being rebased at Cromarty Firth, the battle cruiser squadron was reorganized into a battle cruiser fleet and increased to seven battle cruisers and five *Queen Elizabeth* class super-dreadnoughts and three light cruiser squadrons.[14] And, of course, there had not been complete victory so someone had to be a scapegoat. It turned out to be Rear Admiral Archibald Moore, who was quietly removed from the Grand Fleet rather than court-martialed because "a court martial would have [driven home the lesson] that for the second time in two months, the Grand Fleet had lost the chance of inflicting a decisive defeat through a flag officer complying too rigidly with superior orders instead of using his own judgment and initiative."[15] Perhaps this is true, but one has to recall the higher strategic British goal of not losing the fleet and perhaps this negated the taking of any risk, no matter how great the reward. The objective was to preserve the Grand Fleet against losses, and thus maintain the British distant blockade of the Central Powers. British naval strategy was just as restrictive as was that of the Germans, particularly after the first six months of the war. Ironically the Germans actually had less reason to be restrictive because loss of their fleet was not absolutely going to cost them the war, whereas this was the case with the British. An indecisive major engagement with heavy losses to both sides would have solidified the German fleet's position and done no favors for the already unfavorably viewed Royal Navy at home.

An issue which lies between operational and strategic is one fundamental of an arms race – when in a competition it is essential to give one's team as many resources as the law allows. In this international arms race, there was no law but money and time. Apparently, there was a serious shortage of staff in the Royal Corps of Naval Constructors (RCNC) during the time the British battle cruisers and early dreadnought fleet were designed. This led to shortcuts in the designs of the ships, some of which had adverse consequences. It shows up in the armor plate installed in the *Lion* class and probably in other classes. There is no conclusive evidence, however, that it led directly to the losses later sustained at Jutland. As to other lessons learned and changes made on the British side, there was a realization that battles would be fought at hitherto unprecedented ranges – starting at 20,000 yards or more – and that gunnery control, and indeed elevation of the guns themselves, had to be changed accordingly. There needed to be practice with live ammunition under realistic conditions. Gunnery performance was inadequate at all ranges. "Ignoring *Blücher* they had inflicted only six hits on their enemy counterparts compared to 20 received."[16] Finally, the British believed that the Germans had superiority in scouting by Zeppelins and in threats from torpedoboats and submarines.[17] It was also recognized that there was a disconnect between the Grand Fleet and its needs and the Admiralty's strategy and this needed to be fixed. In fact, there was more a matter of what Patrick Kelly would call "interest group politics" separating the British front commanders from their strategic and political masters. The former would continue to press for fleet actions during the war, especially as the British margin of superiority grew, with concomitant improvements in intelligence processes. Beatty wrote a detailed report to the Admiralty covering tactical changes to be made on 9 February 1915, the most telling section of which involved communications and the need to make certain backup wireless and internal communications from all ships conning towers were redundant and efficient.[18] His second enclosure recognizes the "number of lessons learned are very numerous. Many of them apply to all ships in the Service and involve alterations to machinery . . . the Germans will also have learned valuable lessons, and we can only hope to gain advantage from the battle if we can apply our lessons in a practical matter without delay."[19] Beatty covered issues including zig-zagging, firing while maneuvering, projectiles, lee or weather position, fighting range, director control lighting, tactics, and ships stability (trim). He did not deal with the results of fire in ammunition spaces, as it seemed to have been effectively dealt with by extant British counter-measures. Jellicoe's cover letter to the Admiralty focused on the signaling and communications problems; in it we find reason for Moore's transfer and for what amounts to a reprimand for HMS *Tiger's* performance in the action.[20] Beatty put it this way in his letter to Pelly:

> I wish to emphasize the extreme importance of attaching to the post of second in the line. He is provided when the leader drops out with a golden opportunity to display initiative and take steps for achieving successfully the main object in view – which is the complete destruction of the enemy . . . a disabled ship which has hauled out of the line should not be attacked by four battle cruisers. My signals and standing orders are intended for guidance, as I have often stated, not for rigid obedience if they tend to hinder destruction of the enemy.[21]

Beatty went on to say that *Tiger's* hauling across the bows of *Princess Royal* prevented her from pursuing the enemy and *Tiger's* failure to fire at her opposite number directly led to the heavy concentration of fire on *Lion,* which led to *Lion* being disabled.[22] Beatty also wrote the Second Sea Lord, Admiral Frederick Hamilton, about people problems with *Tiger* and *Indomitable,* but was willing with one exception to let matters lie – albeit with strong direction on how to handle Churchill. Hamilton as Second Sea Lord was responsible for personnel, and thus was less willing to admit the disastrous consequences of the Admiralty policy which resulted in *Tiger* being manned by all the fleet's recovered deserters. The ultimate concerns for history, at least this time for the British side, are contained in the revisions to the *Battle Cruiser Fleet Orders* which Beatty promulgated on 18 February 1915. King George V visited Beatty's squadron at the end of February 1915 to visit ships and wounded. No awards or Orders were given out, but a visit to Beatty's yacht occurred where two of the junior wounded officers were convalescing.[23]

A year later, in a 3 February 1916 appreciation of Dogger Bank lessons, Beatty had one final concern, that it was always the case that a slow ship could not catch a fast one. He then went on to overestimate the German battle cruiser fleet having eight dreadnought class ships by the time of the next encounter against which he would only have four fast second-generation battle cruisers. He also thought (wrongly, as he underestimated her real speed) that bringing *Von der Tann* along on a future sortie would amount to a repeat of the same tactical error *Blücher* represented on 24 January 1915. Finally, there was the matter of armor and the earlier ships were clearly vulnerable. He warned that "if the *Lion* had not had protection from 7" and 9" of armour which burst the projectiles she would have been destroyed."[24] The other lesson is that the British war economy could either produce equipment, ammunition, and supplies for the western front or produce new naval ships and, of these, new battle cruisers were below destroyers and light cruisers in priority. He thought that Hipper would have *Hindenburg* and two *Mackensens* in his command, which both overestimated the capacity of the German economy and misunderstood German war priorities. German priorities were to supply the army and produce U-boats; large surface ships were last by this time. It is also significant that much-praised British intelligence did not know the true state of the German naval order of battle, or had not told Beatty what it knew, or Beatty knew more than he was telling Prime Minister Herbert Asquith exaggerating the case for more battle cruisers. More likely, it was a combination of these factors.[25]

The German side was a different matter altogether. What motivated Ingenohl to send Hipper out in search of such meager returns at such risks? Was it a matter of Ingenohl being conflicted between aggressive admirals and captains, particularly Hipper, and a thoroughly defensive Kaiser and Admiralty which held real power at the time? Knowing what he did not know, why would Hipper have been sent out on a suicide mission for the prize of fishing trawlers? The conventional answer is that the trawlers contained intelligence agents who reported his every move and he wanted this threat removed.[26] The German official history requires a careful reading. Admiral Scheer's account may have been lacking in sources, according to the British official history, which notes that the German asserted the British had lost their dominion over the North Sea, and admits that the Germans might have legitimately thought British losses were greater than they were.[27] The most useful insight in the published history is the war diary of *Seydlitz* and Maurice von Egidy, the German flag captain:

> The plan of the attack did not foresee the probability of encountering important British ships in the North Sea. The actuality of the 24th has on the other hand shown into what an awkward position even fast battle cruiser may get when they are forced to give battle without support from the main fleet. If we had known

our main fleet to be in the rear of us, the commander of the Scouting Forces
would not have found himself in the desperate position where he had to decide
to leave *Blücher* to its fate. We would have carried the ship away in much the
same manner as the British did with *Lion,* which probably was not any worse
damaged than *Blücher* was originally.[28]

This assessment points out the first of a catalog of what-ifs which such
engagements generate. What is known is that when Hipper returned he
wrote: "I have fought to the best of my knowledge and ability and have
done all that is humanly possible despite the unfortunate result which I
believe is the fault of the Fleet."[29] Hipper's chief of staff, Captain Erich
Raeder, the first C-in-C of the German navy in World War II who was on
the bridge of the *Seydlitz* with Hipper for the entire operation said: "To
have stood by the *Blücher* any longer would have risked losing the other
ships and perhaps the entire force. With a heavy heart, Admiral Hipper
countermanded his order and directed a resumption of the withdrawal
southeasterly toward Heligoland. Eyes blurred as the sinking *Blücher*
disappeared in the haze astern."[30]

The *Seydlitz* pulled alongside the quay at Wilhelmshaven to unload
the dead and then proceeded into dock. The dead were frozen in place
and had to be removed from their battle-stations one at a time. The fires
that resulted from the combustion of over 6,000 kilograms of powder
were investigated and the guns pulled out of the two burned-out turrets
and all the machinery overhauled. Captain von Egidy, when told that everything had been done according to regulations, reportedly responded
that "if we lose 190 men and almost the whole ship according to regulations then they are somehow wrong."[31] Indeed, they were to keep the
charges in their protective covers until needed and the same with the
charges themselves. Automatic closing doors were fitted in the magazine hoists and connecting passages between turrets locked in action.[32]
Although the naval and national high commands questioned Hipper's
tactical assignment of *Blücher* to the end of his line, and whether he could
have saved her, they concluded: "Admiral Hipper conducted the whole
matter quite sensibly." Ingenohl, to his credit, said he agreed with Hipper's conduct of the action although he disagreed with some of Hipper's
strategic conclusions.[33] Hipper's observations in his report to Ingenohl
on 27 January included several points, including the erroneous German

assumption Hipper himself had thought correct, that the North Sea was devoid of British heavy ships. In retrospect, this might seem a blindingly obvious observation, but it meant that the Germans now assumed that anytime they went out they would be met by as much force as the British could muster. This mitigated absolute British strategic intelligence advantage, other than the British could still have specific times and places of intercept. Hipper also concluded that the bombardments of the east coast had forced the British to change dispositions to those from which intercept of German forces were easier. This was correct, right down to Humber and Firth of Forth. He also said future operations would have to be conducted with the entire fleet, particularly its most modern warships ready to support the sortie.

Hipper was uneasy about the Second Battle Squadron with its semi-obsolete pre-dreadnoughts being committed to action. A loss would mean 700 good officers and men who could not man new construction. He suggested all pre-dreadnoughts be used either as floating batteries or decommissioned, as they were not battle worthy because of the power of modern artillery.

Additional priority had to be assigned to destroyer flotillas that had to be brought up to strength and always deployed. Further, he thought torpedoboats would be of decisive value in an engagement; even single boats might go unnoticed between the lines and have opportunities against the enemy. The enemy was seriously afraid of torpedoes and could be predicted to act accordingly. Torpedoboat recognition was always a problem and his suggested solution was that German boats be painted red.

Even Hipper thought it was not a good idea to fight more than seventy miles from Heligoland. Any fight would of necessity involve lines of U-boats which could attack both before and after the main action. Fighting in English waters was unrealistic, even suicidal. A trap could be sprung with the appropriate bait in the German Bight, but only on German initiative.

Lastly, either intuiting, or with knowledge of the command problems Beatty had faced, he proposed a standing order for command success should he be killed or disabled: the flag captain would take over the Scouting Group and lead it. After von Egidy, it would fall to the next senior captain. No unnecessary admirals. Hipper did not have a battle cruiser fleet.

Like the British, the Germans felt heads had to roll because of the mistakes made. Hipper wrote in his *Nachlass* on 1 February 1915: "Today I placed before the Fleet Commander the acutely painful question of the loyalty of his captains so that he would understand the consequences of the 24th. I have been very frank with him." The next day Ingenohl was relieved of his command and retired. He said, "I am very sorry about this but there was nothing I could do to help him." Somehow, this reads as sarcasm. In any case, Hipper was not too certain about his own head when he heard Admiral Hugo von Pohl, erstwhile Chief of the Admiralty Staff and an advocate of Kleinkreig, had been appointed. The other casualties were Rear Admiral Paul von Eckerman, the fleet chief of staff, who had been hidden in a battle squadron, and Vice Admiral Wilhelm von Lans, who had actually commanded the rescue force that arrived too late. Hipper need not have worried that the Kaiser was in need of heroes; the Kaiser accepted his explanation for what had happened. Hipper and von Egidy were invited to a late breakfast on the Royal train and accompanied the Kaiser on a tour around Wilhelmshaven on visits to the wounded in hospital and *Seydlitz*. He was awarded the Iron Cross First Class.[34]

The Germans took some corrective action regarding ammunition fires, but they already had two critical advantages: German powder was not in flammable bags or leather cases but rather in brass cartridges; and, the powder itself, although less powerful than lyddite, was much more stable and tended to burn rather than explode.

Hipper's basic recommendation that the fleet conduct operations close to home was followed; sorties with capital ships were only undertaken with maximum ships available and these short-distance sorties were done several times and with increasing frequency until von Pohl died of cancer at the end of 1915. The other thing the fleet did was cover submarine deployments and yield many of its best officers to U-boats, as well as make the future capital ship programs hostage to unrestricted U-boat warfare and divert too many heavy guns from ships under construction to the Army. These actions would have serious consequences but that, too, is another story.

CONCLUSIONS

It is the essence of conflict that violence should occur and the inevitable price that lives should be lost as the objective is the imposition of will of one set of humans on another, otherwise they would not likely think the effort or objective serious. A battle is what happens to make such a process work. But sometimes the actual battle does nothing except to prolong or weaken the will to fight because it makes no real difference in the balance of power. No one wins, no one really loses in absolute terms; this is what happened at Dogger Bank. The wary and bloodied antagonists square off for another round.

To January 1915, the death toll for the navies was already in the thousands. With Admiral Christopher Craddock, *Good Hope,* and *Monmouth,* 1,337 had been lost at Coronel; with Rear Admiral Maximilian von Spee, his sons, and *Scharnhorst* and *Gneisenau,* another 1,400 men were lost at the Falklands. In *Aboukir, Hogue,* and *Cressy,* 1,411 men went to their deaths in the Channel, and in *Formidable* another 547. And these were only the large ships. By January 1915, the Royal Navy had suffered over 3,300 killed in the large ships alone; the Imperial German Navy had lost all its overseas cruisers of all classes and most of its entire inventory of armored cruisers. Including losses in the North Sea and Baltic, these were *Yorck, Friedrich Karl, Mainz, Magdeburg, Dresden, Nürnberg, Königsberg, Leipzig,* and *Ariadne.* The total loss of men from armored cruisers and light cruisers before Dogger Bank was more than 2,236. "At sea the death toll was determined not by the intensity of the fighting but by the size of the ship and how quickly it sank."[35] *Blücher's* loss raised the German total by at least 25 percent. By her sinking, the Royal Navy evened the score to about 3,500 each in the large ships. By the time the war ended, the British naval casualties were over 33,000 dead. German naval casualties were less, but heavily concentrated in the U-boat service. Nevertheless, the navy was still a good place to be compared to the armies of either side, whose casualties mounted to the millions.

The Battle of Dogger Bank was fought on a cold January morning in the North Sea, at distances which were thousands of yards beyond those either side had practiced for. The antagonists were possessed of huge complex machines of unprecedented power, robustness, and speed.

Their communications, however, were hostage to frail radio antennae, flashing lights, and ultimately flag hoist not unlike that used for three hundred years in all fights at sea. Their enemies were weather, smoke, fire time, and human error. The weather was relatively mild until the last and endangered the *Lion*'s survival; it increased the casualty toll among *Blücher*'s survivors. The smoke from both funnels and gunfire made it hard for both sides to see and made the weather gage, so critical for maneuvering in the days of sail, important again, this time for advantage in aiming the new gunfire controls and for being able to judge the actual state of the battle, including real damage to the enemy. Lessons learned called for redundancies in systems on both sides, for more firefighting gear and lights, and breathing apparatus for the combatants. Both commanders recognized the need for clear instructions on succession in the chain of command, and both sides concluded the need for assuming less and knowing more. To some extent, Churchill was right that the battle showed the muscle of British superiority, and when Vice Admiral Reinhard Scheer found himself facing the deployed Grand Fleet on 31 May the following year, that lesson was driven home. Scheer was known to have remarked that "he felt like a virgin with no way out."

The weaknesses and strengths of the German and British fleets were to some extent revealed, but not totally, particularly British vulnerability to explosive destruction. The Germans did adopt their strategy to fighting on their terms, and largely presented little temptation to the British, whose main national efforts were concentrated on two disasters – the Western Front and the Dardanelles. It should be noted that any assertion that the Germans were tied to their anchors after Dogger Bank is much too simple. Hipper and Pohl continued to look for ways to damage the enemy, but without facing suicidal odds. In the rest of 1915, the German fleet did get underway nine times, and numerous smaller operations by cruisers and destroyers were conducted, often in support of U-boats and airships. The British found themselves losing destroyers to the anti-submarine campaign against the first U-boat offensive. Both the battle cruiser fleet and the Grand Fleet moved less and were even less in evidence. This was because: "Fleet operations were subsidiary to the German guerre de course (commerce warfare) and the British counter-measures."[36] Thus it appears that the Germans subsequent to, but not because of, Dogger Bank turned to what Ingenohl and Pohl suggested would work – commerce warfare principally on the backs of a small but rapidly expanding U-boat force into which the best officers from the High Seas Fleet rapidly flowed. Hipper's advice was followed, all the fleet operations, however restricted they might have been if they involved his battle cruisers, were supported by the main fleet, which itself became more and more competent, even if it still contained the obsolescent Second Battle Squadron. They had plenty of time to practice but did not get any reinforcements sufficient to turn the tide. That fact, and the lack of strategic knowledge of the British shortages leading to frozen big ship programs on the other side of the North Sea, meant that the terrible stalemate would continue through and past Jutland and into the American entry into the war.

Of the combatants at Dogger Bank, only the slowly deteriorating wreck of the *Blücher* remains. Sitting upside-down in the mud of the Dogger Bank, she is deep enough to be visited only by mixed-gas divers. The 21 cm turrets are still at the angles at which they burned out shortly before she turned over. She is still a war grave for over 700 German sailors. The First Scouting Group, along with the new *Hindenberg,* once supposed to have 17-inch guns,[37] were all scuttled at Scapa Flow, salvaged, and eventually scrapped. But the *Derfflinger* "with her incredible gift for survival" lay bottom-up off the Hoy throughout the six years of World War II, and was finally towed away and scrapped in 1948.[38] Her bell was turned over to the German navy in 1966. Of the British veterans of Dogger Bank – *Lion, Princess Royal, Tiger, New Zealand,* and *Indomitable* – all succumbed to the Washington Treaty and were scrapped, the last being *Tiger.* There were no civilian casualties in the Battle of Dogger Bank, unlike at Scarborough and Hartlepool, where civilians, women, and children had been lost to shellfire. As Richard Hough put it: "The British public was elated, and as the *Indomitable* towed the battered *Lion* up the Firth of Forth the waiting crowd gave welcome cheers. The newspapers too were elated: 'It will be some time before they go baby killing again' the *Globe* thundered."[39]

Notes

PREFACE

1. Groos, *Der Krieg zur See, Nordsee Bd 1, Karte 6, Entfernungstafel* [German Official History of the War at Sea, North Sea, Vol. 1, Chart 6, Ranges; hereafter: Groos, *Der Krieg zur See,* I–III]. There is also Rudolph Firle, *Der Krieg in der Ostsee, Bd 1, Von Kriegsbeginn bis Mitte März, 1915* (Berlin: E. S. Mittler, 1921), 15–30.

2. These include: Hough, *Naval Battles of the Twentieth Century;* the third chapter covers the battle. Osborne, *Battle of Heligoland Bight;* this is useful for analysis and context. Roberts, *Battlecruisers;* this is a technical and operational history of the British class of ships that fought at Dogger Bank. Staff and Bryan, *German Battle Cruisers 1914–1918* is an analysis of the German ships. Massie, *Castles of Steel;* this is superb and colorful analysis of the entire war, with Dogger Bank covered in two chapters out of thirty-eight. Young, *With the Battle Cruisers;* this reprint, with introduction of the book published in 1921, gives a spectacular view of the battle from the spotting top of HMS *Lion,* the British flagship. See Goldrick, *The King's Ships Were at Sea;* this is the best single analysis, albeit from the UK perspective, and is the most elegant naval literature in this field. Rose, *Power at Sea;* see chapter 6, "Stand-off 1914–1915"; this is good scholarship in the Neptunian/Mahanian context.

3. Staff, *Battle on the Seven Seas.*

4. *Kaisertum* is a word describing the spirit of the times of the Kaiser; it can be more, and incorporate both policy and hubris.

5. Nicholas A. Lambert, "British Naval Policy, 1913–1914: Financial Limitation and Strategic Revolution," *Journal of Modern History,* Vol. 67, No 3, (Sept 1995) University of Chicago Press, 595.

The most interesting and original source in this is the access which Lambert had to Winston Churchill's first draft of *The World Crisis,* the British statesman's apologia for World War I. As Lambert prefers, it is cited as first draft of Sir Winston Churchill's *The World Crisis,* Chartwell Trust, Churchill Papers, and Churchill College Cambridge.

6. Ibid., 596.

7. Halpern, *A Naval History of World War I,* 267ff.

8. Parkes, *British Battleships,* 551.

9. Friedman, *U.S. Cruisers: An Illustrated Design History,* 61–64.

10. Ibid., 63.

11. German sources include *Bundesarchiv/Militararchiv 50/66/10–19. Reichsmarine Amt.* Ship's characteristics books, in detailed form, provide official ship characteristics, performance data, ammunition load outs, speed trials, and schematics, including both plans and elevations for

all German major combatants engaged in Dogger Bank; *Bundesarchiv/Miltararchiv* F 3916 – most of the war diary of the *Von der Tann,* a battle cruiser not at Dogger Bank, but of use for context; *F3885 War Diary of the Flag officer scouting forces, war operations orders 1914–1918; F3899 War Diary of Lutzow, Flagship of FO Scouting forces throughout her existence 1916 only; F3913 SMS Seydlitz War Diary, Flag at Dogger Bank; F3820 War Diary BdA (Flag Officer Scouting Forces) 1914–1918;* PG 76531 is the section of the BdA War Diary dealing with Dogger Bank. It is Band 3. F4062 is the BdA report and analyses of Dogger Bank. F2438/Bd 1 is a conference about battle cruisers at the naval headquarters level. There are some two dozen other files which might apply to the work as outlined below. What is listed above is the absolute minimum.

U.S. National Archives include Record Group 45, Modern Navy, Records of the Office of Naval Intelligence (also available in the Office of Naval Records and Library, Department of the Navy: ONI, *Monthly Intelligence Bulletin,* "The German Official Account of the Battle of Dogger Bank," by CDR Otto Groos. This is a translation of the Naval History account in *Der Krieg zur See.* It goes down to ship's logs extracts.

British sources include: UK National Archives (late Public Records Office). Admiralty 137 Series, File 1943, beginning with BCF reports on 28 August 1914, Battle of Heligoland Bight; also follow up reports through Fleet and Admiralty level; the same for all actions 16 December 1914; Admiralty 137/1022, *Report of the Battle of the Falklands with von Spee's Squadron;* Adm137/1943 *Report of Vice Admiral Sir David Beatty on the Action in the North Sea, January 24, 1915.* Multiple enclosures and German survivor reports; German press report on the action also included. There are additional action reports from the

British side on later actions, Adm 136/1906 which is Jellicoe's Jutland report; Adm 53, ships logs for British ships engaged at Jutland; Adm 53/69093 HMS *Tiger* logs from Dogger bank – actual hand records; *Princess Royal* 24/25 Jan Adm53/55960.

Two books, Brown, *The Grand Fleet,* and Roberts, *Battlecruisers,* cover the British design construction and battle cruiser operations in detail and provide exhaustive archival bibliographies.

12. Kennedy, *Anglo-German Naval Rivalry: A Controlled Process,* 285.

13. von Tirpitz, *Deutsche Ohnmachtspolitk im Weltkrieg,* Anhang 6 [appendix 6].

1. DECISIONS BEYOND THE BATTLEFIELD

1. Staff, *Battle on the Seven Seas,* 83.

2. Kennedy, *Rise and Fall of British Naval Mastery,* 205–37. Kennedy also wrote a short description of the action in "Dogger Bank Clash of the Battle Cruisers," in Fitzsimons, *Warships and Sea Battles of World War I,* 44–52.

3. This is an academically rich and contentious subject, with an extensive and rich historiography. The best historiography on the German Navy and almost any subject related to it is Bird, *German Naval History.* For an update, see Kelly, *Tirpitz and the Imperial German Navy.* The British side is covered by Kennedy, supra.

4. Kelly, *Tirpitz and the Imperial German Navy.* Kelly covers most of this discussion in several places in his work. For Tirpitz as a social Darwinist, see 12.

5. The theme of nationalism is as redolent throughout this period as to lend itself to Hollywood analogies, viz. *Those Magnificent Men in their Flying Machines.* Scheer, *Germany's High Seas Fleet in the World War;* the preface is a national apologia.

6. Hobson, *Imperialism at Sea Naval Strategic Thought.* This is a *tour de force;* critical analysis can be found in 284–96,

"From Maltzahn to Wegener: The German School and Geopolitics."

7. Hillmann represents a post-revisionist school in German naval history, indeed in German history. Hillmann holds that Raeder was building defensively, as indeed was Tirpitz, and that neither had global ambitions. Professor Keith Bird to the author, 28 May 2012.

8. Mitchell, *History of Russian and Soviet Sea Power*, 287. Scheer, *Germany's High Seas Fleet in the World War*, 20.

9. Massie, *Castles of Steel*, 376.

10. Mitchell, *History of Russian and Soviet Sea Power*, 284–87.

11. Wegener, *Naval Strategy of the World War*, 49ff.

12. The insight into the motives behind the operation by the German Fleet on 23 January 1915 is in the German Military Archives (BA/MA) Operations Order itself; the British insight is contained in several places in Chalmers, *Life and Letters of David Beatty*, 168ff., with particular insights also in Keyes, *Naval Memoirs*, I:114–26 – motives of subs and small ships lurking in the narrow seas; 159–69 describes the battle from the small boys' perspective.

13. See Fig. A.2: Appendix 6 to von Tirpitz, *Deutsche Ohnmachtspolitik im Weltkrieg*, [German Appeasement Policy in the World War].

14. Ibid.

15. Richmond, *Sea Power in the Modern World*, 11ff.

16. Ibid., 11.

17. von Tirpitz, *My Memoirs*, 55.

18. Nicholas Lambert, *Sir John Fisher's Naval Revolution* (Columbia: University of South Carolina Press, 1999), 626. Again, the work of Jon Sumida suggests itself, particularly "Machines, Manufacturing, Management, and Money."

19. Halpern, *Naval History of World War I*, 291.

20. Ibid., 294.

21. Ibid., 293. From Scheer, *Germany's High Seas Fleet in the World War*, 222–24.

22. Richmond, *Sea Power in the Modern World*, 305.

23. Ibid.

24. Ibid.

25. Ibid., 307.

26. Ibid.

27. Ibid.

28. The German maximum elevation and effective range varied from class to class. *Blücher* for example had 8.2-inch guns good out to 19,100 meters at 30 degrees. See BA/MA 50/66/17 RMA Deutsche *Kriegsflotte* Band III, *Grosser Kreuzer*, Heft 5 *Scharnhorst, Gneisenau, and Blucher*; for *Von der Tann, Moltke, Goeben*, see Heft vol. 6. *Von der Tann's* maximum range was 18,900 meters at 20 degrees with her 11-inch, 45 caliber main armament; *Moltke's* was 18,100 meters with 11-inch, 50 caliber and only 13.5 degrees elevation. The secondary armament of 5.9-inch guns was effective at 13,500 meters at 20 degrees. *Seydlitz* was the same. *Derfflinger* was not much better. The decision to limit the elevation and therefore effective range of German guns was Titpitz's, based on advice from Scheer, among others.

29. Seligmann, *Naval Intelligence from Germany*, 39.

30. Ibid., 37 and 37n1.

31. Kelly, *Tirpitz and the Imperial German Navy*, 256. This is from PG 66050, and Nachlass 253/22, *Tirpitz Nachlass*, as in Kelly, 256 n127.

32. Ibid., 506n35 from Scheer to Tirpitz 22 August 1906, PG 66080.

33. Ibid., 331.

34. Mackay, *Fisher of Kilverstone*, 376. Brown, *The Grand Fleet*, 58ff. Roberts, *Battlecruisers*, 33ff.

35. Lambert, 598. This new view of Fisher is based on Jon Sumida's analysis of Fisher in his book *In Defense of Naval Supremacy*, cited in Lambert, 598n12. The

bottom line was that it would be cheaper than a balanced fleet.

36. Lambert, 604.

37. Peebles, *Warshipbuilding on the Clyde*, 91–94.

38. Lambert, 616.

39. Ibid., 619. See 619n137–38.

40. Ibid.

41. Ibid., 621. This is all based on primary archival sources.

42. Ibid., 624.

43. Kelly, *Tirpitz and the Imperial German Navy*, 264.

44. Ibid., 327.

45. Ibid., 333.

46. Lord Haldane was Richard Burdon Haldane. He was the German-speaking British War Minister who visited Berlin in February 1912 in an attempt to break the cycle of the Anglo-German arms race. His proposal was based on an Admiralty memorandum which said there was no problem with exchanging detail of order of battle and ships to be built from the British side. The Germans did not see this as a key issue; rather they wanted a political and naval agreement which insured British neutrality in a war with France or Russia. This was unacceptable to the British, the French, and the Russians, all of whom knew of the Haldane Mission. See Marder, *From the Dreadnought to Scapa Flow*, I:229–33; for a more detailed discussion, see Massie, *Dreadnought, Britain, Germany*, 790–817.

47. Marder, 340.

48. Ibid., 343.

49. Ibid., 343.

50. Kelly, *Tirpitz and the Imperial German Navy*, 465; for Scheer's promise, see 429.

51. Churchill, *World Crisis*, 591.

52. d'Eyncourt, "Notes on Some Features of German Warship Construction." There are many sources on both German and British naval programs but this one is useful in that it provides a professional,

postwar look at what was actually done by both sides and when, and may be considered authoritative in that it is after the fact.

53. Tuckmann, *The Proud Tower*, 282.

54. NA/PRO/Adm/116/940B, Dumas to F. Lascelles, Ambassador to Foreign Minister Sir Edward Grey, 4.

55. Marder, I:151–85.

56. Ibid., 152–55.

57. Ibid., 177–78; see also Kelly, *Tirpitz and the Imperial German Navy*, 463. For misperceptions, see Kelly, 278–79.

58. Patterson, *The Jellicoe Papers*, I:18–19.

59. Kemp, *Papers of Admiral Sir John Fisher*, I:341.

60. Patterson, *The Jellicoe Papers*, I:21; for Agadir, see I:22.

61. Scheck, *Alfred von Tirpitz and German Right Wing Politics*, 8.

62. Marder, *From the Dreadnought to Scapa Flow*, I:176.

63. The record of the conference at which *Von der Tann's* essential characteristics were decided is at USNA/T-1022/Reel 1501/PG 66087. The original is now back in the BA/MA at the PG mentioned. This is notable because *Von der Tann* was in the yards for condenser repairs on 24 January 1914. Admiral August von Heeringen supported the 28 cm armament and higher speed of 24 knots on political grounds. Tirpitz said that both political grounds and the 12-inch guns of the *Invincible* made the larger design imperative, this was as of 19 Sept 1906 for the 1907 Ships Program.

64. NA/PRO/Adm 116/866B.

65. Seligmann, *Naval Intelligence from Germany*, 468–73ff.; Tracy, *Collective Naval Defense of the Empire*; see 161–76, Churchill to Herbert Asquith, PM, 14 April 1912, et seq.

66. Tracy, *Collective Naval Defense of the Empire*, 346–47.

67. Gretton, *Winston Churchill and the Royal Navy*, 31ff.

68. Tracy, *Collective Naval Defense of the Empire*, xv.

69. Hobson, *Imperialism at Sea Naval Strategic Thought*. This book is critical for understanding the ideological context of the men who fought the battle, particularly on the German side.

70. This is from a letter to his wife at Hannover Lodge where she had taken interim residency pending his wartime deployment, from Ranft, *The Beatty Papers*, I:111–14.

71. Ibid., I:264, Beatty to his wife, 15 March 1915.

72. Patterson, *Jellicoe Papers*, I:12ff.

2. BUILDING THE
BATTLE CRUISERS

1. Ranft, *The Beatty Papers*, I:97; Beatty to C-in-C Home Fleets, 10 March 1914.

2. John Arbuthnot Fisher, 1841–1920.

3. Mackay, *Fisher of Kilverstone*, 5ff.

4. Patterson, *The Jellicoe Papers*, I:12.

5. Ibid, I:13.

6. Marder, *From the Dreadnought to Scapa Flow*, I:124–25. The rest of the citation goes on to recognize that in 1905, the year of the laying down of the *Dreadnought* and the *Invincible* class battle cruisers, the international situation could change, but that was why a "modified version" of the two power standard was needed which reflected the capabilities of the first two powers in any case. This was the actual situation, before the introduction of dreadnoughts by several powers changed the equation.

7. Marder, *From the Dreadnought to Scapa Flow*, I:406.

8. Hattendorff, *British Naval Documents*, 737–38. See Mackay, *Fisher of Kilverstone*, 208 on boilers, and 282 on involvement in Fisher reforms and naval education. For work involving reform in cross-decking seamen and stokers, a radical idea at the time, see Kemp, *Papers of Admiral Sir John Fisher*, II:126–27.

9. Obituary, *The Times of London*, 30 January 1917.

10. Mackay, *Fisher of Kilverstone*, 389–90.

11. Marder, *From the Dreadnought to Scapa Flow*, I:80n13.

12. Ibid., I:411n10. The witness was Admiral Sir William Fisher who had served as Captain of HMS *St Vincent* in the Grand Fleet under Jellicoe.

13. Ibid., I:408.

14. Patterson, *The Jellicoe Papers*, I:6n1. Fisher to Lord Selborne, 19 October 1904.

15. Mackay, *Fisher of Kilverstone*, 297. Bacon was also the first biographer of Fisher. Bacon, *Life of Lord Fisher of Kilverstone*.

16. John Roberts in Gardiner, *Conway's All the World's Fighting Ships*, 73. "The main belt was 6in [sic and hereafter, meaning inches thick] for a length of 272 feet amidships reducing to 4-in forward and 3-in aft. No side armor was provided between the main and upper decks, and the ammunition hoists for the 7.5in turrets were provided with 7-in armor tubes between these decks reducing to 2-in behind the side armour between the main and lower decks. The 7.5in barbettes were 7in on the outboard side and 3in inboard while the turrets had 8in faces, 6in sides and 4in rears. The 9.2in turrets had 8in faces, and 7in sides and rears, while the barbettes were a uniform 7in, with 3in floors. The forward 0.2in ammunition hoist was protected by a 7in tube from the barbette to the main deck and then reduced to 2in; while aft the tube was 4in only, being entirely behind the side armour. Deck protection was very weak with a ¾in protective deck increasing to 1.5in over the steering gear and a main deck of ¾in amidships with 1in fore and aft. Besides the forward 10in CT they were fitted with and after CT protected by 3in armor, both positions having a 3in communications tube down to the protective deck."

17. Parkes, *British Battleships*, 472.

18. Ibid., 489–91.

19. Ibid., 492.

20. Ibid., 493.

21. See Peebles, *Warship Building on the Clyde*, 60, 67–68; see also Roberts, 25–31, "Years of Economy."

22. Peebles, *Warship Building on the Clyde*, 73.

23. Brown, *The Grand Fleet*, 16. The endorsement was from the pioneer naval architect William Froude whose early work with models and tanks established a global lead for Royal Navy ship design at the height of the Victorian industrial revolution. See also Singer, *History of Technology*, V:386ff., "The development of Applied Hydrodynamics," Froude was *the* pioneer.

24. *Dictionary of National Biography*, entry for John Harper Narbeth, retrieved at www.oxforddnb.com/articles/35/35184 [date viewed 1 November 2012-cegw].

25. For the MVO, see Hieronymussen, *Orders, Medals and Decoration*, 86–91.

26. Obituary, *Shipbuilder and Marine Engine Builder*, vol. 43 (Shipbuilder Press 1936). He was also memorialized in the *Transactions of the Royal Institution of Naval Architects*, vol. 47:2, 245.

27. Ibid., *Transactions*.

28. Patterson, *The Jellicoe Papers*, I:14.

29. Ibid., 30.

30. Ibid. This is from PRO ADD MSS 49035, folio 50.

31. von Tirpitz, *My Memoirs*, 233.

32. Patterson, *The Jellicoe Papers*, I:13. Extract from Jellicoe's autobiographical notes.

33. Numerous works have listed the characteristics of British and German battle cruisers. There are provided for the reader here for convenience and context. The British battle cruisers data are taken in abbreviated form from Roberts, *Battle Cruisers*, which is a fine account of this much maligned category according to Brown, *The Grand Fleet*, 202.

34. Kelly, *Tirpitz and the Imperial German Navy*, 257ff.

35. Ibid.

36. Ibid., 257, 271ff.

37. Ibid., 228, 467.

38. Ibid., 263, 331, 359.

39. Ibid., 257. The Reichsmarineamt Protocol is in 22 Sept 1905, as in Kelly, *Tirpitz and the Imperial German Navy*, 504n127.

40. Kelly, *Tirpitz and the Imperial German Navy*, 272.

41. Paul Schmalenbach, SMS *Blücher*, *Warship International*, #2, June 30, 1971 (London: Naval Records Club, 1972), 171–81. Cite is 174.

42. Kelly, *Tirpitz and the Imperial German Navy*, 253.

43. Ibid., 253, "First News of the Dreadnought," 502–503n103. The source is archival.

44. Ibid., 502–503n103.

45. Deacon, *History of the British Secret Service*, 176.

46. Mackay, *Fisher of Kilverstone*, 321–24. The source is *Fisher Papers*, 4706 Report of the Committee on Designs, 1905.

47. Ibid.

48. Ramsay, *"Blinker" Hall, Spymaster*.

49. Patterson, *The Jellicoe Papers*, I:12.

50. Ibid, I:13.

51. Mäkelä, *Auf den Spuren der Goeben*, 11.

52. Ibid, 11.

53. Seligman, *Spies in Uniform*.

54. Kelly, *Tirpitz and the Imperial German Navy*, 1.

55. Ibid.

56. Forstmeier, *Deutsche Grosskampfschiffe*, 18–19. This is a superb exposition and documentation of the fast battleship or battle cruiser type in its final German iteration.

57. BA/MA 50/66/18, 24.

58. *Germany War Vessels 1914*, NID, 140ff.

59. BA/MA/50/66/18, 24.

60. Marder, *From the Dreadnought to Scapa Flow*, II:36–41.

61. Ranft, *The Beatty Papers*, I:80–81, 97. For unhappiness on the *Goeben* escape and the subsequent Troubridge Court Martial, see 144–45.

62. Ibid., 144–45.

63. BA/MA, *Nachlass Hipper*, N162/1, 17.

64. Kelly, *Tirpitz and the Imperial German Navy*, 382. Kelly cites Halpern, 57ff. on this and more importantly *Nachlass Souchon*, N156/2/32 Tirpitz to Souchon.

65. Kelly, *Tirpitz and the Imperial German Navy*, 282n85.

66. Ibid.

67. Ruge, *SMS Seydlitz/Grosser kreuzer*, II:26.

68. BA/MA N162/1 *Nachlass Hipper*, 4, 23 June 1914. His previous flagship was *Moltke*.

69. Ruge, *SMS Seydlitz/grosser kreuzer*.

70. Breyer, *Schlachtschiffe und Schlachtkreuzer*.

71. Philbin, *Admiral von Hipper*.

72. Ibid., 19ff.

73. Brown and Meehan, *Scapa Flow*, 139.

3. PROLOGUE TO WAR AND BATTLE

1. Gretton, *Winston Churchill and the Royal Navy*, 117.

2. Philbin, *Admiral von Hipper*, 22. For the Mediterranean deployment, see 20n57; for torpedoboat problems, see 21, 58, 59; Hipper to von Trotha, 24 December 1919, *Nachlass von Trotha*, Neidersächsisches Staatsarchiv, Dep 18/132; for torpedo shortages, see BA/MA F3304, Admiral von Ingenohl to Admiral von Tirpitz, 28 Nov 1912.

3. Philbin, *Admiral von Hipper*, 31n87–88, i.e., BA/MA F728/PG65726 Reel 143, *Akten Hochseeflotte, Schlussbericht uber die taktische Tätigkeit der Hochseefltotte im Ubungsyahr 1912*, 21–22, and PG65726, Reel

1247, "Ran an den Feind", 21 December 1913. The evaluation of the tactic is from Marder, *From the Dreadnought to Scapa Flow*, III:181.

4. More will be said of this later, but the observation is in Brown, *The Grand Fleet*, 155.

5. Philbin, *Admiral von Hipper*, 31n89–91. Hipper's own view is from his *Nachlass*, BA/MA, N162, N1/3 25 May 1914. For the Zeppelin, see Douglas Reeman, *The Zeppelin in Combat*, 116.

6. Chalmers, *Life and Letters of David Beatty*, 116–19; quote is on 119.

7. Ranft, *The Beatty Papers*, I:6–7.

8. Ibid., I:7.

9. Ibid. See document 26, I:36–45. Beatty's paper for Winston Churchill on naval dispositions in a war against Germany.

10. Ibid., I:37.

11. Ibid., 47.

12. Chatfield, *Navy and Defense*, 109.

13. Ibid., 119.

14. Chalmers, *Life and Letters of David Beatty*, 120.

15. Ibid., 120.

16. Ibid., 121.

17. Beatty on examining underwater damage to *Lion* where two 12-inch shells from *Derfflinger* hitting almost together had done serious damage. See Patterson, *The Jellicoe Papers*, I.

18. They were doubly short when five additional, but slower *Royal Sovereigns* joined by 1917.

19. *Beatty* and *Jellicoe* Papers NRS.

20. Marder, *From the Dreadnought to Scapa Flow*. The surrender terms resulted in other ships being substituted. The British wanted the entire battle cruiser inventory because they believed that without it the German fleet would have been both hobbled and blind. This thinking was reflective of old school dynamics inside the British Admiralty – perhaps they did not all reflect on how useful the Zeppelin could be as a scouting unit.

21. Surface and Bland, *American Food in the World War*.

22. Ranft, *The Beatty Papers*, I:102, Beatty to his wife, HMS *Lion*, 2 August 1914.

23. Ibid., 107.

24. Ibid.

25. This is covered in Philbin, *Admiral von Hipper*, 37ff., "New Naval Weapons."

26. The definitive work is Osborne, *Battle for Heligoland Bight*; see also Staff, *Battle on the Seven Seas*, 1–27.

27. Captain Sir Basil Liddell-Hart, *Thoughts on War*, 1944, cited in Peter G. Tsouras, *Warrior's Words: A Quotation Book* (London: Cassell Arms and Armour Press, 1992), 180. For an illustration of the actual fog, see Staff, *Battle on the Seven Seas*, 27.

28. Ranft, *The Beatty Papers*, I:108.

29. Halpern, *The Keyes Papers*, I:10, Keyes to Chief of War Staff, 23 August 1914.

30. This general description of the combatants is taken from the relevant German and British sections of Jane, *Jane's Fighting Ships, 1914*.

31. UK National Archives, Adm 53/63076, HMS *Tiger* Log, 24 January 1815.

32. Bowditch, *American Practical Navigator*, 29–40. The abbreviations for weather match precisely those used in the UK logs.

33. BA/MA, F3919/PG 63370 *Vorstoss nach der Dogger Bank is 23.bis.24.I.15. Kreigstagebuch SMS Moltke*. Both sides had standard log inputs for the weather: in the case of *Seydlitz*, and all other German ships it was *Angabe des Orts, Windes, Wetter, Seegang, Beleuchtung, Sichtigkeit der Luft, Mondschein, usw.* [Overview of the area, wind weather, seastate, humidity of the air, state of the moon, and so forth.]

34. N.A., PRO/Adm 137, 1943, typescript from *Admiralty; "Report of Vice Admiral Sir David Beatty on the Action in the North Sea January 24th, 1915"* follows in the same file as 654–89.

35. Groos, *Der Krieg zur See, I*, chart 6, Ranges].

36. Preston, *Battleships of World War I*, 149.

37. Chatfield, *Navy and Defense*, 123–24.

38. Philbin, *Admiral von Hipper*, 51–52.

39. For an example among the German battle cruisers see BA/MA N50/66, *Reichsmarineamt, Deutsche Kriegsflotte, Bd III, Grosse Kreuzer*, 1 and 27. See entry for *Moltke*. For the British *Lion* class, see Roberts, *Battlecruisers*, 41. To find the oil and coal fuel numbers for the entire IAG consult Groner, *Die deutschen Kriegschiffe*, 19–23.

40. See Preston, *Battleships of World War I*, 149ff., for a fuller discussion.

41. One suspects because of lack of money and poor war planning.

42. Groos, *Der Krieg zur See, I*, table 2, Order of Battle of the British Fleet in July 1914 as known to the German Admiralty of the day.]

43. See the figure on endurance for *Moltke* above. Battle cruiser operations were faster and Beatty and Hipper often exercised at maximum speeds. For the British submarine capabilities, see Halpern, *The Keyes Papers*, 2n1. *C, D*, and *E* classes. *C* class; *D* class completed 1910–1912, 550–604 tons, 16 knots surfaced 9–10 knots submerged, 3 tubes, complement 25; *E* class completed 1913–1917, 660–800 tons, 15–16/10 knots 5 tubes, Complement 30.

44. Halpern, *The Keyes Papers*, I:2n1.

45. These boats were deployed in two lines as depicted in Groos, *Der Krieg zur See*, I, chart 33.

46. Rossler, *Die deutschen U-Boote*, 162ff for characteristics. *U-13* and *U-15* were 516 tons surfaced, 691 submerged, 14.9 knots surfaced, 9.5 submerged, 2000 mile range at 14 knots; 4 TT, 6 torpedoes, 29 crew.

47. Ranft, *The Beatty Papers*, I:116–17, Beatty to his wife, 18 August 1914.

48. Patterson, *The Jellicoe Papers*, I:50.

49. BA/MA N162/1/13 *Hipper Nachlass,* 16 August 1914.

50. Chatfield, *Navy and Defense,* 127.

51. Patterson, *The Jellicoe Papers,* I:50.

52. Ibid., I:51.

53. Osborne, *Battle for Heligoland Bight.*

54. Chatfield, *Navy and Defense,* 124.

55. Ibid., 126–37.

56. Philbin, *Admiral von Hipper,* 86.

57. Ibid.

58. Patterson, *The Jellicoe Papers,* I:66. Jellicoe to the Secretary of the Admiralty, 13 September 1914.

59. Groos, *Der Krieg zur See,* II, From the Beginning of September to November 1914 (Berlin, 1922), 66.

60. Ibid., II:242.

61. Jellicoe, *Crisis of the Naval War,* 49–50.

62. Ibid., 136.

63. Note conclusions V through VIII are missing from the published documents and invite further research.

64. Patterson, *The Jellicoe Papers,* I:69–70.

65. Ibid, 72.

66. Ibid. 73, Churchill to Jellicoe, 8 Oct 1914.

67. Philbin, *Admiral von Hipper,* 92ff.

68. Patterson, *The Jellicoe Papers,* I:80.

69. See Ramsay *"Blinker" Hall, Spymaster.*

70. Philbin, *Admiral von Hipper,* 87ff.; see notes.

71. BA/MA F3820/PG 62447 *KtB der BdA, O Sache Kreigsaufgabe 19, Aufgabe der IBdA, KdH,* 28 Oct 1914.

72. *Nachlass Hipper,* 1/41, 28 October 1914.

73. Ranft, *The Beatty Papers,* I:110.

74. BA/MA, *War Diary of the First Scouting Group, Lessons of the Operations on 3 November.* Philbin, *Admiral von Hipper,* 90n41–43.

75. Groos, *Der Krieg zur See,* II, chart 13.

76. *Pachyderm,* or *elephant,* is a term sometimes used to refer to admirals in a less than complimentary way.

77. Philbin, *Admiral von Hipper,* 90–91.

78. *Nachlass Hipper,* 1/44–46, 15 November 1914.

79. Marder, *From the Dreadnought to Scapa Flow,* II:82. The frustration was reflected in a letter from Prime Minister Asquith to Mrs. Edwin Montague, II:82n4.

80. Jellicoe, *Crisis of the Naval War,* 158.

81. Ibid., 156–57.

82. Ibid.

83. See Philbin, *Admiral von Hipper,* 91–96.

84. See Groos, *Der Krieg zur See,* III, chart 1, Operations from 15–16 December 1914.

85. *Nachlass Hipper* 1/48, 24 November 1914. This, if true, indicates the cruiser screen of the Grand Fleet itself. Jellicoe's silence on this is interesting to say the least.

86. Jellicoe, *Crisis of the Naval War,* 161. For the rest of the operation side 164–67.

87. Room 40 was in the process of being set up in early November 1914 and Commander Herbert Hope just joined the operation in November, thus confusion still reigned in that critical operation. See Marder, *From the Dreadnought to Scapa Flow,* II:133, and Ramsay, *"Blinker" Hall, Spymaster,* 57ff.

88. Chalmers, *Life and Letters of David Beatty,* 165.

89. Marder, *From the Dreadnought to Scapa Flow,* II:134.

90. Ibid.

91. Jellicoe, *Crisis of the Naval War,* 176ff.

92. Roskill, *Admiral of the Fleet Earl Beatty,* 92.

93. *Nachlass Hipper* N162/1, 43.

94. Chatfield, *Navy and Defense,* 128–29.

95. Ranft, *The Beatty Papers*, I:175; Beatty to his wife after the victory of the Falklands, 11 December 1914.

96. Ibid.

97. Ranft, *The Beatty Papers*, I:176–96.

98. von Tirpitz, *My Memoirs*, 496.

99. Kahn, *Codebreakers*, 271.

100. *Hipper Nachlass*, entry for 17 December 1914 and subsequent pages.

101. Philbin, *Admiral von Hipper*, 44–51.

102. Jellicoe, *Crisis of the Naval War*, 188.

103. Ibid., 188ff.

104. Johnston, *Clydebank Battlecruisers*, 62–88.

105. Marder, *From the Dreadnought to Scapa Flow*, II:170.

106. Roskill, *Admiral of the Fleet Earl Beatty*, 62–63.

107. Ibid., 96–97.

108. Ranft, *The Beatty Papers*, I:169.

109. Ibid., I:166–67, to Churchill, November 1914. Comments in Beatty's own hand are those in parens.

110. Ibid., I:166–67.

111. Ibid., 168.

112. Ibid., 160.

113. Ibid., 191–92. Beatty to Commanding Officers and the Engineer Captain 1st Battle Squadron, 28 December 1914.

114. Ibid., 170. Commander Henry Parker, R.N.

115. Ibid., 170.

116. Marder, *From the Dreadnought to Scapa Flow*. II:17–18.

117. Roskill, *Admiral of the Fleet Earl Beatty*, 375.

118. Ibid., 166, 21 November 1914.

119. Ibid., 107; actually it was the 9th Cruiser Squadron off Africa; Marder, *From the Dreadnought to Scapa Flow*, II:171.

120. Marder, *From the Dreadnought to Scapa Flow*. I:19.

121. Ibid., 12.

122. Chalmers, *Life and Letters of David Beatty*, xxi.

123. Roskill, *Admiral of the Fleet Earl Beatty*, 375.

124. Ruge, *SMS Seydlitz/grosser kreuzer*, 27.

125. von Waldeyer-Hartz, *Admiral von Hipper*, 123–24. The letter is Hipper to Raeder, 30 June 1926, on the 10th anniversary of the Battle of Jutland.

126. Raeder, *My Life*, 41–42.

127. Ibid., 42.

128. Bird, *Erich Raeder*, 18ff. For the interesting interface of German naval strategy and truth behind controversies, see "Tirpitz. Hipper and Wegener," 26ff.

129. Philbin, *Admiral von Hipper*, 72.

130. Ibid., 101n74–76.

131. Ibid., 102.

132. Ibid., 103. This is also contained in *Nachlass von Levetzow*, Holtzendorff to Levetzow, 7 February 1915.

133. Philbin, *Admiral von Hipper*.

134. *Nachlass Hipper*, 16 October–30 November 1914. There are some later mentions, but for relevance to the combat-worthiness of this new ship, these are the best.

135. See Weir, *Building the Kaiser's Navy*, 145ff.

136. Ibid., 178ff., "Construction outside the U-boat Program."

137. Ibid., 214, table 4.

138. See Philbin, 31, BdA, 3 February 1914, Hipper to Fleet, H.813 M. from BA/MA F728/PG67717.

139. Ibid.

140. Ramsay, see especially 23–73.

141. Patrick Beesley, *Room 40 and British Naval Intelligence 1914–1918* (London: Hamish Hamilton, 1982). This early work is the foundation for our understanding of this WWI activity.

142. Keegan, *Intelligence in War*, 4.

143. Kahn, *Codebreakers*, 267.

144. Ibid., 268.

145. Ibid., 268, citing Churchill, *The World Crisis*.

146. Ramsay, *"Blinker" Hall, Spymaster*, 31.

147. Ibid.

148. Ibid., 30.

149. *Nachlass Hipper*, N162/1, 18 October 1914, 32. Churchill, *World Crisis*, 213, mentions the action, as the Germans having violated the rules of war because they were torn "between the will to wound and the feat to strike . . ." Kahn, *Codebreakers*, 269, for the codebooks recovery. Beyond the trawler, no mention of *Hobart* surfaces in Churchill. See also Kahn, *Seizing the Enigma*, 21–30.

150. Kahn, Codebreakers, 270.

151. Ramsay, *"Blinker" Hall, Spymaster*, 20–21. The source is Beatty to Lady Beatty, Beatty Papers, NMM, and 20 Oct 1914.

152. If there is a fog surrounding the essential question of spy vs. spy in the years leading up to WWI, it is a little thinner around Winston Churchill who was an essential player regardless. See Stafford, *Churchill and Secret Service*, 23–85.

153. Ramsay, *"Blinker" Hall, Spymaster*, 56–57. He cites Churchill and the *Daily Telegraph* series of articles on *Work of the Secret Service* published in the 1930s.

154. Hinsley, *British Intelligence in the Second World War*, I:3.

155. Dorril, *MI6*, 3. See also Haswell, *British Military Intelligence*, 3. More details about the British side of human intelligence in WWI including the *Official Account of the Intelligence Corps in World War I* was lost with many other archives of World War I in World War II bombing raids on London. Deacon, *History of the British Secret Service* provides a complete overview from the Tudors forward, but chapters 12–15 are largely based on secondary sources or published memoirs.

156. Chatfield, *The Navy and Defense*, 109 for respect of intelligence. See Patterson, *The Jellicoe Papers*, I:15, 90, esp. Fisher to Jellicoe, 23 December 1914, and Jellicoe to Admiralty with Beatty enclosure, I:96–97.

157. Roskill, *Admiral of the Fleet Earl Beatty*, 120.

158. Hubatsch, *Der Admiralstab*, 251.

159. Kelly, *Tirpitz and the Imperial German Navy*, 358.

160. Hubatsch, *Der Admiralstab*, 250ff.; Anlagen, 26, 27.

161. Kahn, *Seizing the Enigma*, 271.

162. Ibid., 26–27.

163. Ramsay, *"Blinker" Hall, Spymaster*, 33ff.

164. Kahn, *Seizing the Engima*, 29.

165. By way of an informational aside, there is an odd little document in the records of the German Admiralstab, entitled, *"Denkschrift über die Entwicklung der Druckerei des Admiralstabs der Marine,"* dated Berlin, Dec 1916, at BA/MA/F3302/66705. These are the people who actually had to print the new copies of codes and cyphers and see to their distribution. It provides an overview of all the documents printed during the war up to 1916, by title and the first year seems to have cost 420,000 RM. (April 1914–March 1915). There were 43,000 books and pamphlets done that year alone. They printed the signal books and the codes of the Imperial Navy. See 5–6.

166. Kahn, *Seizing the Enigma*, 30.

167. BA/MA F3902/63272 *KTB SMS Moltke*, 16.12.14, 44 *Bemerkungen zum F.T. Verkehr*.

168. Ibid., see 168 supra.

169. BA/MA F431/PG76974 (or USNA T-1022, Reel 1060) *Akten Betreffened Schriftwechsel uber O Directiven, Kommando der Hochseeflotte Gg437 O.* [Papers concerning the correspondence concerning Operational Directives], 19 January 1914.

4. THE ORDER OF BATTLE

March, *British Destroyers*, vii. Additional data on guns, both German and British, comes from Friedman, *Naval Weapons of World War One*.

1. Gross, *Der Krieg zur See, Nordsee Bd. 3*, 2. [The War at Sea, North Sea, II:2.]

2. Ibid., III:1–2.

3. The data on the German destroyers is from Taylor, *German Warships of World War I*, and Jane, *Jane's Fighting Ships 1914*.

4. Robinson, *The Zeppelin in Combat*, 4–6; see also Groos, *Der Krieg zur See*, III:282–89. This latter indicates L5, 6, and 7 were operationally involved that day but only L5 was at the scene of the action.

5. Groos, *Der Krieg zur See*, III:287.

6. Jane, *Jane's Fighting Ships 1919*, 627, war losses; see also Taylor, *German Warships of World War I*, 131.

7. Taylor, *German Warships of World War I*, 132.

8. Ibid., 133.

9. Parkes, *British Battleships*, 627; Corbett, *Naval Operations, Volume II*, Appendix A, Organization of the Grand Fleet, January 24, 1915, 412–21; Jellicoe, *The Grand Fleet*, 186–98.

10. All data on the battle cruisers capabilities cited here taken from Parkes, *British Battleships*.

11. The date for these ships comes from March, *British Destroyers*; the wartime operational assessments of destroyer performance comes from 234ff.

12. Ibid., 116–20.

13. Ibid., 143–45.

14. Ibid., 133–35.

5. CHASE AND INTERCEPT

1. Groos, *Der Krieg zur See*, III, appendix 8, 282ff.

2. The orders assigning *Blücher* to the First Scouting Group can be found in 15 December 1914, *Admiralstab der Marine*, A10535. Fleet Command to the Kaiser. See U.S. National Archives, Record Group T-1022, Reel 983/PG 76531. This may also be found in the corresponding original in the BA/MA (Federal German Military Archives).

3. For *Blücher*, see BA/MA 50/66/17, 10ff; for Moltke, see 50/66/18, 10ff.

4. *Nachlass Hipper*, comments on speed 20 November, 47. Gary Staff in

Battle on the Seven Seas says *Blücher* actually achieved 25.8 knots on trials and as recently as 3 November 1914 had outrun the turbine equipped *Von der Tann*, 85.

5. Padfield, *The Battleship Era*, 208.

6. Please note all times given after German ships are German time and from the logs; for British ships, who were an hour later, the time is GMT, also from their logs.

7. BA/MA F3919/PG 63370 Log of SMS *Seydlitz* action 23–24 January 1915. The British were on GMT so observed this fire from *Blücher* at 0732 British time. Beatty, Adm 137/1943, enclosure 2, Commodore Tyrwhitt's report, 13.

8. Ranft, *The Beatty Papers*, I, Report; Young, *With the Battle Cruisers*.

9. Massie, *Castles of Steel*, 387–88, quoting Filson Young.

10. Roberts, *Battle Cruisers*, 80–81, table 30, steam trials data for all British battle cruisers.

11. UK National Archives/PRO/Adm137/1943, *Report of Vice Admiral Commanding First Battle Cruiser Squadron February 2, 1915*.

12. Schmalenbach, "SMS *Blücher*," 174ff.

13. Massie, *Castles of Steel*, 388.

14. Ibid., 388–89, quoting Filson Young.

15. Staff, *Battle on the Seven Seas*, 89.

16. Ibid. This is from Korvetten Kapitan Kurt Gebeschus, *Doggerbank*. Gebeschus was a *Blücher* survivor.

6. THE ENGAGEMENT

1. Staff, *Battle on the Seven Seas*, 90.

2. Jane, *Jane's Fighting Ships, 1919*, 507.

3. Padfield, *The Battleship Era*, 208.

4. Staff, *Battle on the Seven Seas*, 92, from the war diary of Lt Gebeschus, *Doggerbank*. Gebeschus was a survivor of the *Blücher*.

5. Young, *With the Battle Cruisers*, 3.

6. UK National Archives, PRO/Admiralty 137/1943, Report of Captain Chatfield, HMS *Lion*.

7. Adm 137/1943, Chatfield.

8. BA/MA F3902/PG63273 SMS *Moltke* war diary, 15 Jan 1915.

9. U.S. Naval Intelligence Division, translation of *The War at Sea*, German Official History, 18 [hereafter: ONI, *The War at Sea*].

10. Adm 137/1943, Chatfield.

11. Ibid.

12. Ibid., 9.

13. Ibid., Report of Rear Admiral Battle Cruiser Squadron.

14. Ibid.

15. Staff, *Battle on the Seven Seas*, 96–97.

16. Schmalenbach, SMS *Blücher*, 180.

17. Adm 137/1943, Rear Admiral Moore, 7.

18. Staff, *Battle on the Seven Seas*, 96.

19. BA/MA F3902, PG 63273, SMS *Moltke* KTB, 24 Jan 1915.

20. Adm 137/1843, Captain de Brock, HMS *Princess Royal*.

21. Adm 137/1943, Captain Pelly, HMS *Tiger*.

22. Ibid.

23. Adm 137/1943, deBrock.

24. Adm 137/1943, Report of Commodore Goodenough, First Light Cruiser Squadron.

25. Adm 137/1943, Captain B. Miller, HMS *Nottingham*.

26. Adm 137/1943, Captain A. Duff, HMS *Birmingham*.

27. Adm 137/1943, Captain T. W. B. Kennedy, HMS *Lowestoft*.

28. BA/MA, N 162/2 *Hipper Nachlass*, 24 Jan 1915.

29. Reeman, *The Zeppelin in Combat*, 4–5.

30. Adm 137/1943, this is from a Home Fleet memorandum 0022A HMS *Iron Duke*, 3 February 1915.

31. Campbell, *Jutland*, 8.

32. BA/MA F3919/KTB SMS *Seydlitz*, 24 January 1915, entry for 1043.

33. Groos, *Der Krieg zur See*, III:211–12.

34. Ibid.

35. BA/MA F3902/PG63273, KTB [war diary] SMS *Moltke*, 24 Jan 1915.

36. Adm 137/1943, Captain Pelly's report, Enclosure Number 6.

37. Adm 137/1943, Captain Chatfield's report.

38. Adm 137/1943, Rear Admiral Moore's report.

39. Ranft, *The Beatty Papers*, I:217.

40. BA/MA *Gefechtsbericht BdA*, 24 Jan 1915 [Battle Report of the Flag officer Scouting Forces].

41. The deployment of U-boats for Hipper's support reflects a high level of confusion on the part of the High Seas Fleet when their assumptions were shown to be completely invalid by British actions. See Groos, *Der Krieg zur See*, , III:203ff.

42. Adm53/55960, Log HMS *Princess Royal*, Sunday, 24 January 1915.

43. Both Beatty's biographers and Arthur Marder support this aspect of his character. See Marder, *From the Dreadnought to Scapa Flow*, II:8n3, and particularly II:12; see also Chalmers, *The Life and Letters of David Beatty*, xxl. An early but even telling nonetheless. See also Roskill, *Admiral of the Fleet Earl Beatty*, 32.

44. Ranft, *The Beatty Papers*, I:217, 218.

45. Ibid., I:219, Moore to Beatty.

46. Chalmers, *Life and Letters of David Beatty*,190.

47. Adm 137/1943 Beatty to Jellicoe, 3; 2 February 2 1915.

48. BA/MA/60/66/17, 11.

49. ONI, *The War at Sea*, 41.

50. *Hipper Nachlass*, 162/2, 15.

51. BA/MA/50/66/10 *Deutsche Kriegsflotte*, 24. The best possible rated speed was about 18 knots for the Second Battle Squadron and 19 knots for the First Battle Squadron. The old pre-dreadnoughts would get into the fight slowly. The fleet

speed for a rescue was 16 knots. The pre-
dreadnought were not a waste of time
in 1915 – their guns ranged as far as their
dreadnought sisters and at 18,850 meters at
30 degrees elevation would have exposed
the King Edward VIIIs who were Beatty's
nearest reinforcement to plunging fire and
a dangerous range gap of almost 6,000
yards.

52. The chronology and events listed
are from the ONI translation of the significant German radio messages during the
battle taken from Groos; see *Der Krieg zur
See*, III. The translation is accurate.

53. Adm 137/1943, Captain Chatfield,
HMS *Lion*, 9.

54. Adm 137/1943, Vice Admiral Beatty,
Gunnery Reports, 27.

55. Adm 137/1943, Captain H. B. Pelly,
HMS *Tiger*.

56. Ibid.

57. Chalmers, *Life and Letters of David
Beatty*,191.

58. Roskill, *Admiral of the Fleet Earl
Beatty*, 117.

59. Ibid.

60. Brown, *Scapa Flow*, 169.

7. THE AFTERMATH

1. Chalmers, *Life and Letters of David
Beatty*, 192, citing Churchill, *The World
Crisis*.

2. See Marder, *From the Dreadnought
to Scapa Flow*, II:188–91 on the Borkum
Sylt ideas.

3. Ibid., II:189n28.

4. Ibid., II:191.

5. Ibid., II:193ff.

6. Churchill, *World Crisis*, 616ff.

7. Jellicoe, *The Grand Fleet*, 197.

8. Ibid.

9. This allows for larger problems of
record. Preston, *Battleships of World War I*,
111. The 12-inch carried were 40 calibre, 51
ton models but would have been equal to
the 28 cm carried on the *Deutschland* and
Braunschweig classes, unless the Germans

chose to use their additional range to tactical advantage.

10. Churchill, *World Crisis*.

11. Corbett, *History of the Great War,
Naval Operations*, II:103. See also insert,
Strategical Plan of the Dogger Bank Action, 24 Jan 1915, for dispositions supporting the posed scenarios.

12. Stafford, *Churchill and the Secret
Service*, 69ff. This motive cannot be absolutely subscribed, but it is the author's
judgment. Ramsay, *"Blinker" Hall, Spymaster*, 72ff. There would be problems.

13. Halpern, *The Keyes Papers*, 46.

14. Bennett, *Naval Battles of the First
World War*, 167.

15. Ibid., 164.

16. Ranft, *The Beatty Papers*, I:203 and
203n1; this is [as cited] from Roskill, *Ad-
miral of the Fleet*, 118–19. Citing N. J. M.
Campbell, *Battle Cruisers, Warship Special
No. 1* (London, 1978) and Marder, *From the
Dreadnought to Scapa Flow*, II:170–72.

17. Ranft, *The Beatty Papers*, I:204.

18. Ibid., I:118–20, Beatty to Admiralty
Numbers.

19. Ibid., I:223.

20. Ibid., documents 124 and 125.

21. Ibid., I:246, Beatty to Pelly.

22. Ibid.

23. Roskill, 120–21.

24. Ranft, *The Beatty Papers*, I:282–86,
and 286n145, Beatty to Asquith.

25. This suggests there are opportunities for additional research into the state of
British Naval intelligence on some of these
second tier issues.

26. Massie, *Castles of Steel*, 375.

27. Corbett, *History of the Great War
Naval Operations*, II:101–102.

28. ONI, *The War at Sea*, 47.

29. Philbin, *Admiral Hipper*, 113. For the
sources, see 113n115.

30. Raeder, *My Life*, 56.

31. Staff, *Battle on the Seven Seas*, 102.

32. Ibid; see also Ruge, SMS *Seydlitz/
grosser kreuzer*, 31, 33–40.

33. Philbin, *Admiral Hipper,* 112.

34. Ibid., 113–17.

35. Gilbert, *The First World War,* 127.

36. Marder, *From the Dreadnought to Scapa Flow,* II:342.

37. Ibid., II:380–81n86.

38. Brown and Meehan, *Scapa Flow,* 139.

39. Hough, *Naval Battles of the Twentieth Century,* 201.

Bibliography

PRIMARY SOURCES

The logs and after action reports for both Admiral Beatty and Admiral Hipper are available. The construction details of the ships on both sides, including the compromises, are also available. Eyewitness reports and prisoner interrogations are available. Intelligence and orders from higher commands as well as fleet level war diaries are also available on both sides. Three archives are involved: the Federal German Military Archives, Bundesarchiv/Militararchiv, Freiburg im Breisgau, Germany; the UK National Archives (formerly the Public Record Office), Kew, London, UK; and the U.S. National Archives, Washington, DC. The latter has microfilm copies of the German records which are more easily available to North American scholars.

German Sources

BA/MA, *Bundesarchiv/Militararchiv* F 50/66 10–19. *Reichsmarineamt.* Ship characteristics books. In detailed form, these provide official ship characteristics, performance data, ammunition load outs, speed trials and schematics, including both plans and elevations for all German major combatants engaged in Dogger Bank.

BA/MA, 50/66/17, *Blücher.*

BA/MA, 50/66/18, *Deutsche Kriegsflotte,* RMA.

BA/MA, *Nachlass Hipper,* N162/1.

Bundesarchiv/Miltararchiv F 3916 – *KtB Kriegstagebuch* [War Diary of the Battle Cruiser] SMS *Von der Tann,* a battle cruiser not at Dogger Bank, but of use for context. *BA/MA F3885 KtB der BdA/ Kreigstagebuch der Befehlshaber Aufklarungschiffe* [War Diary of the Flag Officer Scouting Forces, War Operations] *orders 1914–1918.*

F3820 *KTB der BdA Kreigstagebuch Befehlshaber der Aufklärungschiffe Dogger Bankschlacht,* F4062 [War Diary of the Flag Officer Scouting Forces, Dogger Bank Report] 1914–1918/ PG 76531. This is the section of the BdA war diary dealing with Dogger Bank. [Band 3]. F4062 is the BdA battle report and analysis of Dogger Bank.

F3899 *Kriegstagebuch SMS Lützow.* Flagship of flag office scouting forces throughout her existence (1916 only).

F3913 *KTB SMS Seydlitz* [war diary], German flagship at Dogger Bank.

F2438/Bd 1 *Grosserkreuzer.* This is a record of Imperial German Navy conferences regarding battle cruisers including highest German government participation at the chancellor level.

US National Archives, Washington, DC

Record Group 45, *Modern Navy Records of the Office of Naval Intelligence.* (Also available in the Office of Naval Records and Library, Department of the Navy.) *Monthly Intelligence Bulletin.* "The German Official Account of the Battle of Dogger Bank, by Cmdr. Otto Groos." This is a translation of the German official naval history in *Der Krieg zur See,* Vol. III. It goes down to ship's logs extracts.

British Sources

UK Admiralty Library, CA 0121, Naval Intelligence Division. *Germany War Vessels 1914, NID.*

UK National Archives (late Public Record Office), Kew.

Admiralty 137/1022, report of the Battle of the Falkland's with von Spee's squadron.

Admiralty 137/1943, beginning with Battle Cruiser Squadron (later Fleet) reports on 28 August 1914, Battle of Heligoland Bight; also follow-up reports through Fleet and Admiralty level; all actions 16 December 1914; Beatty to Jellicoe, 2 February 1915; Vice Admiral Beatty, gunnery reports; reports of Captain Chatfield (HMS *Lion*), Rear Admiral Moore, Captain Pelly (HMS *Tiger*), de-Brock, Commodore Goodenough (First Light Cruiser Squadron), Captain B. Miller (HMS *Nottingham*), Captain A. Duff (HMS *Birmingham*), Captain Kennedy (HMS *Lowestoft*), and Captain Pelly (enclosure number 6)

Adm 53, ships logs for British ships engaged at Dogger Bank and later at Jutland.

Adm 53/55960, HMS *Princess Royal* logs, 24/25 Jan 1915. Provides texture and first line record of events.

Adm 53/63076, HMS *Tiger* log, 24 January 1815.

Adm 53/69093, HMS *Tiger* logs from Dogger Bank – actual hand records.

Adm 136/1906, Jellicoe's Jutland report.

Adm 137/1943, report of Vice Admiral Sir David Beatty on the Action in the North Sea, 24 January 1915. Multiple enclosures and German survivor reports; German press report on the action also included. There are additional action reports from the British side on later actions.

PUBLISHED WORKS

Assman, Kurt. *Deutsche Schiksalsjahre Historische Bilder aus dem zweiten Weltkreig und seiner Vorgeschichte.* Wiesbaden: Eberhard Brockhaus, 1951.

Bacon, Admiral Sir Reginald. *The Life of Lord Fisher of Kilverstone.* 2 vols. London, 1929.

Barnett, Corelli. *The Swordbearers: Supreme Command in the First World War.* Bloomington: Indiana University Press, 1975.

Bennett, Goeffrey. *Naval Battles of the First World War.* New York: Scribner's, 1968.

Bird, Keith. *Erich Raeder: Admiral of the Third Reich.* Annapolis: Naval Institute Press, 2012.

———. *German Naval History.* New York and London: Garland, 1985.

Bowditch, Nathaniel. *American Practical Navigator.* Washington: USGPO, 1928.

Bracken, Paul, Ian Bremmer, and David Gordon, eds. *Managing Strategic Surprise: Lessons from Risk Management and Risk Assessment.* Cambridge: Cambridge University Press, 2008.

Brassey, Earl of, and John Leyland. *Brassey's Naval Annual 1915 War Edition.* London: Wm. Clowes and Sons, 1915.

———. *Brassey's Naval Annual 1919.* London: Wm. Clowes and Son, 1919.

Breyer, Siegfried. *Battleships and Battle Cruisers 1905–1970.* New York: Doubleday, 1978.

———. *Schlachtschiffe und Schlachtkreuzer 1905–1970*. München: J. F. Lehmanns Verlag, 1970.

Brown, Malcolm, and Patricia Meehan. *Scapa Flow*. London: Penguin Allen Lane, 1969.

Brown, David K. *The Grand Fleet: Warship Design and Development 1906–1922*. Annapolis: Naval Institute Press, 1999.

Bruce, George. *Sea Battles of the 20th Century*. London: Hamyln, 1975.

Burt, R. A. *British Battleships 1889–1904*. Annapolis: Naval Institute Press, 1988. Definitive for *King Edward VII* class.

Burt, R. A., and W. P. Trotter. *Battleships of the Grand Fleet: A Pictorial Review of the Royal Navy's Capital Ships in World War One*. Annapolis: Naval Institute Press, 1982.

Campbell, John. *Jutland: An Analysis of the Fighting*. Annapolis: Naval Institute Press, 1986. Dogger Bank is covered in the introduction.

Cannadine, David. *In Churchill's Shadow: Confronting the Past in Modern Britain*. Oxford: Oxford University Press, 2003.

Cecil, Lamar. *Wilhelm II, Prince and Emperor 1859–1900*. Chapel Hill and London: University of North Carolina Press, 1999.

———. *Wilhelm II, Emperor and Exile 1900–1941*. Chapel Hill and London: University of North Carolina Press, 1996.

Chatfield, Admiral of the Fleet, Lord. *The Navy and Defense: The Autobiography of Admiral Lord Chatfield*. London: William Heinemann, 1942.

Chalmers, Rear Admiral W. S. *The Life and Letters of David Beatty, Admiral of the Fleet*. London: Hodder and Stoughton, 1951.

Churchill, Sir Winston S. *The World Crisis*. New York: Charles Scribner's, 1949.

Corbett, Sir Julian S. *History of the Great War, Naval Operations*, (new edition). London: Longmans, Green and Co., 1929.

Costello, John, and Terry Hughes. *Jutland 1916*. New York: Holt Rinehart and Winston, n.d..

Custance, Admiral Sir Reginald. *A Study of War*. Washington and London: Kennikat Press, 1924.

Deacon, Richard. *A History of the British Secret Service*. New York: Taplinger, 1969.

d'Eyncourt, Sir Eustace T. "Notes on Some Features of German Warship Construction," *Proceedings of the Institution of Naval Architects*, spring meetings of the sixty second session, paper read 16 March 1921, 1–15.

Dorril, Stephen. *MI6: Inside the Covert World of Her Majesty's Secret Intelligence*. London: The Free Press, 2000.

Fischer, Fritz. *Griff nach der Weltmacht die Kriegzielpolitik des Kaiserlichen Deutschland 1914/18*. Dusseldorf: Droste Verlag, 1956. Also available in translation.

Fitzsimons, Bernard. *Warships and Sea Battles of World War I*. New York: Beekman House, 1973. Great drawings.

Forstmeier, Friedrich. *Deutsche Grosskampfschiffe, 1915–1918: Die Entwicklung der Typenfrage im Ersten Weltkrieg*. Munich: J. F. Lehmann's Verlag, 1970.

Friedman, Norman. *Naval Weapons of World War One: Guns, Torpedoes, Mines and ASW Weapons of All Nations, An Illustrated Directory*. Barnsley, Yorkshire: Seaforth Publishing, 2011.

———. *U.S. Cruisers: An Illustrated Design History*. Annapolis: Naval Institute Press, 1984.

Frost, H. H. *The Battle of Jutland*. Annapolis: Naval Institute Press, 1936, 1964.

Gardiner, Robert. *Conway's All the World's Fighting Ships*. Annapolis: Naval Institute Press, 1979.

Giese, Fritz E. *Kleine Geschichte der deutschen Flotte*. Berlin: Haudeverlag, 1966.

Gilbert, Martin. *The First World War: A Complete History*. New York: Henry Holt, 1994.

Goda, Norman J. W. *Tomorrow the World*. College Station, Texas: Texas A&M Press, 1998.

Goodall, S. V. "The ex-German Battleship Baden." *Proceedings of the Institution of Naval Architects*, spring meetings of the sixty second session, paper read 16 March 1921, 15–32. Discussion follows at 34–48.

Greger, Rene. *The Russian Fleet, 1914–1917*. London: Ian Allen, 1972.

Gretton, Vice Admiral Sir Peter. *Winston Churchill and the Royal Navy*. New York: Coward McCann, 1968.

Gröner, Erich. *Die deutschen Kriegschiffe, 1815–1945*. Munich: J. F. Lehmann's Verlag, 1966.

Groos, Otto. *Der Krieg zur See, Nordsee, Erster Band, Von Kriegsbeginn bis Anfang September 1914*, Berlin: E.S. Mittler&Sohn, 1922. [*The War At Sea, North Sea*, Vol. I, "From the Beginning of the War until September 1914"].

———. *Zweiter band, Von Anfang September bis November 1914*. Berlin: E.S. Mittler&Sohn, 1922. [Vol. II, "From the Beginning of September to November 1914"].

———. *Dritter Band, Von Ende November 1914 bis Anfang Februar 1915*. [Vol. III, "From the End of November 1914 to the beginning of February 1915"]

Görlitz, Walter. *The Kaiser and his Court: The First World War Diaries of Admiral Georg Alexander von Muller*. London: MacDonald, 1961.

Halpern, Paul G. *A Naval History of World War I*. Annapolis: Naval Institute Press, 1994.

———. *The Keyes Papers Selections from the Private and Official Correspondence of Admiral of the Fleet Baron Keyes of Zeebrugge, Vol. I, 1914–1918*. London: Navy Records Society, 1972.

Hansen, Hans Jürgen. *The Ships of the German Fleets, 1848–1945*. New York: Arco, 1975.

Von Hase, George. *Kiel and Jutland*. London: Skeffington and Son, n.d. Von Hase was gunnery officer of SMS *Derfflinger*.

Haswell, Jock. *British Military Intelligence*. London: Weidenfield and Nicolson, 1973.

Hattendorf, John B., et al., eds. *British Naval Documents, 1204–1960*. London: Naval Records Society, 1990.

———. *Ubi Sumus? The State of Naval and Maritime History*. Newport, R.I.: Naval War College Press, 1994.

Hieronymussen, Paul. *Orders, Medals and Decoration of Britain and Europe*. London Blandford, 1970.

Herwig, Holger H. *Luxury Fleet: The Imperial German Navy, 1888–1918*. London: Allen and Unwin, 1980.

———. *The German Naval Officer Corps: A Social and Political History, 1890–1918*. Oxford: Clarendon Press, 1973.

Hinsley, F. H. *British Intelligence in the Second World War*. 5 vols. London and Cambridge: HMSO and Cambridge University Press, 1979–1990. The first volume derives lessons from the First World War back to Room 40.

Hitler, Adolph. *Mein Kampf*. Important because it criticized the numbers, speed and armament of German ships in surprising detail.

Hobson, Rolf. *Imperialism at Sea Naval Strategic Thought: The Ideology of Sea Power and the Tirpitz Plan, 1875–1914*. Boston: Brill Academic Publishers, 2002.

Hythe, Viscount. *The Naval Annual 1913* [reprint]. New York, Arco Publishing, 1970.

Hough, Richard. *Naval Battles of the Twentieth Century*. Woodstock and New York: Overlook Press, 2001.

———. *Dreadnought: A History of the Modern Battleship.* London: Michael Joseph, 1965.

Hubatsch, Walther. *Der Admiralstab und die obersten Marinebehörden in Deutschland 1848–1945.* Frankfurt am Main: Bernard und Graefe, 1958.

Hurd, Archibald, and Henry Castle. *German Sea Power: Its Rise, Progress, and Economic Basis. With Maps and Appendixes Giving the Fleet Laws, Etc.* London: John Murray, 1913.

———. *The British Fleet in the Great War.* London: Constable, 1919.

Jane, Fred T. *Jane's Fighting Ships 1914.* London: Sampson Low Marsden and Co., 1914.

Jane, Fred T., with Oscar Parkes. *Jane's Fighting Ships 1919.* London: Sampson Low Marsden and Co., 1919.

Jellicoe, Viscount John Rushworth of Scapa, Admiral of the Fleet. *The Grand Fleet 1914–1916, The Grand Fleet, Its Creation Development and Work.* London: Cassell and Co., 1919.

———. *The Crisis of the Naval War.* London: Cassell, 1920.

Johnston, Ian. *Clydebank Battlecruisers: Forgotten Photographs from John Brown's Shipyard.* Annapolis: Naval Institute Press, 2011.

Kahn, David. *The Codebreakers: The Story of Secret Writing.* London: Weidenfield and Nicolson, 1967.

———. *Seizing the Enigma: The Race to Break the German U-Boat Codes, 1939–1943.* New York: Barnes and Noble, 1998.

Keegan, John. *Intelligence in War: Knowledge of the Enemy from Napoleon to Al-Qaeda.* New York: Knopf, 2003.

Kelly, Patrick J. *Tirpitz and the Imperial German Navy.* Bloomington and Indianapolis: Indiana University Press, 2011.

Kemp, P. K. *The Papers of Admiral Sir John Fisher.* Vol. I. London: Navy Records Society, 1960. [See entry for Patterson volume II].

Kennedy, Paul. "The Development of German Naval Operations Plans Against England, 1896–1914." *English Historical Review,* January 1974, 48–77.

———. "Dogger Bank: Clash of the Battle Cruisers." *Beekman History of the World Library, Warships and Sea Battles of World War I.* London: Phoebus Publishing, 1973.

———. *The Rise and Fall of British Naval Mastery.* London and Basingstoke: Macmillan, 1983.

———, ed. *The War Plans of the Great Powers 1880–1914.* London: Allen and Unwin, 1979.

Keyes, Sir Roger. *The Naval Memoirs of Admiral of the Fleet Sir Roger Keyes.* London: Thornton Buttersworth, 1935.

MacKay, Ruddock. *Fisher of Kilverstone.* Oxford: Clarendon Press, 1973.

Mäkelä, Matti E. *Auf den Spurren der Goeben.* Munich: Bernard und Graefe Verlag, 1979.

March, Edgar, *British Destroyers: A History of Development, 1892–1953.* Annapolis: USNI, 1966.

Marder, Arthur J. *From the Dreadnought to Scapa Flow,* 5 vols. London and New York: Oxford University Press, 1965–1973.

Massie, Robert K. *Castles of Steel: Britain, Germany, and the Winning of the Great War at Sea.* New York: Random House, 2003.

———. *Dreadnought: Britain, Germany and the Coming of the Great War.* New York: Random House, 1991.

Mitchell, Donald W. *A History of Russian and Soviet Seapower.* London: Andre Deutsch, 1974.

Osborne, Eric W. *The Battle of Heligoland Bight.* Bloomington and Indianapolis: Indiana University Press, 1995.

Patterson, A. Temple, ed., *The Jellicoe Papers,* Vol. I, *1893–1916.* London: Navy Records Society, 1966.

———. *The Jellicoe Papers,* Vol. II, *1916–1935.* London: Navy Records Society, 1968.

Padfield, Peter. *The Battleship Era.* London: Rupert Hart Davis, 1972.

———. *The Great Naval Race: Anglo-German Naval Rivalry, 1911–1914.* New York: David Mackay, 1974.

Parkes, Oscar. *British Battleships: A History of Design Construction and Armament,* New and revised edition. London: Seeley Service, 1970.

Peebles, Hugh B. *Warship Building on the Clyde: Naval Orders and the Prosperity of the Clyde Shipbuilding Industry, 1889–1919.* Edinburgh: John Donald, 1987.

Pears, Commander Randolph. *British Battleships, 1892–1957: The Great Days of the Fleets.* London: Putnam, 1957.

Philbin, Tobias R. *Admiral Hipper: The Inconvenient Hero.* Amsterdam: Gruner, 1982.

———. *König Class Battleships, Warship Profile 37.* London: Profile Press, 1973.

von Pohl, Admiral Hugo. *Aus Aufzeichnungen und Briefen.* Berlin: Karl Siegismund, 1920.

Preston, Antony. *Battleships of World War I.* London: Arms and Armour Press, 1972.

Ranft, Bryan Mcl., ed. *The Beatty Papers: Selections from the Private and Official Correspondence of Admiral of the Fleet Earl Beatty, Vol. I, 1902–1918.* London: Navy Records Society, 1989.

———. *The Beatty Papers, Vol. II, 1916–1927.* London: Navy Records Society, 1993.

Quarm, Roger, and John Wylie. *W. L. Wyllie, Marine Artist 1851–1931.* London: Chris Beetles Ltd, 1981.

Raeder, Erich. *My Life.* Annapolis: Naval Institute Press, 1960.

Ramsay, David. *"Blinker" Hall, Spymaster: The Man Who Brought America into World War I.* Stroud, Gloucestershire: History Press, 2009.

Reeman, Douglas. *The Zeppelin in Combat: A History of the Combat Airship Division, 1912–1918.* Henley-on-Thames: G. T. Foulis, 1971.

Richmond, Sir Herbert. *Sea Power in the Modern World.* Baltimore: Waverly Press, 1934.

Ritter, Gerhard. *The Sword and the Scepter: The Problem of Militarism in Germany,* Vol. II, *The European Powers and the Wilhelminian Empire, 1890–1914.* Coral Gables: University of Miami Press, 1970.

Roberts, John. *Battlecruisers.* London: Chatham, 1997.

Roskill, Stephen. *Admiral of the Fleet Earl Beatty, the Last Naval Hero: An Intimate Biography.* New York: Atheneum, 1981.

———. *Churchill and the Admirals.* New York: William Morrow, 1978.

Rose, Liske A. *Power at Sea: the Age of Navalism 1890–1918.* Columbia: University of Missouri Press, 2007.

Rose, Susan, ed. *The Naval Miscellany,* Vol. VII. London: Navy Records Society, 2008.

Rössler, E. *Die deutschen U-Boote und ihre Werften Band 1.* Munchen: Bernard & Graefe Verlag, 1979. [The German U-boats and their Builders, volume 1]

Ruge, Friedrich. *In Vier Marinen Lebenerinnerungen als Beitrag zur Zietgeschichte.* Munich: Bernard & Graefe, 1976.

———. *SMS Seydlitz/grosser kreuzer, 1913–1919, Warship Profile 2.* Windsor: Profile Publications, Warships in Profile, 1973.

Raffael Scheck. *Alfred von Tirpitz and German Right Wing Politics, 1914–1930.* Atlantic Highlands, N.J.: Humanities Press, 1998.

Scheer, Admiral Reinhard. *Germany's High Sea Fleet in the World War.* London: Cassell, 1920.

Schmalembach, Paul. "SMS *Blücher.*" *Warship International,* no. 2, June 30, 1971, 71

Seligmann, Matthew S. *Naval Intelligence from Germany: The Reports of the British*

Naval Attaches in Berlin, 1906–1914. London: Navy Records Society, 2007.

———. *Spies in Uniform British Military and Naval Intelligence on the Eve of the First World War,* Oxford: Clarendon Press, 2006.

Singer, Charles et al., eds., *A History of Technology, Vol. V, The Late Nineteenth century, 1850–1900.* New York and London: Oxford University Press, 1958.

Smith, Thomas S. A. "German Accounts of the Principal Naval Actions, 1914–15." *RUSI Journal 1916.* 910–20.

Staff, Gary. *Battle on the Seven Seas: German Cruiser Battles, 1914–1918.* South Yorkshire: Pen and Sword Maritime, 2011.

Staff, Gary and Tony Bryan. *German Battlecruisers, 1914–1918.* North Hampshire: Osprey, 2011.

Stafford, David. *Churchill and Secret Service.* New York: Overlook Press, 1997.

Stoessinger, John G. *Why Nations Go to War.* London: St Martin's Press, 1992.

Sumida, Jon. "Machines, Manufacturing, Management, and Money: The Study of Navies as Complex Organizations and the Transformation of Twentieth Century Naval History." In *Doing Naval History: Proceedings of the Second Yale–Naval War College Conference.* Newport, R.I.: NWC Press, 1995.

Surface, Frank M. and Raymond L. Bland, *American Food in the World War and Reconstruction Period Operations of the Organizations Under the Direction of Herbert Hoover, 1914–1924.* Stanford: Stanford University Press, 1931.

Taylor, John C. *German Warships of World War I.* Garden City, N.Y.: Doubleday, 1970.

Thomas, Charles S. *The German Navy in the Nazi Era.* Annapolis: Naval Institute Press, 1990.

von Tirpitz, Admiral Alfred. *Deutsche Ohnmachtspolitik im Weltkriege: Politische Dokumente.* Hamburg and Berlin: Hanseatische Verlagsanstaldt, 1926.

———. *My Memoirs.* London: Hurst and Blackett, 1919.

Tracy, Nicholas. *The Collective Naval Defense of the Empire, 1900–1940.* London: Ashgate Press for the Navy Records Society, 1997.

von Trotha, Vize Admiral Adolph *Admiral von Tirpitz, Flottenbau und Reichsgedanke.* Breslau: Korn Verlag, 1933.

Weir, Gary H. *Building the Kaiser's Navy: The Imperial Naval Office and German Industry in the von Tirpitz Era, 1890–1919.* Annapolis: Naval Institute Press, 1992.

Tuckmann, Barbara. *The Proud Tower.* New York: Macmillan, 1962.

Wegener, Vice Admiral Wolfgang. *The Naval Strategy of the World War.* Translated with introduction and notes by Holger H. Herwig. Annapolis: Naval Institute Press, 1989; original German edition, 1929.

Wyllie, John, and Roger Quarm. *W. L. Wyllie, Marine Artist, 1851–1931.* London: Chris Beetles, 1982.

Wylie, William Lionel, and M. F. Wren. *Sea Fights of the Great War: Naval Incidents during the First Nine Months.* London: Cassell and Co., 1918. Contains the Wylie sketches of the action.

Young, Filson. Editing and notes by James Goldrick. *With the Battle Cruisers.* Annapolis: Naval Institute Press, 1988.

Waldeyer-Hartz, Hugo. *Admiral von Hipper.* London: Rich and Cowan, 1933.

Index

TOBIAS R. PHILBIN is Adjunct Professor of Information Assurance at the Graduate School of Management and Technology of the University of Maryland. He has also taught at the Virginia Military Institute, the U.S. Naval War College. He received his PhD in War Studies from Kings College London. He is author of *Admiral von Hipper: The Inconvenient Hero, The Lure of Neptune: German-Soviet Naval Collaboration and Ambitions, 1919–1941,* and *Warships for the King: Ann Wyatt (1658–1757) Her Life and Her Ships.* He is a retired naval reserve Commander and served almost 30 years as a civilian in the U.S. intelligence community.